This Language, A River

This Language, A River

A HISTORY OF ENGLISH

K. AARON SMITH AND SUSAN M. KIM

broadview press

BROADVIEW PRESS – www.broadviewpress.com
Peterborough, Ontario, Canada

Founded in 1985, Broadview Press remains a wholly independent publishing house. Broadview's focus is on academic publishing; our titles are accessible to university and college students as well as scholars and general readers. With over 600 titles in print, Broadview has become a leading international publisher in the humanities, with world-wide distribution. Broadview is committed to environmentally responsible publishing and fair business practices.

Library and Archives Canada Cataloguing in Publication

Smith, K. Aaron (Kelly Aaron), 1965-, author
       This language, a river : a history of English / K. Aaron Smith and Susan M. Kim.

Includes bibliographical references and index.
ISBN 978-1-55481-362-9 (softcover)

       1. English language—History—Textbooks. 2. Textbooks. I. Kim, Susan M., author II. Title.

PE1075.S65 2017   420.9   C2017-907025-8

Broadview Press handles its own distribution in North America:
PO Box 1243, Peterborough, Ontario K9J 7H5, Canada
555 Riverwalk Parkway, Tonawanda, NY 14150, USA
Tel: (705) 743-8990; Fax: (705) 743-8353
email: customerservice@broadviewpress.com

Distribution is handled by Eurospan Group in the UK, Europe, Central Asia, Middle East, Africa, India, Southeast Asia, Central America, South America, and the Caribbean. Distribution is handled by Footprint Books in Australia and New Zealand.

Broadview Press acknowledges the financial support of the Government of Canada through the Canada Book Fund for our publishing activities.

Edited by Juliet Sutcliffe

Book design by Chris Rowat Design. Cover image: WoutervandenBroek

PRINTED IN CANADA

To our students

Contents

Acknowledgments

We would like first to express our gratitude first to our editor, Marjorie Mather, for her energetic support for this project, and for her knowledgeable guidance through the processes. We are grateful to the anonymous reviewers for Broadview for their generous and rigorous comments on the manuscript, and to Juliet Sutcliffe for the careful copy editing of the manuscript. In addition, thank you to Sharon Rowley, who tested out an early version of the manuscript in her class and provided a number of corrections, and to Bill Schipper, who first directed us to Broadview.

Thanks are due to the Department of English and the College of Arts and Sciences at Illinois State University, which supported the collaborative teaching and research that made this book, and many other projects, possible for us. We would like to thank our colleagues in the Department of English, and especially Susan Burt, Irene Brosnahan, Chris Breu, Susan Kalter, Katherine Ellison, Brian Rejack, Roberta Trites, Amy Robillard, Ricardo Cruz, and Carol and Ed Lind for their help, encouragement, and friendship.

We would like to express our gratitude to our teachers, especially to S. Lee Hartman, Geoffrey Nathan, Margaret Winters, Joan L. Bybee, Christina Von Nolcken, and Kostas Kazazis. And to Thomas Cable, Robert Stevick, Hal Momma, and Michael Matto for their support.

From Aaron:
It isn't possible to thank everyone who has played some role in the development of this book. Here I would also like to recognize my closest friends, whose conversations (and fights) about language, linguistics, and life have benefited me greatly: Jack Kiefer (Chris), Susan M. Kim, and Dawn Nordquist. And finally, I would like to thank my husband, Moriki Tomihara: you're too good for me—people have said so for years.

From Susan:

Thank you to my other long-time collaborators, my friends Asa and Ashlie. And to my family: to my father for the model of dedication and persistence he has provided for me; to my sister for always sending the noise; to Rayma for the perfect salads just when you need them; to David, my favorite brother; to Nick; to Thomas, Ella and Jasper, for the home they have made for me. And to Aaron and Moriki, also my family.

Finally, we thank the students of English 241 and English 310, to whom this book is dedicated, for the ongoing inspiration and engagement they provide.

Preface: About This Book

The book is a history of the English language. It is *a* history. As such it is one of many, many other histories of the English language. It is certainly not the only possible, or the only "correct," history. We have attempted here to present a history of the English language that will provide students with fundamentals both for future study and for the teaching of English in secondary schools. While in a few places we argue, based on our own research, for revision of certain of the received facts about the history of English, the history provided here is based on the most widely accepted accounts of the development of English among scholars, although the selection of topics and the placement of those topics within the overall narrative reflect our unique viewpoints.

In this book, we emphasize that language changes, and that studying the history of language means being attentive to its description at any given moment, and understanding the ways it changes between one point in time and another.

We are also concerned with not only *what* changes, but also *why* these changes occur. Answering the question of why a language changes in a certain way means examining both the ways that all languages tend to develop, regardless of outside-linguistic pressures, and the ways in which politically, economically, socially, and culturally specific pressures on a specific language may influence that change.

We recognize that, in order to engage with work of this sort, readers of this book will have to approach it differently from the way they may approach the reading for other studies in the humanities:

1. Studying the history of the English language requires learning or relearning grammar fundamentals as well as certain fundamental concepts in linguistics. It is impossible to examine how changes in the language have occurred if we do not share a literal and conceptual vocabulary for doing so: we cannot talk about changes in the sound system of the language, for example, until we have established a technical vocabulary for describing the sounds of language. This work will require careful reading of technical material, and

considerable memorization. For this reason, we have included exercises and answers to those exercises as a way of encouraging readers to review the material in small segments, and to remain as active as possible in their reading of the book and their acquisition of these terms and concepts.

2. Studying the history of the English language requires learning or relearning some of the history and geography of England and those countries in which English is now used. It is impossible to talk about how the Norman Conquest affected the development of the English language if we do not also talk about when, where and why the Conquest happened. As with the terms and concepts discussed above, we have included exercises throughout the book (with answers at the end) which focus on the details of this historical material as a way to encourage readers to review the material in small segments, and to remain active in their engagement with it.

3. An active command of the fundamental concepts is necessary for understanding the analysis that is in many ways the most rewarding aspect of the study of the history of English. This book presents data—on techniques for describing language, on language at given moments, on historical situations—with the aim of *using* that data, and encouraging its readers to use that data, in an analysis of how and why English has changed in the ways that it has in the last millennium and a half.

We see living language and language change as a dynamic process that moves constantly and infinitely in complex ways. We have thus attempted to present concepts and data as clearly as possible and to integrate them into our developing analysis at every stage. For us, as we hope for you too, the challenge—and the pleasure—of the study of the history of English lies precisely in the ways in which it brings together so many different kinds of intellectual work in approaching an understanding of the language we use, sometimes without even thinking about it, every day.

CHAPTER ONE

Introduction

ALL LIVING LANGUAGES CHANGE, ARE CHANGING, AND WILL CONTINUE TO CHANGE

A rather large industry has developed around a desire to slow or even halt changes in the English language, but such an enterprise is impossible. As long as a language is spoken by living human speakers, like all things humans do in a social context, it will change over time. The only languages that can be said to be no longer changing are dead languages, languages that no longer have living native speakers. Even some dead languages change, however, if they continue to have cultural importance beyond their status as living languages. Even into the present day, Latin is used in certain official capacities, and while no one now speaks Latin as a native language, even in the limited contexts in which it is now used, Latin is still changing. For example, in 2003 the Vatican released a new Latin dictionary in which *motorcycle* was listed as *birota automataria levis*. We can be certain that no one was speaking Latin as a native language when the first motorcycle was produced.

TWO WAYS OF DESCRIBING LANGUAGE: SYNCHRONIC AND DIACHRONIC APPROACHES

Historians of a language trace changes in that language across time. To do so they must consider the language both synchronically and diachronically. **Synchronic** approaches to describing a language involve description and analysis of the language at a single moment in time. An example of a synchronic statement about English is the following:

In Present-Day English (PDE), the future is expressed with *will* + verb. For example, in the sentence *I study*, the action occurs at the present time. But when the verb is combined with *will*, in *I will study*, the action will occur in the future.

Synchronic should not be understood to mean "at a moment in the present time." It simply means at a single time, present or past. The following is also a synchronic statement, here concerning a single moment of time in the past:

> In early Old English (OE), the future was expressed with the present tense form, together with a future adverb like *tomorrow* or in a context in which a future inference was strongly available. For example *iċ leorniġe* means *I study* in OE. The same form, *leorniġe*, however, may be translated into PDE as *will study* if it occurs in a context that suggests the future, as in *tomergen iċ leorniġe*, (*tomorrow I will study*).

Synchronic statements are descriptions or analyses of language at a specific point in time. That point in time may be narrowly or broadly conceived (a specific year, or a period of the language that may have lasted centuries), but it is a single and specific point. Any history must include synchronic data and analysis. But as a history, it must also link synchronic descriptions or analyses across time. **Diachronic** approaches link synchronic descriptions or analyses. An example of a diachronic statement about English might link the two synchronic statements we provided above:

> Between early OE and PDE, a future periphrasis (multiple-word construction) with "will" emerged and became increasingly obligatory in future contexts. For example, OE *iċ leorniġe* > PDE *I will study*.

A history of a language may certainly be presented as a series of synchronic and diachronic descriptions and analyses. But while it is essential to attempt to understand *what* happened, it is just as important to ask *why* it happened, what motivated the changes. If, as you were reading the examples above, you were asking yourself *why*: "Why did a future periphrasis with *will* emerge?" or "Why didn't one exist in early Old English?" or "Where did the *will* in that periphrasis come from?" or "Why does the Old English have *leorniġe* while the PDE has *study*—where did the word *study* come from?" then you were already asking about the motivations for language change.

WHY LANGUAGE CHANGES: INTERNAL AND EXTERNAL MOTIVATIONS

We can divide the motivations for language change into two broad categories. Later in this discussion, we will complicate this division slightly. But for now, we will consider one kind of motivation for language change to be internal, and the other external. **Internal motivations** for language change have to do with the ways that languages, all languages, work. We call them internal because they are internal to language: they are not about the lives—social, cultural, or political—of their speakers so much as about what speakers do with language.

For example, the future auxiliary (or helping verb) *will* comes from the OE verb *willan*, which meant *to want, to desire*. So originally when a speaker of early OE used the verb *will*, as in *Ic wille leornian*, the sentence meant *I want to study*. Such statements about future desires carry with them an implication of future intention. Such implications may become conventionalized as the intended meaning, at which time we can say that the use of *will* is about future intention, as in *I will see you in my office at noon*. Another important step in the development of *will* as a future marker was that the part of the meaning of *will* involving intention also gave rise to a meaning involving prediction; if someone intends to do something or intends for something to happen, he or she is essentially making a prediction about the future. Consequently, certain statements with *will* have the meaning of future prediction, as in *He will be here soon*.

While it may be tempting to impute conscious effort to such an orderly and explainable change, to do so would be misleading. Strictly speaking, the OE verb *willan* became a future auxiliary because of certain natural forces within the language itself (although, like all changes, this change is certainly propelled by the fact that language is used by speakers). Notice how desire, intention, prediction and futurity were always part of the meaning of *will*, but over time, different parts of those meanings came into focus. Only our ability to go back and retrace the steps of that refocusing gives that change the appearance of orderly and conscious change. To speakers at any given moment in the history of a language, language is simply being used for communication. While the unconscious choices of those speakers follow certain principles and show patterns of change over time, those same speakers are not generally aware of the changes they are enacting.

How do we know though that the change from *willan* to *will* is due to natural forces within the language? Why couldn't we hypothesize that for some reason English speakers became more interested in the future and therefore developed a future **auxiliary verb**? Three things make any such account based on conscious decision or need highly unlikely.

First, grammatical development of the kind just described rarely occurs consciously. Yes, grammarians write books that attempt to tell us how we should use grammar, but those attempts at prescribing conscious grammatical usage are largely unsuccessful in the face of natural, subconscious changes. Many present-day grammar books still discuss the use of *who* versus *whom*, for example, yet very few English speakers observe or understand the difference. The distinction between *who* and *whom* promises to continue to fade, much to the chagrin of many grammarians. As we will discuss later, the loss of the distinction between *who* and *whom* is part of a larger set of changes that have been occurring in English for more than a thousand years. No matter how powerful a given user of English might be, he or she is unlikely to be able to counteract the tendencies of a thousand years of language change.

Second, it is not true in any sense that speakers of OE did not have a way to talk about the future before the development of *will* into a future auxiliary. In a famous OE poem, "Deor," for example, the narrator predicts over and over again that the hardships of the present time will pass. Only a narrator with a clear concept of the future could do so. The OE prognostic texts, perhaps even more clearly, include techniques for predicting the future, an activity only possible if a clear concept of the future exists.

Third, the development of a verb meaning *desire* into a future marker is not unique to the English language. In fact, very similar developments can be shown in a number of other languages, among them Italian, Danish, Inuit, Buli, Nimboran, Bongu, Dakota, and Tok Pisin.[1] The apparent universal availability of this change in such a broad array of human languages suggests strongly that it is related to commonalities of language use and cognition among humans generally, and not just about the use of English or the English experience.

Students of English may be tempted to think of English as special or dear. And in some respects it may be. But from a linguistic standpoint, internal changes like the development of future *will* indicate that English is similar to at least some of the 6,000–7,000 or so other languages of the world.

But language change is also motivated by dynamics specific to the lives of its speakers. **External motivations** for language change have to do with those dynamics. External motivations include pressures like the prestige of one dialect over another, or economic advantage or imposition, as in the global spread of English during and after the colonial period, or language contact, as now exists between Spanish and English in the American Southwest, or political domination, as was the case during the Middle English (ME) period.

Probably the most dramatic, most catastrophic from some perspectives, most exciting from others, external event in the history of English is the Norman Conquest. The Norman Conquest occurred in the year 1066. The Normans, who successfully conquered England, did not speak English. They spoke a dialect of Old French. Consequently, for generations after the Norman Conquest, the ruling class in England spoke not English but a dialect of French. For several hundred years after that, French dominated high culture in England. French was the language of royal courts, but also of courts of law. While Latin remained the language of the Church, in the generations after the Conquest increasingly powerful ecclesiastical positions, and hence also educational positions, in England were held by speakers of French.

Not surprisingly, the **lexicon** (the set of non-grammatical words) in English expanded dramatically in both size and nature during the four hundred years after the Conquest to include as many as 10,000 borrowings from various French dialects. And not surprisingly, these borrowings very often reflect the social relations between

---

1   Joan Bybee, Revere Perkins, and William Pagliuca, *The Evolution of Grammar: Tense, Aspect, and Modality in the Languages of the World* (Chicago: U of Chicago P, 1994), 243ff.

speakers of French and speakers of English in England. One of the most famous of these examples is the introduction of a number of words like *beef* and *poultry*, words for meats that came to exist in English alongside the words for the animals from which the meat comes. Speakers in many languages of the world identify meat by the name of the animal, as in Spanish *carne de cerdo*, literally "meat of the pig." The borrowing of French words for meat gives English an interesting set in which the word for the animal is the retained native word from Old English but the word for the meat of that animal is a borrowed French word. So, for example:

From French	Native
beef	cow
pork	swine
poultry	chicken
venison	deer

The borrowings from French are not words for things that simply did not exist in England before the Normans conquered it. These borrowings, or changes in the lexicon of the language, are motivated not by internal dynamics, but by external pressures. They reflect the social domains in which English and French were used. Farming and tending animals remained a job of the conquered classes, the English, and so the names of the animals persisted in English. Activities more closely associated with or conceived of as part of high culture, fell within the domains of French and so the terms used for the meats were often borrowed from French.

If we return to our example with *leorniġe* and *will study*, and the question "Why does the OE have *leorniġe* while the PDE has *study*—where did the word *study* come from?" we might, given this context, propose an external motivation: that *study* as a verb might have entered into English from French during the period after the Conquest when speakers of French dominated high culture and when speakers of French were likely to have occupied positions of authority in the Church, and hence also in the educational institutions. In fact, *study* as a verb does come into English at exactly this period. The Oxford English Dictionary cites the earliest written occurrence of the word *study* in a text from around 1300: *He lynede adoun vpon his boc, þo he ne miȝte <u>studie</u> nomore.* "He leaned down upon his book because he could not study anymore."[2]

Of course, *leorniġe* has not disappeared from English. Certainly people both learned and studied in England before the Conquest. The introduction of the borrowed word *study* into the lexicon of English does not reflect the need for a term for a new concept. Rather, it reflects the social relations between speakers of French and speakers of English in the period after the Conquest.

---

2 *Oxford English Dictionary Online*, s.v. "study."

As we noted above, we must slightly complicate the distinction between internal and external motivations for language change. We divide the motivations for language change roughly into internal and external motivations for clarity of presentation. However, it is important to keep in mind that internal and external motivations for language change often work simultaneously. The fact that language is used in social exchange provides the impetus even for those types of change we might conveniently label as internal, a point we hinted at before. At other times, internal and external change might work against each other, and there may be multiple motivations for any given instance of language change.

The following history of English will engage in both synchronic and diachronic description and analysis of English, using data ranging from the earliest reconstructions of its precursor languages to transcripts of our own speech. We will ask not only how English has changed over the last thousand or so years, but also what might have motivated those changes.

EXERCISES

1.1   Identify the following statements as synchronic or diachronic.

a. In OE, the suffix -*es* on a noun could indicate that that noun was possessive.

b. In OE, the pronoun *þu* (*thou*) was singular, meaning *you* as one person. The pronoun *ge* (*ye*) was plural, meaning *you* as more than one person.

c. In the OE and early ME periods, the distinction between *thou* and *ye* was one of number (singular or plural), but by the Early Modern English (EModE) period, the distinction between the two forms developed from one exclusively involving number into one also involving politeness: the *thou* forms were used for addressing not only a singular addressee but also intimates and inferiors; the *ye* forms were plural, but could also be used as polite forms for showing respect or addressing superiors, both singular and plural in number.

d. The OE -*es* suffix on nouns is retained in PDE as the possessive -*s*.

1.2 Identify the following motivations for language change as internal or external.

a. When there is a dominant pattern, forms in a language tend to be pulled towards that pattern. So, for example in the history of English, most verbs in the language have become "regular." That is, they take -*ed* to make the past tense, *walk–walked*. So when new verbs appear in the language, they almost always follow this regular pattern, as with *text–texted*.

b. Scandinavians settled in England at the end of the ninth century. This settlement was permanent and resulted in intermarriage and close daily contact between speakers of Norse (Scandinavian) and English. At least a thousand words entered the lexicon of English from Norse in the centuries following this settlement. In addition, even some grammatical words are introduced into English from Norse.

CHAPTER TWO

Grammar Fundamentals

We cannot discuss the structure of language without a shared basic vocabulary for doing so. The following chapter, a basic guide to the grammar of English, provides definitions and explanations of terms and concepts fundamental to language study. Students' familiarity with the terms and concepts discussed in this chapter will vary considerably. As a result of significant differences in pedagogical approaches to language in secondary schools, for some students, this chapter will be a review of material they learned years ago, but for others this chapter will be a first introduction to terms and concepts like "subject" and "relative clause." We will refer to the terms and concepts in this chapter throughout the book. If these are new terms and concepts to you, take the time now to become comfortable with them. Do remember, however, that any time you encounter one of these terms in a later chapter, you can always return to this chapter, or the glossary, to refresh your understanding of it.

PARTS OF SPEECH

There are seven parts of speech in English: noun, verb, adjective, adverb, preposition, conjunction and interjection, with related categories such as pronoun, auxiliary verb, and determiner. Each is treated below.

INTERJECTION

Interjections are emotive expressions that one utters in surprise, pain, glee, etc.

> <u>Ouch</u>! You are on my foot!
> <u>Oh</u>, I forgot you were there!

Interjections are syntactically independent of the utterances following them, and in many treatments of grammar they are largely ignored, as they will be here.

THE NOUN

Many have learned that a **noun** is a "person, place, or thing." In order to account for abstract notions, nouns such as *liberty* or *bereavement*, one often adds that a noun may represent an idea. Although, strictly speaking, identifying a noun as a "person, place, thing, or idea" is a semantic approach (that is, it involves the meaning of the word) and as such can cause some problems, the characterization of a noun as a "person, place, thing, or idea" often works fairly well. In fact, even students with little formal grammar instruction are highly successful in identifying nouns based on this definition.

But since "noun" is a structural category in language, one should also be able to identify nouns based on the grammatical patterns they enter into. In English, for instance, nouns can occur with the definite article *the*.

The <u>market</u>, the <u>lion</u>, the <u>sugar</u>, and the <u>liberty</u> are now ours.
We noticed the <u>amazement</u> over the <u>transformation</u>.

One way we might begin to define "noun" without taking a semantic approach is to note that, unlike other parts of speech, nouns can follow the definite article. So, for example, consider the sentence:

The _____ ate breakfast.

Any word that can occupy the blank in that sentence will be a noun.[1]
We should note, however, that some nouns, particularly proper nouns, i.e., those denoting the name of something, like *Bob, Canada, Illinois State University*, etc., do not regularly occur with the definite article, unless there is ambiguity among multiple references with the same name.

<u>Canada</u> (never *the Canada) is that country north of the United States.
But
He just isn't the <u>Bob</u> I married nine years ago.[2]

Nouns are also inflected for number. That is, nouns can change their form to indicate that they are plural. Most nouns in English indicate that they are plural by adding the suffix –*s* to the end of the word.

I have one cat.
She has two cat<u>s</u>.

---

1 Sometimes an adjective with a suppressed noun may seem to occur in this position, e.g., *The rich get richer.*
2 An asterisk in this context indicates that the sentence, form, or phrase is not one that a speaker of writer of English would likely produce.

I take one sugar in my tea.
He takes three sugar<u>s</u> in his tea.

Note that in the last sentence, *sugar* is a subclass of nouns sometimes called non-count nouns because substances like sugar cannot be counted in the way that one would count, say, pencils or cats. In such cases, the plural marker –*s* will change the referent away from the substance to the packaging of that substance, thus *sugars* = *packets of sugar* or *waters* = *glasses/bottles of water*. Or in some instances, the plural on such non-count nouns will refer to types/species of the noun, thus *rices* = *types of rice* as in *We serve various <u>rices</u> from around the world*. Some non-count nouns, particularly abstract nouns like *astonishment*, do not easily occur in the plural. The plural form of *astonishment* in the following sentence, for example, is highly unlikely.

After so many surprises and so many <u>astonishments</u>, the band fell apart.

Because most nouns are inflected for number with the suffix –*s*, we can be fairly confident that if the word can occur in the phrase

One _____, two _____-s

it is a noun.

As with other grammatical categories, in order to determine whether a word is a noun, a verb, an adjective, etc., we can develop a hypothesis based on a semantic definition, but applying the formal tests (like occurrence with the definite article or the plural -*s* for nouns) will help to confirm or reject that hypothesis.

A Note about Irregular Plurals

Of course some nouns in English have an irregular plural. These "irregularities" often reflect older patterns in the language. From a historical viewpoint these plural forms are not irregular at all. These irregular plural forms include:

-en	oxen
Ø[3]	deer, sheep
-ren	children
vowel change	men, mice, geese

In addition to these older English patterns, there are also several plurals based on the plural form in the languages from which the nouns were borrowed.

---

3   Ø indicates that the grammatical category may be manifested by the absence of an overt marker.

From Latin

-us	→	-i	syllabus → syllabi, focus → foci, fungus → fungi
-um	→	-a	datum → data, forum → fora
-a	→	-ae	alumna → alumnae, formula → formulae, vertebra → vertebrae
-ex	→	ices	index → indices

From Greek

| -on | → | -a | criterion → criteria |
| -is | → | -es | crisis → crises |

From Hebrew

| Ø | → | -im | cherub → cherubim, seraph → seraphim |

From French

| -au | → | -aux | fabliau → fabliaux |

Many of these plurals from languages other than English are replaced with the regular English -s/-es plural, e.g., *syllabuses*. The use of one or the other plural in such instances is often a matter of style and personal preference rather than grammatical imperative.

THE PRONOUN

Treated here along with the noun is the pronoun. We will look at four types: personal pronouns, demonstrative pronouns, indefinite pronouns, and relative pronouns.

Personal Pronouns

Personal pronouns are referring words. They may refer to entities present in the discourse, e.g., *you* or *I/we*. Otherwise, they refer to a noun that has already been used in the sentence or group of sentences. (This kind of pronoun use has anaphoric reference.)

Jane started her new job last week and she loves it.

The pronoun *she* refers back to the noun *Jane* in the first part of the sentence.

In some other instances a pronoun is deployed before its referent (the noun it refers to), often for stylistic effect. (This kind of pronoun use has cataphoric reference.)

As he slipped into the darkened room, John could smell the vampire's presence.

In this instance the pronoun *he* refers to the noun *John*, which appears in the second clause.

Pronouns and Case

Case is a term used in the description of noun systems in which nouns or pronouns change their form depending on how they are used in a sentence. Thus in a case system, a noun or pronoun will have a different form depending on its use as a subject, object, possessor, etc.

Personal pronouns in Present-Day English (PDE) often show case. Case is a key concept in the study of many languages: Russian, Latin, Ancient Greek, Japanese, Korean, etc. It is also a very important concept to understand for the study of the history of English.

Consider the following sentence:

Sally sold seashells, but <u>she</u> didn't sell many before the police kicked <u>her</u> off the beach.

In this sentence both the pronoun *she* and the pronoun *her* refer back to *Sally.*

But while both *she* and *her* refer back to *Sally, she* and *her* obviously have different forms. These different forms indicate that the pronoun has different grammatical functions in the sentence. Specifically, *she* is the subject of the verb *didn't sell,* and *her* functions as the direct object of the verb *kicked . . . off.*

Personal pronouns in English are divided into three cases: subjective, objective, and possessive. Consider the pronoun *he/him/his* for example, in the following sentences. In each of these sentences, the pronoun *he/him/his* refers to the same person, Sergio.

<u>Sergio</u> is talented.
<u>He</u> works hard.
We all admire <u>him</u>.
Those beautiful quilts are <u>his</u>.

But in each of these instances, the pronoun has a different grammatical function. *He* is the subject of the sentence *He works hard. Him* is the direct object of the sentence *We all admire him. His* indicates possession in the sentence *Those beautiful quilts are his.* Each function has a unique pronoun form.

Case	Pronoun Form
subjective	he
objective	him
possessive	his

Person and Number

Pronouns can also be organized according to their **person** (**first**, **second**, or **third**) and **number** (**singular** or **plural**). The first-person pronouns refer to the speaker(s) or writer(s). The second-person pronouns refer to the person(s) being spoken or written to. The third-person pronouns refer to a person or persons being spoken or written of.

> First-person pronouns: I, we
> Second-person pronouns: you
> Third-person pronouns: he, she, it, they

Pronouns can indicate number. That is, they can be singular or plural. *I* is singular. *We* is plural. *They* is the plural of *he*, *she*, or *it*. *You* is both singular and plural, at least in Standard English: many other varieties of English use a distinct plural (*y'all*, *y'unz*, *youse*, etc.).

Additionally, singular pronouns in the third person (*he*, *she*, and *it*) are distinguished for gender: masculine, feminine, or neuter. Note, however, that English is unlike many languages (such as Spanish, French, German, etc.) in which gender is grammatical. **Grammatical gender** involves a system in which all nouns in the language belong to a gender class. PDE has **natural gender** in that the gender of a noun is based on animacy. When animacy is considered, living things, like people, pets and domesticated animals, are referred to as *he* or *she*. All inanimate nouns, as well as nouns denoting animals for which the biological gender is unknown, are referred to as *it*.

A summary of the personal pronoun forms, organized according to case, gender, and number, follows.

Summary of the Personal Pronouns

Personal pronouns: subjective forms (used when the pronoun is functioning as a subject)

	Sing.		**Pl.**
1st person	I		we
2nd person	you		you
3rd person			
Masc.	he	All genders	they
Fem.	she		
Neut.	it		

Personal pronouns: objective forms (used when the pronoun is functioning as the direct object, indirect object, or object of a preposition)

	Sing.		**Pl.**
1st person	me		us
2nd person	you		you
3rd person			
Masc.	him	All genders	them
Fem.	her		
Neut.	it		

Personal pronouns: possessive forms (used when the pronoun "possesses" something)

	Sing.		**Pl.**
1st person	mine		ours
2nd person	yours		yours
3rd person			
Masc.	his	All genders	theirs
Fem.	hers		
Neut.	its		

Demonstrative Pronouns

Demonstrative pronouns are deictic words (pointing words) that express relations of distance to the speaker/writer. Demonstrative pronouns are either proximal (near) or distal (away from) and either singular or plural. This four-way relationship yields the following demonstrative pronouns for PDE:

	Sing.	**Pl.**
Proximal	this	these
Distal	that	those

Here, you can have this. (spoken while extending an object to another person)

Give me a few of those! (referring to a portion of the books a friend is carrying)

While PDE has a two-place (proximal and distal) deictic system, languages can certainly have more than two places. Spanish has a three-place deictic system (*este, ese, aquél*), and English used to have a third deictic, *yon*, as in the Christmas carol:

…'round yon virgin, mother and child

Yon is still found in the adverb form *yonder* in some varieties of PDE.

Indefinite Pronouns

In every instance we have discussed so far, the pronouns have referred to a specified entity. *She*, for example, referred to the specific human being, *Sally*. *Those* referred to books carried by a friend. Some pronouns, however, can refer to unspecified entities. Such pronouns are called **indefinite pronouns** and they include the following: *someone, somebody, anyone, anybody, something, anything, everyone, everybody.*

Somebody ate my porridge.

Don't say anything you might regret later.

Note that in these sentences *somebody* and *anything* do not refer to specified nouns but to any member within very broad noun classifications. *Somebody* can be any human being.

Relative Pronouns

The **relative pronouns** are *who(m)*, *which*, *that*, and ∅.

We elected the candidate who was a better speaker.

In the sentence above *who* is a relative pronoun. Its reference is to *candidate*.

We elected the candidate who was a better speaker.

Relative pronouns are used to introduce relative or adjective clauses the function of which is to describe a noun. Thus a relative pronoun in English not only refers to a noun but also redeploys that referent in the form of a pronoun within an adjective clause. For this reason, a relative pronoun does double duty, referring to a noun while at the same time having a grammatical function in its own clause. That is, in the sentence above, *who* refers to *candidate* but also serves as the subject in the clause *who was a better speaker*.

THE NOUN PHRASE

In the opening parts of this section, we looked at nouns as single entities, but in grammar it is necessary to consider nouns on another level as well, the level of the phrase. A **noun phrase** (NP) is made up of a noun and the words that cluster around it.

Consider the following sentences:

The big dog chased the squirrel.
We had an excellent dinner.

I terrified <u>that mean old cat</u>.
She was pleased with <u>her recent grade</u>.

In each of the underlined NPs, there is a head noun, which we recognize to be the most important word of the cluster: *dog, dinner, cat, grade.*

In each case there are other kinds of words that occur with that noun and modify it. *Dog* occurs with the definite article *the* and with the adjective *big*; *dinner* occurs with the indefinite article *an* and with the adjective *excellent*; *cat* occurs with the demonstrative *that* and with the two adjectives *mean* and *old*; and *grade* occurs with the possessive determiner *her* and with the adjective *recent*.

One way to understand the structure of these groups of words is by examining them in the form of diagrams, like the following.

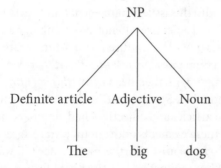

Therefore in the sentence, *The big dog chased the squirrel*, the subject of the sentence is the single word *dog* on one level, but the entire phrase *the big dog* on another.

If we can think about grammatical information, like subject, as a property of the NP, we can also understand phenomena like agreement to operate within the entire NP as well. In many languages, like Spanish and English in its earlier stages, all of the members of the noun phrase agree in number and gender.

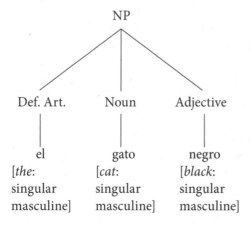

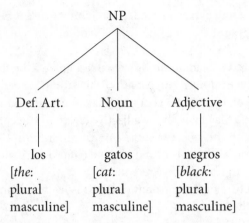

It may seem that in Modern English (ModE) this issue of agreement is not particularly relevant, since the definite article *the* and adjectives do not show singular and plural. However, demonstrative determiners (not to be confused with demonstrative pronouns discussed above) do have singular and plural forms: *this–these, that–those*. Demonstrative determiners in English do agree with their head noun (*this* book/*these* books). Early varieties of English acted more like Spanish in that there were many singular and plural forms for the definite article, and adjectives had singular and plural forms as well. In Old English (OE) these elements of the noun phrase agreed with the noun similarly to the way they do in Spanish. Furthermore, since OE was a case language in which nouns (like PDE pronouns) had distinct case forms, the definite article and adjectives agreed with their head nouns not only in number and gender, but also in case. Again, it is at the level of noun phrase that these grammatical alignments occur.

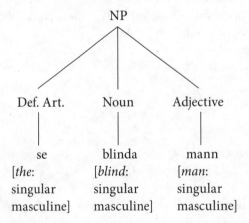

Note that here the phrase *se blinda mann* agrees in gender and number, and that it also agrees in case; that is, the forms of these words indicate that the noun phrase is a likely subject of a sentence.

It is also possible for a noun phrase to be made up of a pronoun alone, and that is the reason that the category pronoun is treated along with the noun and elements of the noun phrase here.

NP

Pronoun

me

THE VERB

The most common semantic characterization of a **verb** is that it is a word that shows an action. This is, however, an exceedingly poor way to think of the verb. It is true that a number of verbs denote an action:

He <u>kicked</u> the ball.
Romeo <u>kissed</u> Juliet's hand.
Alicia <u>ran</u> in the race.

There are many words that can denote action and some of those words are not verbs:

Her <u>speech</u> won the heart of every listener.

Speech refers to the action of speaking. However, *speech* is not a verb but a noun.

A second problem is that there are verbs that do not denote an action at all:

Hansel <u>is</u> the son of neglectful parents.
Renate <u>loved</u> the theater.

Neither the verb *is* nor the verb *loved* denotes an action. *Is* denotes a linking relationship between *Hansel* and *the son*, and *loved* in the second sentence refers to an experience not an action.

If we must have a semantic definition for verb, we would have to indicate that a verb is a word that denotes an action, relation or state and further concede that not only verbs denote these meanings. Defining verbs in this way results in a definition so broad that it really isn't very helpful. Considering the structural behavior of verbs allows us to be much more definitive.

The first structural property that we can consider is that of tense. Each finite verb in English must indicate tense: either past or present. If a word can be made past or present, it is a verb.

Consider the following list:

scanner, coffee, beautiful, very, type

Only one of these words can be changed from present to past: *type* → *typed*. There is no **scannered*, **coffeed*, **beautifuled*, or **veryed*: these words are not verbs.

Of course there are other structural properties of verbs which can be used as tests of this sort. Verbs can take an *-ing* inflection: *typing*, but not **coffeeing*, **scannering*, **beautifuling*. They also take an *-s* inflection in the third-person singular: *he types*, but not **he coffees*, **he scanners*, **he beautifuls*. (This last test is really just another test with tense, but in this instance in the present tense.)

Tense

Although it is one of the grammatical terms many people feel comfortable with, **tense** is actually a difficult concept in many grammatical traditions. The difficulty arises because the term *tense* has frequently been used both for indicating general time of an utterance and for denoting all kinds of marking on a verb, some that have nothing to do with time.

Traditionally the term tense has been limited to suffixes on the verb that denote general time like present or past. In this way of thinking, English only has two tenses, present and past:

She plays basketball.
She played basketball.

Some are inclined to expand the term tense so that it can encompass time expressed by auxiliary verbs as in:

She will play basketball.

From a pedagogical standpoint there is no great harm in considering auxiliary verb *will* + a verb as a future tense. However, in this book, we will encourage the limiting of the term tense to suffixes on the verb, because as will be seen later on, the appearance of just two tenses, as defined here, is typical of English and the languages that it is historically related to.

Aspect

Much of what is called tense, even in some school grammars, is actually a more specific verbal category called **aspect**. Aspect refers to the finer distinctions concerning the temporal information of a verb. For example, consider the two sentences:

> He <u>runs</u> every day at three pm.
> He <u>is running</u> now.

In both sentences the verb indicates an action in the present time, but in the first sentence it is in the present tense while in the second it is in the present **progressive**. Progressive is an aspectual category that refers to actions that are ongoing. In the second sentence, the action of running is happening now. In contrast, in the sentence *He runs every day at three pm*, the action is habitual.

Auxiliary Verbs

Consider the following sentences:

> He <u>plays</u>.
> He <u>is playing</u>.
> He <u>has been playing</u>.

In the first sentence, we can recognize that the verb is *plays*. In the second sentence, a form of the verb *play*, i.e., *playing*, is combined with an auxiliary verb, here a form of the verb *be*. In the third sentence, a form of the verb *play* is combined with two auxiliary verbs, forms of *have* and *be*.

A main verb together with its auxiliaries can be thought of as a **verb phrase**, similar to the noun phrases discussed in the previous section:

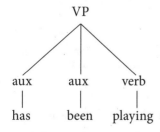

There are four subclasses of auxiliary verbs in English: **HAVE-auxiliary**, **BE-auxiliary**, DO-auxiliary, and modal auxiliaries.

The HAVE-auxiliary

The auxiliary verb *have* is used in the **perfect** forms. Perfect forms tend to express completion of the action of the verb.

Present Perfect

Maria <u>has seen</u> the last of the summer wine.
The Oakridge Boys <u>have</u> not <u>had</u> a single in many years.

Past Perfect

Pat and Chris <u>had known</u> each other for several years before they tied the knot.

The BE-auxiliary

The auxiliary verb *be* is used in the progressive forms. Progressive forms tend to express the ongoing nature of the action of the verb.

Present Progressive

I <u>am sending</u> this via e-mail.
The tomatoes <u>are rotting</u> on the counter.

Past Progressive

Damian <u>was walking</u> down Broadway when he was spotted by the talent scout.
They <u>were planning</u> a new landscaping project but decided against it.

The auxiliary verb *be* is also used in the **passive** forms.

Present Passive

Lately Bob <u>is tormented</u> by guilt because of the lies he told his family.
Cheryl and Tania <u>are</u> often <u>entrusted</u> with the confidences of their friends.

Past Passive

Last year, Arthur <u>was given</u> the most prestigious prize in his field.
Even though I <u>was asked</u> to participate, I refused on moral grounds.

The DO-auxiliary

The DO-auxiliary is sometimes referred to as a "dummy" auxiliary since it does not add to the meaning of the verb form in the way that *have* and *be* are thought to. Auxiliary *do* is used when negating a verb in the simple present or simple past or forming a question in those tenses:

I live in Seattle.   I <u>do</u> not live in Seattle.   <u>Do</u> you live in Seattle?
I spoke to Raheema yesterday.   I <u>did</u> not speak to Raheema yesterday.
<u>Did</u> you speak to Raheema yesterday?

Auxiliary *do* can also be used to add emphasis to a sentence: *No, really I <u>do</u> love you. It's just that....*

The PDE verb system is summarized in the chart below.

ACTIVE	Simple	Progressive	Perfect	Perfect-progressive
Past	took	was taking	had taken	had been taking
Present	takes	is taking	has taken	has been taking
Future I	will take	will be taking	will have taken	will have been taking
Future II	is going to take	is going to be taking	is going to have taken	is going to have been taking

PASSIVE	Simple	Progressive	Perfect	Perfect-progressive
Past	was taken	was being taken	had been taken	had been being taken
Present	is taken	is being taken	has been taken	has been being taken
Future I	will be taken	will be being taken	will have been taken	will have been being taken
Future II	is going to be taken	is going to be being taken	is going to have been taken	is going to have been being taken

(Some of the longer verb forms in the above chart are often avoided in writing for stylistic reasons.)

Generating the Forms of the Verbs

When one learns a verb in English, one commonly learns to recite three forms of that verb:

write   wrote   written
see   saw   seen

These three forms are called the principal parts of the verb. These parts are:

1. Base form   *write*
2. Simple past   *wrote*
3. Past participle   *written*

From these three forms one is able to generate each of the verb forms listed in the above chart.

Modal Auxiliaries

A third subclass of auxiliary verbs is the group of modal auxiliaries: *will*, *would*, *may*, *might*, *can*, *could*, *shall*, *should*, *must*. Modal auxiliaries express subtle mood nuances within the verb phrase: ability, obligation, possibility, permission or desire.

Ability:	*He <u>can</u> speak 17 languages.*
Weak obligation:	*You <u>should</u> give the money back.*
Strong obligation:	*You <u>must</u> enclose a check with the order.*
Possibility:	*They <u>might</u> show up later.*
Permission:	*You <u>may</u> come along if you would like.*

A Note on Modal Auxiliaries and the Subjunctive

Many languages express some of these nuances through changes in the verb form. Those who have studied other languages will recognize that some of the nuances expressed through the modal auxiliaries in PDE are expressed through the use of the subjunctive mood in other languages, as was the case in earlier stages of English. While the subjunctive mood in English is no longer a very robust grammatical or semantic category, our system of modal auxiliaries has taken on much of the load of the subjunctive. Consider the very nuanced meanings conveyed in the following:

(Upon hearing a knock at the door):	
Well, that <u>will</u> be John.	Absolute certainty
Well, that <u>must</u> be John.	High certainty
Well, that <u>should</u> be John.	Some certainty
Well, that <u>could</u> be John.	Low certainty
Well, that <u>might</u> be John.	Uncertainty

English modals are very frequent. The use of modal auxiliaries is much more important to a full description of English than many grammatical traditions have acknowledged, and they are quite important for the history of English.

THE ADJECTIVE

An **adjective** is often defined as a word that describes or modifies a noun.

A <u>black</u> cat
The <u>square</u> stone

In these noun phrases *black* describes *cat* and *square* describes *stone*. With adjectives, the semantic definition tends to work pretty well. However, in terms of structural behavior, adjectives are easily definable because they show comparative and superlative forms, either through changes to the word (*big* → *bigger*) or through the arrangement of words (*beautiful* → *more beautiful*).

Degree

Positive Degree

The **positive** degree of an adjective describes a noun without comparison to any other noun, such as in the examples, *a black cat* or *the square stone.*

Comparative Degree

The **comparative** degree is used when comparing exactly two nouns according to some quality.

> Jack is <u>taller</u> than Raymond.
> Dogs are <u>more sociable</u> than cats.

Here *Jack* is ascribed more of the quality "tallness" than *Raymond* is. In terms of the quality "sociability," *dogs* are said to have more of it than *cats* do.

These sentences also show another formal aspect of the comparative: sometimes the comparative degree is marked with an inflectional ending –*er*, as in *taller.* That is, the comparative can be **synthetic**. (Grammatical relationships expressed by word-forming processes can be described as synthetic.) In other instances, the comparative is marked syntactically through a **periphrastic** construction with the adverb *more*, as in *more reliable.* (A periphrastic construction is one which involves more than one word.) The general patterns for using -*er* or *more* are given below, after the presentation of the superlative degree.

Superlative Degree

The **superlative** degree is used to compare more than two nouns.

> Jack is the <u>tallest</u> of all the students.
> Agatha is the <u>most reliable</u> of all my friends.

Jack is ascribed the most of the quality "tallness" out of a set of several students. *Agatha* is said to have the superlative degree of "reliability" among all of the speaker's friends. As with -*er* and *more* in the comparative degree, the superlative degree is formed either with the inflectional suffix -*est* or with the adverb *most.*

-er/-est or more/most?

The choice of the suffixes (-*er*/-*est*) or the adverbs (*more*/*most*) is another area of English grammar in which there has long been considerable variation. Unsurprisingly, and commensurate with grammarian attempts to prescribe correct usage, much anxiety has arisen concerning the forms. Most grammars give rules of usage more or less in accordance with the patterns described below.

Adjectives of one syllable build the comparative and superlative forms with the addition of the inflectional suffixes *-er* or *-est* respectively.

big	→	bigger ... biggest
tall	→	taller ... tallest
high	→	higher ... highest
thick	→	thicker ... thickest
slow	→	slower ... slowest
red	→	redder ... reddest

Adjectives with more than two syllables build the comparative and superlative forms with the adverbs *more* and *most* respectively.

beautiful	→	more beautiful ... most beautiful
excellent	→	more excellent ... most excellent
violent	→	more violent ... most violent
pernicious	→	more pernicious ... most pernicious
tumultuous	→	more tumultuous ... most tumultuous

In regard to those adjectives with two syllables the most uncertainty arises. Two-syllable adjectives that end in *-y, -er, -le, -some,* or *-ow* can combine with the suffixes *-er* and *-est* in the comparative and superlative:

sunny	→	sunnier ... sunniest
tender	→	tenderer ... tenderest
humble	→	humbler ... humblest
handsome	→	handsomer ... handsomest
narrow	→	narrower ... narrowest

While *sunnier* and *sunniest* do not seem objectionable, one also hears *more sunny* and *most sunny* quite frequently. *Tenderer/tenderest, humbler/humblest,* and *handsomer/handsomest,* however, are often rejected by English speakers as wrong-sounding; preference seems to be for *more tender, most humble, more handsome,* etc.

Part of this confusion stems from the fact that number of syllables may be a secondary factor in the development of rules for the choice between *-er/-est* and *more/most.* The patterning is also sensitive at least in part to the etymological origin (the historical source) of the adjective. Adjectives that have been in the language since OE felicitously combine with the older suffixes *-er/-est*. These older adjectives tend to be of one syllable, or to end in suffixes like *-y, -er, -le,* and *-ow*. Adjectives that entered the language later as borrowings from languages like French or Latin combine more easily with the later-developed syntactic patterns using *more* and *most*. These borrowed adjectives tended to be multisyllabic.

In PDE, since a great many of those older OE adjectives are of one syllable or had ended in *-iġ* (which becomes *-y*), *-er,* or *-le,* etc., and since adjectives borrowed later tend to be multisyllabic, it appears that the rule for choosing *-er/-est* or *more/most* is about syllable length. But in many cases, the rule reflects the historical development of these patterns and the etymological history of the adjectives. The fact that forms like *evilest,* as in *the evilest man on earth,* do not sound completely objectionable may reflect the fact that *evil* is an OE word, OE *yfel*. However, there are also ample instances where the origin of the adjective does not seem to predict its comparative/ superlative pattern and even multisyllabic borrowed adjectives have appeared and do appear with -er/-est: *pleasanter, crueler, sincerer, politer.*

Attributive and Predicate Adjectives

Another structural behavior of adjectives is that they may occur in attributive or predicative position. An **attributive adjective** occurs in the position in front of the noun it modifies:

He wore a <u>green</u> jacket.

A predicate adjective appears after a linking verb, like the **copular verb** *be*, and states some quality about the noun that is functioning as the subject of the verb:

His jacket is <u>green</u>.

Some adjectives cannot appear in both positions. *Utter* can only occur in attributive position:

He is an utter fool.
Not
*His foolishness was utter.

Similarly, *alive* can only occur in predicative position:

The monster was alive.
Not
*An alive monster can be quite dangerous.

THE DETERMINER CLASSES

Determiners occupy the initial position in a noun phrase, and they modify the head noun of that phrase. (For this reason they could be treated as a subclass of adjectives, but here we treat them in their own section. The determiners in English include the definite and indefinite articles, the demonstrative determiners, and the possessive determiners.

The Definite and Indefinite Articles

The Definite Article
The form of the **definite article** in PDE is the invariable form *the*.

> The blanket was left crumpled on the floor.

The Indefinite Article
The **indefinite article** in PDE has two forms, *a* and *an*. Most students have learned the rule that *a* is used before consonants and *an* is used before vowels. However, it is very important to remember that the distribution of *a* and *an* depends on consonant and vowel sounds, not letters.

> an apple
> a desk

But also:

> a university
> an honor

A precedes *university* because the noun begins with a consonant sound while *an* occurs before *honor* because the <h> is silent.

Demonstrative Determiners
Demonstrative determiners have the same forms as the demonstrative pronouns and, like the demonstratives pronouns, they are also used to establish distance.

	Sing.	**Pl.**
Proximal	this	these
Distal	that	those

The difference then between demonstrative pronouns and demonstrative determiners is their syntactic positioning, the place of the word in a phrase or sentence. A demonstrative pronoun refers to an entity (often an entire proposition) and assumes a noun function:

<u>That</u> is the worst movie ever.

That refers to the movie under discussion (probably one just viewed or mentioned) and functions as the subject of the sentence.

In contrast, the demonstrative determiner does not refer to an entity but rather modifies a noun.

<u>That</u> movie was very good.

That, in the sentence above, is a determiner of *movie*.

Possessive Determiners

Possessive determiners are determiners in so far as they occupy the initial position of the noun phrase and modify the head noun. But they also have pronominal qualities. That is, they both modify the head noun in a noun phrase and refer to a possessor, which, like pronoun antecedents, will already have been established in the context.

I sold <u>my</u> car.
The rabbits stored <u>their</u> food.

The forms of the possessive determiner are:

		Sing.		**Pl.**
1st person		my		our
2nd person		your		your
3rd person				
Mas.		his	All genders	their
Fem.		her		
Neut.		its		

Quantifiers

Quantifiers belong to a functional category related to the class of determiners. Quantifiers are words that express some notion of quantity concerning the noun in the noun phrase. Quantifiers include: *none, some, many, much, all, several, a few, a number*, etc. Quantifiers appear at the beginning of the noun phrase, with or without the linking preposition *of*:

<u>All</u> the books were collected and distributed to the children.
Or
<u>All of</u> the books were collected and distributed to the children.

Quantifiers may also be used as pronouns in the case that the noun referred to has been established in the discourse:

<u>All</u> were collected and distributed to the children.

THE ADVERB

The word class traditionally called **adverb** is not as coherent as the other parts of speech. The problem is that the functions of the various members of the traditional adverb class are quite different. Thus an adverb is said to modify a verb, an adjective, another adverb or an entire clause. We will treat each of these functions separately.

Modifying a Verb

An adverb may modify a verb, adding information concerning time, place/direction, manner, or frequency.

Time
I will call you <u>tomorrow</u>.
Allan saw the play <u>yesterday</u>.
We will have a new plan <u>soon</u>.
<u>Next</u>, the band will play "Over There."

Place/Direction
Let's stop and rest <u>here</u> for a while.
Seymour walked Patience <u>home</u> after the party.
We are heading <u>uptown</u> to meet some friends.

Manner
Matt spoke <u>quickly</u> but <u>precisely</u>.
Drive <u>safely</u>!

Many adverbs of manner end in *-ly*. In such cases, the adverb is derived from an adjective: *quick* → *quickly, precise* → *precisely, safe* → *safely*. However, some adverbs of manner are identical to the corresponding adjective: *fast, hard*.

The train moved <u>fast</u> along the new rails.
It rained <u>hard</u> last night for about two hours.

Frequency

Those dogs <u>always</u> bark when a plane passes over.

We take the train into the city <u>often</u>.

I have <u>never</u> heard such nonsense in all my life!

Adverbs that modify verbs tend to occur in syntactic positions close to the verb; time adverbs, which have a lot of flexibility, are exceptional in this respect:

> Yesterday, the mail was late.
> Or
> The mail was late yesterday.

However, sometimes in very literary registers, the adverb modifying a verb will be placed at the beginning of the sentence (this is particularly the case with frequency adverbs), and this placement may cause a syntactic rearrangement.

> We have seldom required more than 200 pages of reading in a single night.
> →   Seldom have we required more than 200 pages of reading in a single night.

Modifies an Adjective or Another Adverb

Essentially, when an adverb modifies an adjective or another adverb, it is stating a degree of the quality expressed by that adjective or adverb. Thus these adverbs are commonly called degree adverbs. Degree adverbs include: *really, very, too, absolutely, exceedingly, frightfully, immensely, totally,* etc.

> The cake arrived <u>really</u> late and we feared it wouldn't arrive at all.
> The <u>frightfully</u> high doorway dwarfed even the tallest entrant.

Modifies an Entire Clause

Adverbs modifying an entire clause often give a speaker's/writer's view about the situation expressed in that clause.

> <u>Hopefully</u>, the stock market will rally in the next week.
> <u>Unfortunately</u>, we couldn't get tickets at such a late date.

THE PREPOSITION

A **preposition** is often a small word that is used to establish a specific relationship of a noun to the rest of the clause in which it appears. Prepositions may also be compound, that is, composed of several words, e.g., *in spite of.* (On the notion of the prepositional phrase, and for a provisional list of simple and compound prepositions, see Object of a Preposition, pp. 53–54.)

The relationships expressed by prepositions include the following:

Existence at single point in time: *on, at, in*
>   *The newlyweds left for Vegas <u>on</u> Monday.*

Duration of time: *since, by, for, during, in/within*
>   *They have been very happy <u>since</u> the performance.*

Sequence of time: *before, after*
>   *I will call <u>after</u> the meeting.*

Position: *in, on, at, over, above, under, underneath, beneath, below, near, next to, alongside, beside, between, opposite*
>   *The picture hangs <u>above</u> the door.*

Direction: *to, from, toward(s), in, into, on, onto, up, down, around, through, past, by, up to*
>   *We walked <u>past</u> the old school.*

Cause: *because of, for the sake of, on account of*
>   *The peasants rebelled <u>on account of</u> the new taxes.*

Concession: *in spite of, notwithstanding, regardless of*
>   *Amy still loved her couch <u>regardless of</u> the rips and tears in it.*

Condition: *in case of, in the event of*
>   *<u>In case of</u> fire, break glass.*

Purpose: *for, for the purpose of*
>   *They left <u>for</u> unspecified reasons.*

Accompaniment: *with, along with, together with*
>   *<u>Together with</u> my best friend, I visited Paris.*

Addition: *as well as*
>   *We ate quesadillas <u>as well as</u> chicken salad.*

Comparison: *as, like*
>   *Millie had eyes <u>like</u> stones.*

Instrument: *with*
> *The cable guy loosened the connection <u>with</u> a wrench.*

Means: *with, by means of*
> *Anybody can achieve his/her goals <u>with</u> hard work and integrity.*

Manner: *with, without*
> *They completed the task <u>with</u> alacrity.*
> *Sammy always arrived on time <u>without</u> fail.*

Source (including material and origin): *of, from, out of*
> *He is <u>from</u> France.*
> *Moriki made the necklace <u>from</u> silver.*
> *This handle is made <u>out of</u> pure cherry wood.*

Separation: *from*
> *You have to remove the seeds <u>from</u> the pepper before dicing it.*

Possession: *of*
> *The hideout <u>of</u> the Williams Gang is famous.*

THE CONJUNCTION

Conjunctions are words used to join words, phrases or clauses to other words, phrases or clauses. Obviously, the function of some conjunctions overlaps with that of other parts of speech, such as prepositions and certain types of adverbs that modify an entire clause. Conjunctions are divided into two main types: coordinate conjunctions and subordinate conjunctions.

Coordinate Conjunctions

Coordinate conjunctions include the additive *and*, the concessive *but*, and the disjunctive *or* (*nor*). These conjunctions may be used to link words.

Could you pass me the <u>bread</u> <u>*and*</u> <u>butter</u>.

I was always <u>elated</u> <u>*or*</u> <u>sad</u> with no indifferent feelings at all.

Coordinate conjunctions may also link phrases.

Get <u>out of my dreams</u> <u>*and*</u> <u>into my car</u>.

The fustian cowboy *and* the scantily dressed tightrope walker began a duet.

Coordinate conjunctions may also link clauses.

You don't have to go home *but* you can't stay here.

I will have satisfaction *or* I will write a letter to your boss.

Subordinate Conjunctions

Subordinate conjunctions, such as *while, although,* etc., are used to introduce subordinate or dependent clauses. Dependent clauses include adverb clauses, relative (or adjective) clauses, and noun clauses. These dependent clause types and the subordinate conjunctions used to introduce them are taken up later in this chapter.

FUNCTIONAL VERSUS LEXICAL WORDS

In the preceding treatment, pronouns, determiners, and auxiliary verbs were treated within the larger categories of nouns, adjectives, and verbs, respectively. However, pronouns, determiners, and auxiliary verbs, as well as conjunctions and certain adverbs, like degree adverbs, and prepositions, according to some grammars, are function words, while nouns, non-auxiliary verbs and adjectives are lexical words.

Function words express the grammar of a language in so far as they might refer to a noun phrase previously mentioned, as does a pronoun: *Mike slept all day. I think he had a fever.* The pronoun *he* in this example refers to the noun *Mike.* Or, function words might be used to identify whether a noun is definite or indefinite within the discourse: *the dog ~ a dog.*

Lexical words, on the other hand, express the content of an utterance; they are, generally speaking, less abstract than are function words. Consider the following sentence:

The dog has returned.

Words like *the* and *has* are function words. Their job is to express grammatical meanings like definiteness in the noun or perfective aspect in the verb phrase. *Dog* and *returned,* however, are lexical; they convey concrete, referential meanings. In fact the lexical content of this sentence is so concrete that one has a good idea of the meaning of the sentence from the words *dog* and *returned* alone.

The distinction between lexical and function words is important for the study of the history of a language for several reasons. One reason is that lexical and function words differ in terms of how frequently or easily new words may be developed in each. New nouns, verbs, and adjectives are constantly emerging: *Obamacare* (noun), *to facetime* (verb), *bootylicious* (adjective). New function words are less common, at least within the lifespan of a single generation. Another important difference between lexical and function words is that new lexical words are often consciously added to the language; if someone invents a new gadget, he or she names the gadget intentionally. New function words cannot generally be consciously legislated.

For example, it is common to recognize several possible gender configurations beyond the traditional male–female binary. We understand some persons to be transgender, cisgender, transitioning, etc. Some have advocated a new set of pronouns to include all such gender identities. To date, however, such an extended pronoun system has not taken root, and despite the many and varied gender possibilities, speakers continue to identify definite, human, third-person, singular referents as *he* or *she*:

Chaz Bono is now 48 years old. He used to appear on his mother's and father's variety show in the 1970s.

Even though Chaz Bono was born female, he identifies as male, and so one would make the choice of using *he* (and its forms) to refer to him.

EXERCISES

The following exercises are intended to provide an opportunity to review the basic concepts and terms covered in the preceding pages. Answers to the exercises can be found at the back of the book. Be sure to review the relevant sections if necessary. For example, if you misidentify a noun in #1, be sure to review "The Noun" on pp. 22–23.

2.1   Identify the part of speech for each word in the following sentence.

Example: The dog bites.
    the   determiner
    dog   noun
    bites   verb

That large man in the yellow hat spoke loudly about monkeys and literature.
that   _____
large   _____
man   _____

in   _____

the   _____

yellow   _____

hat   _____

spoke   _____

loudly   _____

about   _____

monkeys   _____

and   _____

literature _____

2.2 **Fill in the blanks with an appropriate word and identify the part of speech of that word.**

    a. The _____ ran down the street. (part of speech _____)
    One _____but two _____-s. (part of speech _____)

    b. The _____ cat (part of speech _____)
    My cat is _____-er than yours (part of speech _____)
    but his cat is the _____-est of all. (part of speech _____)

    c. Today I _____. Yesterday I _____-ed.
    (part of speech _____, _____)

    I am _____-ing a letter. (part of speech _____)

2.3 **Identify the person, gender (if relevant), and number of the following pronoun forms. Remember that some forms can be both singular and plural.**

    a. she _____ _____ _____
    b. we   _____ _____
    c. they _____ _____
    d. I   _____ _____
    e. you _____ _____ _____

2.4 Identify the following determiners as definite article, indefinite article, possessive determiner, or demonstrative determiner.

    a. a/an   _____
    b. his   _____
    c. that/this   _____
    d. our   _____
    e. the   _____

2.5 Identify the tense of the following verb forms as present or past.

    a. goes   _____
    b. walked   _____
    c. feel   _____
    d. is   _____
    e. has   _____

2.6 Identify the following forms as progressive or perfect.

    a. is going   _____
    b. has gone   _____
    c. was talking   _____
    d. has talked   _____
    e. will be talking   _____
    f. will have gone   _____

2.7

    a. What is the present participle of the verb *talk*?   _____
    b. What is the past participle of the verb *talk*?   _____
    c. What is the present participle of the verb *go*?   _____
    d. What is the past participle of the verb *go*?   _____

2.8

    a. Identify the prepositions in the following sentence.

       On the table you will find a list of things you should buy at the grocery store.

b. Identify the conjunctions in the following sentence.

Talitha and Connor like baseball and hockey, but neither of them is planning to go to sports camp or even to play on the teams next year.

2.9 **Perform the following functions on the sentence below. Note that performing some of these functions will entail changing other words in the sentence to maintain agreement.**

The big dog goes to his good doghouse and sleeps soundly.

a. Put the adjectives in the superlative degree.
b. Make the nouns plural. Note that the change will require you to alter the forms of the verbs and the possessive determiner as well.
c. Put the verbs in the simple past.

2.10 **Which form of the pronoun (subjective, possessive, or objective) would you use in the following sentences?**

a. *This box belongs to her but this one is _____.*
b. *_____ go running every morning at 6.*
c. *The sailor gave _____ a pat on the back.*

BASIC SYNTACTIC RELATIONS FOR NOUNS

By "syntactic relations for nouns" we mean the grammatical roles that nouns play in their sentences. The basic syntactic relations for nouns are the following: subject, direct object, indirect object, object of a preposition, and subject complement.

SUBJECT

A particular difficulty in learning the syntactic functions for nouns is that they are often defined semantically, a problem we encountered earlier in definitions of parts of speech. For instance, the **subject** is often said to be "what the sentence is about." Hence, in the following sentence,

<u>Sandwiches</u> are often made of bread and meat.

Sandwiches is the subject of the sentence, and it is in fact "what the sentence is about."

While this kind of semantic definition will work for some sentences, there are many sentences for which it will not. Consider the following sentence:

As for vacations, <u>I</u> never take them.

What is this sentence about? One could easily say that it is about *vacations*, but *vacations* is not the subject of the sentence (it is the object of the preposition *as for*). The subject of this sentence is the subjective first-person pronoun *I*.

Another common semantic definition of the subject is that the subject is "the noun that is performing the action of the verb." Hence, in the sentence

<u>Solita</u> carried the dictionary.

Solita, the subject of the sentence, performs the action of the verb *carried*.

But semantic definitions of syntactic phenomena are usually insufficient. Consider:

<u>Jack</u> heard a noise.

While "Jack" is the subject, it can hardly be said that he has "performed" any action. If anything we would say that he is the experiencer of the noise. Therefore, it is a good practice to begin identifying the subject according to certain of its structural behaviors.

Subject–Verb Agreement

The subject is the noun with which the verb agrees in number.

Subject	Verb
<u>Jack</u>	<u>has</u> taken three years of French.
<u>The exchange students</u>	<u>have</u> taken three years of French.
<u>Jack and Jill</u>	<u>have</u> taken three years of French.

In the first sentence, the subject *Jack* is in the third-person singular and therefore requires the singular form *has*. In contrast, the subjects of the second and third sentences, *students* and *Jack and Jill* (a compound subject) are third-person plural and thus take the form *have*. Of course this test is of limited value for ModE since our verbs do not conjugate as much as verbs do in some other languages.

Syntactic Position

The subject is the noun that appears to the immediate left of the verb in a simple declarative sentence.

Subject	Verb
<u>Jack</u>	<u>wrote</u> a letter about the incident to the newspapers.
<u>Maria</u>	<u>decided</u> to take more linguistics courses.

There are a few situations that can complicate this description. First, it may happen that certain material may intervene between subject and verb:

<u>Jack</u>, in anger, <u>wrote</u> a letter about the incident to the newspapers.
<u>Maria</u>, who had been a math major, <u>decided</u> to study linguistics.
<u>The problem</u>, clearly, should be reassessed.

In the first instance, *Jack* is still the noun immediately to the left of the verb *wrote*: *in anger* is a prepositional phrase. In the second sentence *who had been a math major* is a relative clause and can be removed, thus revealing *Maria* as the noun immediately to the left of the verb *decided*. In the third sentence, an adverb, *clearly*, intervenes between the subject and the verb in order to express the speaker's/writer's opinion.

DIRECT OBJECT

The **direct object** is largely semantically and syntactically coherent. Semantically, the direct object is a patient of the verb, which means that it is the noun that is affected by the action expressed in the verb (and in the case of direct objects, the verb is almost always an action-type verb). Syntactically, the direct object is the noun that will become the subject in a passive transformation; that is, the noun that will become the subject if we make the verb passive. For example:

The locusts destroyed <u>the crops</u>.
direct object

→   *<u>The crops</u> were destroyed by the locusts.*
    subject

In the first sentence, *the crops* is the thing that was destroyed. Also it is the noun phrase that becomes the subject when the sentence is made passive.

INDIRECT OBJECT

An **indirect object** can only occur when there is a direct object present. And only a limited number of verbs can take a direct object and an indirect object.

In any sentence with an indirect object (and thus also a direct object), there are two noun phrases after the verb. The indirect object will always be the first noun phrase of the two. Consider the following sentence:

Bill	*gave*	*Renate*	*the letter*
	verb	NP 1	NP 2

Note that there are two noun phrases after the verb. The first noun phrase, *Renate*, is the indirect object. The second, *the letter*, is the direct object.

Bill	*gave*	*Renate*	*the letter*
	verb	indirect	direct

A good syntactic test for the indirect object is that the indirect object can be transformed into a prepositional phrase with *to* or *for* following the direct object without changing the meaning of the sentence:

> Bill gave <u>Renate</u> the letter.
→ Bill gave the letter <u>to Renate</u>.

> Andrew bought <u>Tony</u> a sweater.
→ Andrew bought a sweater <u>for Tony</u>.

As the examples in the above sentences also illustrate, the indirect object is almost always animate, usually a person or people. (Note carefully: the nouns *Renate* and *Tony* are no longer indirect objects after the transformation; they have become objects of the prepositions *to* and *for*. Because of the problematic inclusion of semantics into grammatical description, some grammatical traditions are confused about this fact.)

OBJECT OF A PREPOSITION

The noun following a preposition in a prepositional phrase is the **object of the preposition**. Some examples:

in the car
at a dog park
under some tables
next to an abandoned house

The grammatical concept of the prepositional phrase tends to be intuitive for English speakers. Once a preposition is identified, locating its object is a relatively simple matter.

The following is a list of some common prepositions in English. (See also "The Preposition," pp. 43–45.)

Simple prepositions: *about, across, after, against, around, at, before, behind, beside, between, beyond, by, despite, down, during, except, for, from, in, inside, like, near, of, on, over, past, since, through, till, to, toward, under, until, up, within, without,* etc.

Compound or complex prepositions: *according to, ahead of, along with, apart from, away from, because of, contrary to, due to, instead of, next to, on to, out from, out from under, prior to, regardless of, subject to, thanks to, together with, up against,* etc.

SUBJECT COMPLEMENT

A linking verb connects the subject with information in the predicate. Among the most common linking verbs are *to be, to become, to appear,* and *to seem.*

> The gardener <u>was</u> a good chess player.
> A good teacher <u>can become</u> a great teacher.
> The boy <u>appeared</u> sad after the death of his goldfish.
> The girl <u>seemed</u> happy after the success of the concert.

Note that in each of these sentences, the noun or adjective following the linking verb restates something about the subject. Another way to say this is that the noun or adjective in the predicate completes (complements) the subject: it is the **subject complement**.

OBJECT COMPLEMENT

Similar to the subject complement, which completes the subject, objects may take a complement, as in the following sentence:

> The subcommittee named Reda its president.

In the sentence, *Reda* is the direct object of the verb *named* and *its president* is an **object complement** since it "fills out" information concerning the office to which Reda was named. Object complements may be adjectives too:

> Colleen considered her classmates <u>smart</u>, but she didn't trust their dedication.

In the above sentence, one may use *to be* between the complement and the adjective:

Colleen considered her classmates *to be* <u>smart</u>, but she didn't trust their dedication.

APPOSITIVE

A noun phrase in any position can be expanded by another noun phrase following it. In PDE this phrase, known an **appositive**, is usually set apart by commas in writing and by a lowered and separate intonation contour in speech. The use of apposition is a significant feature of much early literature in English.

<u>Greg Hanson</u>, *<u>our newest board member</u>*, brings experience to the team.
We read a book about <u>"The Wanderer,"</u> *<u>an Old English poem</u>*.

EXERCISES

2.11 **Identify which of the following describes the subject, the direct object, the indirect object, and the object of the preposition.**

   a. The noun phrase with which the verb agrees in number, and most often the noun phrase immediately to the left of the verb is the

   _____.

   b. The noun phrase which immediately follows a preposition and makes a prepositional phrase with it is the_____.
   c. When two noun phrases follow the verb and are not in apposition or joined by a conjunction, the first noun phrase is the _____. The second is the _____.

2.12 **Identify the subject, the direct object, the indirect object, and the object of the preposition in the following sentence.**

   The captain of the ship gave the child a toy.

   a. Subject   _____
   b. Direct object   _____
   c. Indirect object   _____
   d. Object of the preposition _____

2.13 The following two sentences are both made up of a noun phrase, a verb, and another noun phrase. In both sentences, the second noun phrase is *a doctor*. What is the difference between the syntactic function of *a doctor* in the first sentence and the syntactic function of *a doctor* in the second?

a. *The woman is a doctor.*
b. *The woman sees a doctor.*

2.14 The following two sentences are equivalent in meaning. What is the difference between the syntactic function of the noun phase *the golfer* in the first sentence and the syntactic function of the noun phrase *the golfer* in the second?

a. *The pro gave the golfer a good tip.*
b. *The pro gave a good tip to the golfer.*

SENTENCES

Sentences fall into three basic categories: simple sentences, compound sentences, and complex sentences.

SIMPLE SENTENCES

In a **simple sentence** there is a single subject and a single predicate. The predicate is made up of the verb, its modifiers, and its objects:

<u>I</u>	<u>saw Mick</u>.
subject	predicate

<u>The forlorn lover</u>	<u>cried over the breakup of his affair</u>.
subject	predicate

Sometimes the predicate or the subject may be compounded. However, such sentences are still considered simple since the entire subject is doing the entire predicate (as opposed to one part of the subject performing one part of the predicate and the other part of the subject performing the other part of the predicate).

<u>Jack </u>and <u>Jill</u> went up the hill.
Samantha <u>turned on the television</u> and <u>watched the news</u>.

COMPOUND SENTENCES

A **compound sentence** is one in which one or more simple sentences are joined with a coordinate conjunction (*and, or, nor, but*):

> *I have seen the truth* and *it is good.*
> *We wanted to go to Nevada* but *the campground was closed.*
> *You can stay and be part of the solution* or *you can leave and represent all that is wrong with your generation.*

Compound sentences are said to be paratactically arranged because their arrangement involves placing equivalent entities side by side.

COMPLEX SENTENCES

In a **complex sentence** a subordinate clause is contained within the main clause. A clause contains a subject and a predicate. We can think of a simple sentence as a single independent clause. But some clauses cannot stand alone. Consider, for example,

> She became a veterinarian.
> and She became a veterinarian because she loved dogs.

She became a veterinarian contains a single subject and a single predicate: it is a simple sentence. In the second sentence, *She became a veterinarian because she loved dogs*, the first clause, *she became a veterinarian*, is the main clause. The second clause, *because she loved dogs*, while it contains a subject, *she*, and a predicate, *loved dogs*, begins with a word, *because*, which establishes a dependent relationship to the main clause. *Because she loved dogs* is a subordinate clause in this sentence: it cannot stand alone as a complete sentence.

There are three types of subordinate clauses: adverb clauses, adjective clauses/relative clauses, and noun clauses, all of which we review in the following sections.

Adverb Clauses

Adverb clauses modify some aspect of the predicate, usually the main verbal idea. These clauses may indicate:

Time
Mike left <u>after they had given out all of the prizes</u>.
Wilhelmina saw the movie <u>before she actually read the review</u>.

Concession

The squirrel remained in the mighty oak <u>although the tree had stopped producing acorns</u>.

Cause

I wrote to the company <u>because they should know about my concerns</u>.

Place

Maryanne started up right <u>where Jason had left off</u>.

Condition

I will call you <u>if you are home before dinner</u>.

The word that introduces the adverb clause is called a subordinate conjunction (see p. 46). Some common subordinate conjunctions used to introduce adverb clauses are:

Because, after, before, while, as, even though, although, since, if, unless, so (that), where(ever), when(ever), etc.

However, certain of these subordinate conjunctions can also be prepositions. Consider:

I left *before they arrived.*
I left *before the party.*

In the first sentence, *before* is an adverb clause subordinator and it is followed by its clause (the group of words with the subject *they* and predicate *arrived*). In the second sentence, *before* is a preposition and it is followed by a noun phrase, *the party*, its object.

I left	*before*	*they*	*arrived.*
	subordinate conjunction	subject	verb

I left	*before*	*the party.*
	preposition	object of the preposition

Relative Clauses

A **relative clause**, sometimes also called an adjective clause, modifies a noun. The word that introduces a relative clause is called a relative pronoun. Which relative pronoun is used depends on a number of criteria. If the noun being modified is not animate (and especially not human), the relative pronouns *that* or *which* may be used:

We bought a computer that had over 20 GB of RAM.
The school _which I attended in 1974_ has now closed.

If the noun being modified is an animate being and human, the relative pronoun _who/whom_ is used, although _that_ is frequently used as well.

The bank teller _who works in Window J_ will be able to help you.
My best friend, _whom you met last month_, is leaving for Russia next Monday.

The two examples above also illustrate case. The difference between _who_ and _whom_ is that _who_ is used when the relative pronoun is the subject or subject complement and _whom_ is used when it is the direct or indirect object or the object of a preposition. In the grammatical sense, _who_ is subjective; _whom_ is objective. In this way, note that _who_ in the clause _who works in Window J_ is the subject of the verb _works_ while _whom_ in the clause _whom you met_ is the direct object of _met_. No reasonable language authority insists on maintaining the difference between _who_ and _whom_ in PDE.

Pied Piping and Preposition Stranding
PDE shows a lot of variation when the relative pronoun is the object of a preposition. One major variation is between stranding the preposition at the end of its clause (preposition stranding) and placing it in front of the relative pronoun (pied piping). In the following example, the preposition is stranded at the end of its clause:

The student _who/whom I gave the paper to_ is not responsible for any of the errors.

Other times the preposition is placed in front of the relative pronoun, in which case we say it has been pied-piped to the front of its clause.

The student _to whom I gave the paper_ is not responsible for any of the errors.

When the preposition is pied-piped to the beginning of the clause, the relative pronoun for animate referents, especially people, must be _whom_ and the relative pronoun for things must be _which_. If not the sentence is ungrammatical:

The student to whom I gave...
not   *The student _to who/that I gave_...

The house in which they live...
not   *The house _in that they live is_...

Relative Pronoun Deletion
Relative pronouns in English may sometimes be deleted when the relative pronoun is not the subject of its clause: *I gave Mary the book that you recommended* or *I gave Mary the book you recommended.*

Noun Clauses
Noun clauses are subordinate clauses that function as nouns, i.e., as subjects, direct objects, etc. Consider the sentences:

Do we have to turn the paper in on Friday? I am unclear about that.

The word *that* in the second sentence is a demonstrative pronoun and it is the object of the preposition *about.* Its referent is the entire first sentence, a questioning of whether or not the paper must be turned in on Friday. We can combine these two sentences such that the question is embedded within the second sentence:

I am unclear about whether we have to turn the paper in on Friday or not.

Now the question is a noun clause within the main sentence.

Note that after that sentence's conversion into a noun clause, its function is still that of the demonstrative pronoun before the replacement, i.e., the object of the preposition *about.* We distinguish three types of noun clauses, depending on the type of underlying sentences they derive from.

Type I: Noun Clauses Derived from Statements
A noun clause derived from a declarative statement (not a question but a statement of fact) is introduced by the subordinate conjunction *that.*

Jack helps the elderly. I noticed that.
→   I noticed *that* Jack helps the elderly.

When the noun clause derived from a statement is functioning as a direct object, the subordinate conjunction *that* may be omitted.

I notice *that* Jack helps the elderly.
or   I notice Ø Jack helps the elderly.

When a noun clause derived from a declarative statement is the object of a preposition, English uses *the fact that* as a complex subordinator.

    Jack helps the elderly. We talked about that.

→   We talked about <u>*the fact that* Jack helps the elderly</u>.

The fact that can also appear in other contexts. For example, *it* varies with *that* in introducing Type I noun clauses as subjects:

> <u>*That*</u> *the company moved its headquarters out of the city surprised everyone.*
> <u>*The fact that*</u> *the company moved its headquarters out of the city surprised everyone.*

In fact, many speakers find the use of *that* to introduce a noun clause as a subject to be odd, and prefer *the fact that* or some other way of expression. Other expressions like *the idea that*, *the concept that*, etc. may also be used in such contexts, but *the fact that* appears to have become more general in that usage.

Type II: Noun Clauses Derived from Yes/No Questions

A noun clause derived from a yes/no question (i.e., a question for which the appropriate answer is *yes*, *no*, or *maybe*) is introduced with the subordinator *if* or *whether*.

    Will Jack be there? She always asks that.

→   She always asks <u>*whether* Jack will be there</u>.

or   She always asks <u>*if* Jack will be there</u>.

If the noun clause derived from a yes/no question is functioning as the subject, only *whether* should be used in formal English.

    Is it raining? That is important.

→   <u>Whether</u> it is raining or not is important.

Type III: Noun Clauses Derived from Wh- Questions

A noun clause derived from a *wh-* question (*who*, *where*, *when*, *how*, etc.) uses the same *wh-* word as the word to introduce the noun clause.

    Where is France? Selma asked me that.

→   Selma asked me <u>*where* France is</u>.[4]

    Who is to blame? I don't know that.

→   I don't know <u>*who* is to blame</u>.

---

4 The verb in the embedded noun clause may be shifted to agree with the tense of the main verb: *Selma asked where France was.*

EXERCISES

2.15 Identify the main clause in each of the following sentences.

    a. After Jennifer finished the book, she loaned it to Marguerite.
    b. The parrot and the budgie ate the birdseed after they finished the worms.
    c. Although Jonathan ran very fast, Machiko was able to catch him easily.
    d. When the clock chimed, the whole mantle shook.

2.16 Identify the relative clauses in each of the following sentences.

    a. The movie that we saw last week is still playing at the theater today.
    b. The poster is concealing a door which provides an emergency exit.
    c. Marcus is a collector who really knows his antiques.
    d. Fluffy is the only dog I love.

2.17 Rewrite each of the following pairs of sentences, replacing the demonstrative pronoun (*that*) in the second sentence with a noun clause constructed from the first sentence. For example:

> *The house was haunted. The plumber did not know <u>that</u>.*
> → *The plumber did not know that the house was haunted.*

    a. The cat was sleeping. That pleased the mouse.
    b. The fish could sing. That surprised many people.
    c. Can the parrot speak Italian? Carla is always asking that.
    d. Where is the remote? I need to know that.

CHAPTER THREE

Before English

Our study of the history of the English language begins well before there is any English language to speak of. In fact, it doesn't even begin in the geographical territory that would come to be known as England. Instead it begins at around 4,000 BCE (fifth to fourth millennium BCE) in what is modern-day Russia and the Ukraine among a group of people who are believed to have spoken a more or less single language known as Indo-European (IE). Most scholars believe that the original homeland of these Indo-Europeans was located north of the Caspian Sea and the Caucasus mountains in the Pontic-Caspian Steppe zone, shown in Figure 3.1.

FIGURE 3.1   **Probable homeland of the Indo-Europeans.**

THE INDO-EUROPEAN HOMELAND

The evidence in support of locating the Indo-European homeland in the place indicated on the map comes from both archeological and linguistic evidence. As a number of scholars have pointed out, languages descended from this original Indo-European language show common words for snow and freezing, words that give us an indication of the climate of the Indo-Europeans. In addition, certain common words for various kinds of animals (*bear, wolf, boar, bees*) and plant-life (*birch, oak, willow, apple*), and especially the lack of vocabulary for animals and plants from eastern Asia (*palm tree, camel, dates, banyan tree*), point us to an original location in Europe in a temperate climate.

There have been many theories about the homeland of the Indo-Europeans, positing that the Indo-Europeans might have originated in northern Europe, in the Balkans, or in Asia Minor, among other places. In the early 1970s, however, the archeologist Marija Gimbutas (1921–94) linked the Indo-Europeans with the culture of the Kurgans, a culture then being explored through archeological excavation in the Steppe region. One aspect of the attractiveness of the **Kurgan hypothesis** lies in the congruency between the cultural and technological life of the Kurgan people and the words shared in the languages descended from their supposed language, Indo-European. Thus commonly shared words like *wheel, plow,* and *axle* in many IE languages correspond to the fact that these Kurgan peoples were agricultural and cultivated the land, as opposed to living as gatherers. Also, it is quite clear from the discovery of burial sites that the Kurgan people who made them had a religion and a belief in an afterlife. One of the main figures of that religion has been identified as a sky god, associated with thunder. This sky-god shows up under the related names of Zeus, Jupiter, Tiw, etc. in various Indo-European languages, as does the figure of a dawn goddess, associated with spring, surviving in the Greek figure of Eos, for example, and in English the word *Easter.*

No one piece of the evidence for the connection between the Kurgan peoples and the IE language is conclusive. Instead it is the total of the body of evidence that is most compelling. Certainly Gimbutas's Kurgan hypothesis, with some modifications, remains the most influential even today. The inferential nature of the hypotheses on the origins of the Indo-European people extends to hypotheses concerning their original language as well. In fact, the question of what might be the original IE language predates the identification of the people who might have spoken such a language—a language that remains, for us, a theoretically reconstructed language based on no direct written evidence of that language.

HISTORICAL RECONSTRUCTION AND PROTO-INDO-EUROPEAN

Given that there is no direct written evidence of IE, one may well ask how we know, or how we think we know, anything about it. The answer is that we are able to build up elaborate hypotheses about past languages (or parts of languages) that we have no direct evidence for through a methodology known as linguistic reconstruction.

Sir William Jones (1746–94), a scholar and British judge in eighteenth-century India, is most often cited as the first scholar to observe that many of the older and contemporary languages of Europe and India were remarkably similar and to propose on the basis of such similarities that those languages are related to each other in that they share a common ancestor language, which no longer survives. In an address to the Asiatick Society in Calcutta in 1786, Jones remarked:

> The *Sanscrit* language, whatever be its antiquity, is of a wonderful structure; more perfect than the *Greek*, more copious than the *Latin*, and more exquisitely refined than either, yet bearing to both of them a stronger affinity, both in the roots of verbs and the forms of grammar, than could possibly have been produced by accident; so strong indeed, that no philologer could examine them all three, without believing them to have sprung from some common source, which, perhaps, no longer exists; there is a similar reason, though not quite so forcible, for supposing that both the *Gothic* and the *Celtic*, though blended with a very different idiom, had the same origin with the *Sanscrit*; and the old *Persian* might be added to the same family.[1]

While Jones's 1786 address is very often cited as the first articulation of the idea that this group of languages may once have shared a common ancestor, the notion that Greek, Latin, and even Sanskrit were related was not new and versions of this idea had been around for some time before Jones. It is a fact about the writing of history/histories that changes in intellectual ideas or even periods of history are often construed as abrupt and identified with a single historical figure or with a single event rather than as part of a complex, messy, and ongoing set of events or intellectual exchanges. Still, it is true that after 1786 the search for the original IE language became a major scholarly pursuit and many scholars developed hypotheses about the "common source" for Latin, Greek, Sanskrit, etc.

If the year 4,000 BCE is correct, or even somewhat correct, as a date for the existence of the Indo-European peoples and their language, then we are dealing with a time depth of such great proportion that it is hard to be absolutely certain of anything. It is, however, clear that Jones's proposal was right; many of the languages

---

1 Philip Baldi, *An Introduction to the Indo-European Languages* (Carbondale, IL: Southern Illinois UP, 1983), 3.

used in vast tracts of Asia, nearly all of Europe, and in more recent years carried to North and South America and many Atlantic and Pacific islands, are related. Even a very casual survey of some of these languages shows not only a significant number of clearly related lexical items, but also, and more importantly, shared grammatical structures. Consider for example these words for family relationships in Present-Day English (PDE), Latin, Classical Greek, and Sanskrit, the ancient language of India referred to in Jones's address.

English	Latin	Greek	Sanskrit
mother	māter	métēr	mātár
father	pater	patér	pitár

These words are very similar, with similar meanings, and similar patterns of sounds. It is quite possible, of course, that two completely unrelated languages may have similar words as a result of borrowing, something that happens between languages all the time. For example, English and Japanese do not share a common source in their histories but English uses words like *sushi*, *samurai*, and *futon*, all of which have been borrowed from Japanese. But notice an important difference between words like *sushi* and *samurai* on the one hand, and words like *mother* and *father* on the other. *Sushi* and *samurai* are very intricately tied to Japanese culture and the borrowing of those words is as much a borrowing of the culture as it is a borrowing of the words. Another way of thinking about this is that there was no reason for the words *sushi* and *samurai* to exist in English before their borrowing, because there were no such things as *sushi* and *samurai* among English speakers before their introduction into English from Japanese culture.

However, most languages of the world, regardless of the culture in which the language is spoken, have words for *mother* and *father*, although the exact connotations and boundaries of what might constitute such designations show considerable cultural variability, e.g., stepfather, surrogate mother, a beloved aunt, etc.

Still, *mother* and *father* are relatively ubiquitous words, and more or less semantically coherent words for very basic family relationships are unlikely to be borrowed; the similarities in the words for *mother* and *father* in English, Latin, Greek, and Sanskrit instead suggest a relationship among the languages: a "common source." Certainly a more extensive sampling of other lexical items unlikely to be borrowed (words for numbers, for example) affirms such a hypothesis.

The terms for *mother* and *father* provide a good example of how the comparative method works. Not only does the comparison of the words allow us to infer relatedness, but it also gives us a way of projecting backward and hypothesizing what the original words for *mother* and *father* might have been in the parent language, again in this case, **Proto-Indo-European** (PIE). Using *mother* as a starting point (and leaving English out of the equation for the present time), we note that the forms in

Latin, Sanskrit, and Greek all begin with an *m-*. So it would seem pretty obvious that the original PIE word for *mother* would also begin with an *m-*.

Next we note that all of the words have a vowel following *m-*; however, Latin and Sanskrit have an *-a-* while Greek has *-e-*. Invoking the majority principle, we would hypothesize that the vowel of the original should be *-a-*. However, our reconstruction cannot not rest on the majority principle alone; it is also necessary to investigate how likely our hypothesis is. In the case of reconstructing an -ā- for the original IE vowel, we are claiming that an IE -ā- changes to *-e-* in Greek. It turns out that when we look at other sets of words in Latin and Sanskrit that have -ā-, the Greek reflex is *-e-*. It also so happens that even some dialects of Greek retain the IE -ā-, as in Doric *māter*.[2] These facts, and others, allow us to conclude comfortably that the origin IE vowel was indeed -ā-. Continuing in this way, we would end up with a proto-form, *matér (note that in historical linguistics an asterisk before the word means that the word is reconstructed; an accent indicates where the stress falls on the word). This is the form that many scholars agreed was the most likely word for *mother* in PIE. (Later evidence has suggested that the vowel *a* is a much more complex reflex, the details of which are beyond the scope of this book.)

While the similarity among words that are unlikely to be borrowed provides good evidence for relatedness, similarities in elements of grammar among putatively related languages is equally if not more compelling. Consider, for example, the forms of the verb *to be* in the present tense in English, Old English, Gothic, Latin, Greek, and Sanskrit.[3]

English		Old English	Gothic	Latin	Greek	Sanskrit
(I)	am	eom	im	sum	eimi	asmi
(you)	are	eart	es	ei	asi	asi
(he)	is	is	ist	est	esti	asti
(we)	are	sind	sijum	sumus	esmen	smas
(you)	are	sind	sijuÞ	estis	este	stha
(they)	are	sind	sind	sunt	eisi	santi

Although the forms in PDE are less obviously similar to those in Latin, Greek, and Sanskrit, the forms in Old English (OE) and Gothic (a language spoken in Europe around 500 CE) are clearly too similar to have come about by accident. For example, you can easily recognize across the languages the *-m* in the forms corresponding to the PDE *am*, and the *-s-* in the forms corresponding to the PDE *is*.

---

2   Andrew L. Sihler, *New Comparative Grammar of Greek and Latin* (Oxford, Oxford UP, 1995), 50–51.

3   Albert C. Baugh and Thomas Cable, *A History of the English Language* (5th edition) (Upper Saddle River, NJ: Prentice Hall, 2002), 20.

Through historical comparison scholars have reconstructed both the grammar and the lexicon of the ancestor language for this group of related languages. This group of related languages, which includes English, is known as the Indo-European family of languages. Figure 3.2 shows the present-day geographical distribution of IE languages.

FIGURE 3.2   Present-day geographical distribution of Indo-European languages. Reprinted with the permission of George Boeree.

It is important to keep in mind as one examines the present-day distribution of IE languages that while it is possible to generalize about geographical distribution and language relatedness, such generalization can be very misleading. Given the fact that French, Spanish, German, and Swedish are all IE languages, for example, one might generalize that most languages now spoken in Europe are IE, and that is somewhat true. But it is also true that *not all* languages now spoken in Europe are IE. While Finland is geographically very close to Sweden and Russia, Finnish is *not* an IE language. Similarly, while Turkey is geographically very close to Greece and Iran, and both Greek and a number of Iranian languages are IE, Turkish is not an IE language.

It may also be tempting to generalize about language relatedness and geographical distribution and to posit that languages that are spoken in geographically proximal regions tend to be related, as for example are French and Spanish. But again, this generalization can be very misleading. Basque, another non-Indo-European language, is spoken in a region spanning both French and Spanish territories. Furthermore, even though the geographical distance is much greater between England and Iran than that between England and Finland, English as a language is actually related to Farsi, the official language of Iran, but it is *not* related to Finnish.

THE GENETIC MODEL

The use of terms like *related* and *family of languages* results from the dominan̄
phor for discussing languages that develop from a common source, the **genetic
model**. In such a model, a language is said to descend from a parent language (as
a daughter language, and languages that descend from the same parent are called
sister or cognate languages. Most linguists and language historians do not exploit the
genetic model beyond the parent, daughter, sister designations. Few scholars today
will talk of grandparent, cousin or aunt languages, for example).

Another fairly common way to discuss development from a common source
is the tree metaphor in which one talks of roots, branches and stemming. Figure
3.3 presents a tree of the Indo-European languages. In that figure, as you can see,
Indo-European is made up of several "branches" of ever-smaller sub-groupings until
finally the ends of the branches list out the various individual languages.

FIGURE 3.3   Tree of the Indo-European languages.

Currently, family relationships among languages are expressed in less literal diagrams, like that in Figure 3.4.

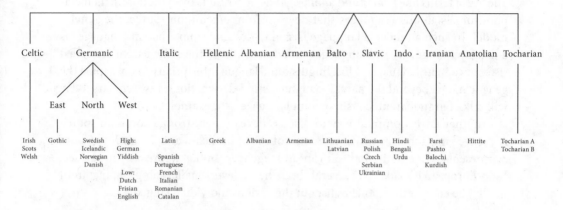

FIGURE 3.4   The Indo-European languages.

One problem with both the genetic and the tree models is that these models, as metaphors, are often extended from the languages they represent to the people who speak or spoke them. That is, upon learning that English is a **Germanic** language, one may be tempted to hypothesize that *speakers* of English are genetically descended from speakers of the "parent" languages. While it is possible that *some* speakers may be genetically descended from those Germanic peoples, there is no necessary relationship whatsoever between the genetics of a particular speaker and the language that person speaks. A Chinese child, adopted from infancy by monolingual English-speaking US parents has no predisposition for Chinese. That child will speak English as a native language and could only learn Chinese as a second language. (Some people still believe somewhat romantically that such children somehow "remember" the language of their birth and culture; they do not.) When we employ the genetic model to talk about languages, we are *not* talking about the genetics of the speakers of those languages.

STRUCTURE OF PROTO-INDO-EUROPEAN

Proto-Indo-European differed from the structure of PDE in some notable ways. In fact, the structure of PIE was more like that of Latin or Ancient Greek than that of many modern European languages, although the discovery of certain very old IE branches, like Anatolian, which includes Hittite, has led some scholars to claim that earlier reconstructions of PIE may have reflected an over-reliance on Greek, Latin, and Sanskrit. In this section, we do not attempt to give you a comprehensive view of all of the structures in PIE, and you should know that much of the reconstructed grammar of PIE is highly controversial among scholars. Instead we offer an overview of some elements of the structure of the noun and verb systems. We have chosen these elements not only because they are elements of PIE many scholars will agree upon,[4] but also because we will return to these structural elements in our work with the subsequent history of English.

PIE NOUNS

Number

PIE distinguished three numbers: singular, plural, and **dual**.

Singular	referring to one only as in *horse*
Plural	referring to more than one as in *horses*
Dual	referring to two and only two of something

Although the dual persists into OE, it does not exist in PDE. However, the remnants of the dual remain in words like *both* and *either* that have to do with just two things, *both horses, either sister.*

Gender

Later PIE likely distinguished three genders: neuter, feminine, and masculine. Earlier PIE may have only distinguished two genders, common and neuter. Many readers are probably familiar with the notion of gender from languages that they have studied. For instance, in Spanish, nouns that end in -*o* are generally masculine and nouns that end in -*a* are generally feminine, for example *caballlo* (horse, masc.) and *mesa* (table, fem.). Gender is a very important structural category in the history of English, one which has undergone significant changes. As we will discuss later, gender in OE was very much like gender in Spanish, French, Latin, German, and Russian. However, because it changed some time in the Middle English (ME) period, for Modern English (ModE) speakers, the notion that a table is feminine is difficult because gender terms like masculine, neuter, and feminine are no longer broad, classificatory terms as they are in, say, Spanish.

Case

One of the most significant subsystems of nouns in PIE is that of case. Case is a very important concept for studying the history of English. Essentially, case is a system

---

4 Baldi, *An Introduction to the Indo-European Languages*, 3–23.

in which a noun or pronoun (and often the words that modify it, like adjectives or definite articles) changes form according to whether it is being used to show a noun phrase as the subject, direct object, indirect object, object of a preposition, etc. (See again Chapter 2, p. 25.)

Although in ModE case is formally observable only among some pronouns, other languages have more elaborate case systems in which full nouns change their form according to whether they are used as subject, direct object or some other function. In Latin for instance, the word *lupus* (wolf) has the form l-u-p-u-s when it is the subject, as in the following sentence:

Lupus   vīdit   agricolam
wolf   saw   farmer
The wolf saw the farmer.

However, the form of the word when it is the direct object is l-u-p-u-m, as in the following sentence:

Agricola   vīdit   lupum
Farmer   saw   wolf
The farmer saw the wolf.

While ModE doesn't have a case system as elaborate as that of Latin, at earlier stages of its history, English did signal case in a way not unlike that in the Latin example. An intriguing part of the history of English is the fact that this case system was lost. We will discuss why it was lost and the effects of that loss on other parts of the language in subsequent chapters.

PIE VERBS

The structure of the PIE verb is somewhat controversial. Earlier scholars believed that the verbal system of PIE was like that of the older IE languages, such as Ancient Greek, Latin, and Sanskrit. If that is true, the PIE verb system was very different from that of PDE.

We can get a sense of what the Ancient Greek verb system was like in the following synopsis for the verb *grapho* (to write). ("Synopsis" here means a verb paradigm [i.e., pattern] in which all of the forms are given based on a single person category. In other words, this synopsis gives all of the forms of the verb *to write* in Ancient Greek conjugated in the third-person singular.)

Active Voice

	Present	Imperfect	Future	Aorist	Perfect	Pluperfect
Indicative	graphei	egraphe	grapsei	egrapse	gegraphe	egegraphei
Subjunctive	graphēi			grapsēi		
Optative	graphoi		graphoi	grapseie		
Participle	graphōn		grapsōn	grapsas	gegraphōs	
Imperative	graphetō			grapsatō		
Infinitive	graphein		grapsein	grapsai	gegraphenai	

Middle and Passive Voice

	Present	Imperfect	Perfect	Pluperfect
Indicative	graphetai	egrapheto	gegraptai	egegrapto
Subjunctive	graphētai			
Optative	graphoito			
Participle	graphomenos		gegrammenos	
Imperative	graphesthō		gegraphthō	
Infinitive	graphesthai		gegraphthai	

Middle Voice

	Future	Aorist
Indicative	grapsetai	egrapsato
Subjunctive		egrapsētai
Optative	grapsoito	grapsaito
Participle	grapsomenos	grapsamenos
Imperative		grapsasthō
Infinitive	grapsesthai	grapsasthai

Passive Voice

	Future	Aorist
Indicative	graphēsetai	egraphē
Subjunctive		graphēi
Optative	graphēsoito	grapheiē
Participle	graphēsomenos	grapheis
Imperative		graphētō
Infinitive	graphēsesthai	graphēnai

A few of the terms in the synopsis of the Greek verb will be familiar to you, while a few others might be less so. We will pause for a moment to supply some of the terms which may be less familiar to you. Most of these terms will be repeated later in this book in our description of the historical stages of English.

In a sentence in the **active voice**, typically the subject is the doer of an overt action upon some affected entity. (*Dmitri kicked the ball.*)

In a sentence in the **passive voice**, the affected entity of an active sentence is transformed into the subject of the passive verb form. The doer of the action is optionally expressed in a *by* phrase. (*The ball was kicked by Dmitri.*)

The **middle voice** conceptualizes the action as a process and makes the affected entity into the subject. Some consider sentences like *The window broke* to be a kind of middle voice construction in English. Others, however, do not include the middle voice in a description in English.

The **indicative** is a grammatical mood that refers to situations that the speaker asserts as true in the real world.

The **subjunctive** is a grammatical mood that refers to situations that the speaker asserts as hypothetical, probable, or contingent.

The **imperative** is a grammatical mood in which the speaker exerts control over an outside agent, for example a command. (*Dimitri, throw the ball!*)

The **optative** is a grammatical mood used to make a wish. In ModE we make optative statements in the following ways, along with some other expressions:

May all your wishes come true.
Would that he loved me. (archaic)

The **aorist** is a verbal category that places a verb in the past without regard to its beginning, end, or other relations of temporal relevance.

One thing that is quite clear from the synopsis is that there are a lot of verb forms and verbal categories in Greek. However, other IE languages, like the Germanic languages, as well as some very old IE languages like Hittite, have comparatively simplified verbal systems, as the synopsis for the Gothic verb *nasjan* (to save) shows below.

Active

	Present	Past
Indicative	nasjiþ	nasida
Subjunctive	nasjái	nasidēdi
Imperative	nasjadáu	
Participle	nasjands	
Infinitive	nasjan	

Passive

	Present	Preterite
Indicative	nasjada	
Subjunctive	nasjáidáu	
Imperative		
Participle		nasiþs
Infinitive		

It is obvious that the Gothic system is considerably simpler than that of Ancient Greek. In light of these two extremely different types of systems among Indo-European languages, opinion on the PIE verbal system is now split between those who posit an elaborate system, like that of Greek, and consequently believe that languages like Gothic lost many of the verbal inflectional categories of PIE, and those who posit a simple verbal system for PIE and view the system of Greek to have been built up from that original simple system. In yet another view, the complexity of the PIE verbal system may have been somewhere between that of Greek type and that of the Gothic type, complexifying in the former and simplifying in the latter.

We certainly cannot solve this complex issue, but we will note that the discussions concerning the complexity of verbal systems in IE focus pretty exclusively on inflectional suffixes and ignore another very important way that notions of time, mood, voice, and aspect are expressed in languages: periphrastically. For example, you might notice that several of the cells in the Ancient Greek paradigm are blank. In some instances, such as the middle/passive perfect subjunctive, the category was signaled in Ancient Greek through *gegrammens ei*, a verbal construction in which the first word is a participle and the second word is a form of an auxiliary verb. You can contrast this type of periphrastic construction to the way that past tense in PDE is expressed through a suffix attached directly to the verb, as in *walked*. We say that *walked* is an inflectional form. However, like the Greek construction *gegrammens ei* just discussed, progressivity or ongoing action is expressed by an auxiliary verb together with the *-ing* participle of the verb in PDE, as in *is writing*. As covered in Chapter 2, *is writing* is called a periphrastic construction.

It is an interesting fact about the study of language and language histories that these kinds of periphrastic constructions have been so little studied despite the fact that they have such a central role in IE languages. Consider for instance that it is impossible in English to express *he is riding his bike right now* without using the progressive. You cannot use any other verb form with the adverbial expression *right now*. In other words, the periphrastic progressive is obligatory in that sentence. Obviously, the development and use of periphrasis is centrally important in understanding changes in the English verb system, a system that was originally similar to that of Gothic. The development of periphrasis is important in other areas of the historical study of English grammar as well.

EXERCISES

3.1 Which of the following is *not* an IE language?

    a. Swedish, Danish, or Finnish?
    b. Greek, Persian, or Turkish?
    c. Hindi, Basque, or Pashto?

3.2 Which of the following is *not* related to English?

    a. Pashto, spoken in present-day Iran, Afghanistan, and India.
    b. Urdu, spoken in present-day Pakistan and India.
    c. Finnish, spoken in present-day Finland.
    d. Manx, spoken until the end of the twentieth century on the Isle of Man.

3.3 True or false?

    a. English is an Italic language, like Latin.
    b. English is a Celtic language, like Scottish.
    c. English is a Germanic language, like Swedish.
    d. English is a Balto-Slavic language, like Lithuanian.

3.4 True or false?

    a. English has Latin as its "ancestor" language.
    b. English has Greek as its "ancestor" language.
    c. English has Hebrew as its "ancestor" language.
    d. English has Sanskrit as its "ancestor" language.

3.5 Consider the following sentences in Latin:

Discipulus   amat canem.
The student loves the dog.

Canis   amat discipulum.
The dog loves the student.

Note that in the first sentence, the form of the Latin word meaning *student* is *discipulus*, but in the second it is *discipulum*. What concept explains why the noun takes these different forms in these sentences?

3.6 Which of the following are *periphrastic* constructions in PDE?

    a. walked
    b. is walking
    c. have walked
    d. will be walking
    e. walks

CHAPTER FOUR

Introduction to Phonetics and the International Phonetic Alphabet

OVERVIEW

A major goal of the historical study of a language is to describe changes in linguistic structure on all levels: that is, to describe changes in morphology, syntax and phonology. Because **morphology** has to do with the way that words and their parts are composed and **syntax** has to do with the meaningful order of words, these two levels of description are very often analyzed using the conventional **orthography** (writing system) of the language in the period under investigation. **Phonology**, however, deals with the sounds of the language for which conventional orthographic systems cannot provide adequate description. Think, for example, of all of the sounds that can be represented by the letter <s> in conventional spelling: the sound in *Sarah*, the sound in *cheese*, the sound in *pleasure*. Conversely, think of the many different ways the sound [f], the first sound in the word *fish*, can be spelled in conventional spelling: *fish*, *phenomena*, *enough*....

In order to study the sounds and the changes in the sound system of a language (i.e., the language's phonology), we employ phonetics. Phonetics is the study of human speech sounds. Note that phonetics is not language-specific; phonetics covers all human speech sounds in whatever language they might occur, although obviously not all human languages have the same inventory of sounds. Therefore, it is possible to talk about the phonetics of Mandarin, Swahili, or English. The description below focuses on sounds important for the historical study of English.

There are many more sounds in English than there are letters in the conventional alphabet. Furthermore, as illustrated above, the English spelling system has many apparent irregularities, with some letters representing many sounds, identical sounds represented by different letters, "silent" letters, etc. (Note that these irregularities can be called "apparent" irregularities because spellings that may seem illogical to us today frequently have logical historical motivations.) But the problem of using orthography to study the sounds of a language is not unique to English; this problem exists for all languages, even those like Spanish, in which spelling and pronunciation are more tightly correlated.

The inadequacy of language-specific orthographies for the study of the sounds of language has given rise to the development of technical alphabets. Many students are familiar with such alphabets from dictionaries, in which the pronunciation of a word is often given in parentheses after the word's entry. The phonetic spellings in dictionaries vary significantly. One dictionary might represent the **vowel** in *cat* as ä, another as ă, yet another as *a*, and still yet another as æ. For consistency, linguists developed a phonetic alphabet that has become the standard system for representing human speech sounds. This alphabet is known as the International Phonetic Alphabet, or the IPA.

In IPA, there is a one-to-one correspondence between a symbol and the sound it represents. Thus all the various sounds conventionally represented by <s> in *Sarah*, *cheese* and *pleasure* are all spelled differently in IPA: the sound conventionally spelled with <s> in *Sarah* is represented by the IPA symbol [s]; the different sound conventionally spelled with <s> in *cheese* is represented by the IPA symbol [z]; and the sound conventionally spelled with <s> in *pleasure* is represented by the IPA symbol [ʒ]. Likewise, the sound of the first consonant in *fish*, conventionally spelled with an <f> (*fish*), a <ph> (*phenomena*), or a <-gh> (*enough*), is always written in IPA as [f].

Again it should be remembered that even though the focus here is on English, IPA symbols are constant across language: [f] is used in any language where that sound is made whether it is English *fish*, Spanish *fiebre* (fever), German *Vater* (father), or Mandarin *fángzi* (house). (Note that an initial <v> in German is pronounced [f], underscoring the fact that language-specific orthographies often mask phonetic similarities between languages.) Most IPA symbols are familiar to those with knowledge of the Roman or Greek Alphabets.

SYMBOLS

In this section the IPA symbols are provided beside words that exemplify the sounds represented by those symbols. In the first subsection are the consonant symbols which are identical in form to letters used in the Roman alphabet. These symbols are presented in alphabetical order. The second subsection contains the IPA symbols for consonants not found in the Present-Day English (PDE) alphabet. The third subsection presents the symbols for vowel sounds.

CONSONANTS: IPA SYMBOLS BASED ON THE ROMAN ALPHABET

IPA symbol	sample word
b	boy
d	do
f	fish
g	game
h	hat
j	yard
k	kitten
l	laugh
m	mop
n	nap
p	pin
s	sample
t	token
v	vest
w	water
z	zoo

CONSONANTS: IPA SYMBOLS NOT FOUND IN THE ROMAN ALPHABET

IPA symbol	sample word
ʃ	shoe
ʒ	azure
tʃ	cheese
dʒ	judge
θ	thin
ð	that
ŋ	finger
ɹ	rather
ʔ	oh-oh (see below for a description of this sound)

Note that in many textbooks [r] is used instead of [ɹ]. As discussed below, these symbols represent different sounds in IPA.

VOWELS

IPA symbol	sample word
ɑ	f<u>a</u>ther
æ	b<u>a</u>t
ɛ	b<u>e</u>t
e	b<u>ai</u>t
ɪ	<u>bi</u>t
i	b<u>ea</u>t
ɔ	b<u>ough</u>t
o	b<u>oa</u>t
ʊ	b<u>oo</u>k
u	b<u>oo</u>t
ʌ	b<u>u</u>tt
ə	<u>a</u>bout
y	French t<u>u</u>; German f<u>ür</u> ·
[ɑi]	r<u>i</u>ght
[ɑu]	h<u>ou</u>se
[oi]	b<u>oy</u>[1]

It is particularly in the vowel system that the inadequacy of English spelling for consistent representation of sounds is most obvious. Notice that the IPA vowel symbols are often much closer to the sounds represented by the conventional spelling of Spanish or German vowel sounds, for example, than they are to the sounds represented by the conventional spelling of English. Notice, too, that there are several more vowel sounds than the five orthographic vowels <a, e, i, o, u>. Given these mismatches between English spelling and phonetic spelling, vowels sometimes present a special challenge to English speakers when they first study phonetics.

As we indicate in the chart, [ɑ] represents a low, back vowel like the *a*-sound in *father*. In many language textbooks [a] is used instead. However, strictly speaking, [a] in IPA represents a more fronted low vowel, found in some varieties of East Coast US and UK English.

---

1   The examples are based on Standard US pronunciation. Dialects in the US and around the world will show much variation in the pronunciation of any one of these words.

DESCRIBING THE SOUNDS OF ENGLISH

THE CONSONANTS

The sounds called **consonants** are produced by stopping or constricting the flow of air through the vocal tract.

The image below illustrates the vocal tract. The physical structures of the apparatus involved in the production of English sounds are: lips, teeth, alveolar ridge, palate, velum, glottis, larynx, nasal cavity. (Note that many languages make use of other physiological structures. The pharynx, for example, is important for describing the sounds of Arabic.) It is important to know the physiological regions of the vocal tract well in order to understand how they are involved in speech.

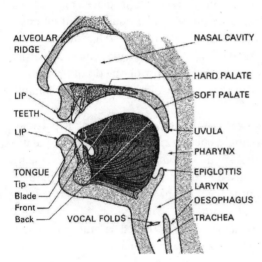

FIGURE 4.1   Vocal Apparatus.

Consonants can be described by:

1. the **place of articulation** (where the vocal tract is closed or constricted),
2. the **manner of articulation** (whether the flow of air is stopped or constricted),
3. and **voicing** (the state of the vocal folds in the glottis).

Place of Articulation

Consonants in English have as their places of articulation the lips, teeth, alveolar ridge, palate, velum, and glottis.

When a consonant has the lips as its place of articulation, it is called a **labial**. Consider the sound [b], as in the word *about*. When that sound is made, the speaker's lips are placed together. Thus [b] is a labial. More specifically, it is a **bilabial**; that is, making the sound [b] involves both lips. Bilabial consonants in English include [p, b, m, w].

When a consonant sound has the upper row of teeth and the lower lip as its place of articulation, it is called a **labiodental**. The sound [f], as in *fish* is a labiodental. Labiodental consonants in English include [f, v].

Dental consonants also involve the teeth. Dental sounds in English are really **interdental** consonants because they are produced with the tongue located between the teeth as the place of articulation. The sound [ð], as in *they*, is an example of an interdental consonant. Interdental consonants in English include [ð, θ]. Note that while interdental consonants appear in many languages other than English (e.g., certain varieties of Spanish, Greek, etc.), many languages have dental sounds that are not interdental but instead involve articulation with the tongue placed on the back of the teeth. In the Romance languages, for example, [d̪ t̪] are such dental sounds.

The alveolar ridge is the structure just behind the upper front teeth. Sounds which have the alveolar ridge as the place of articulation are called **alveolar** consonants. The sound [d], as in the first consonant in *dog*, is made by putting the tip of the tongue and the alveolar ridge in contact. [d] is an alveolar consonant. Alveolar consonants include [t, d, s, z, ɹ, n, l].

A number of consonant sounds involve both the alveolar ridge and the palate in their place of articulation. Not surprisingly, such sounds are called alveo-palatal consonants. The sound [tʃ], as in the first sound of *church* for example, is made by first touching the tip of the tongue to the alveolar ridge, and then moving the point of contact between the tongue and the mouth back to the palate. [tʃ] is an alveo-palatal. Alveo-palatals include [tʃ, dʒ, ʃ, ʒ].

Sounds with the palate as their place of articulation are called **palatal** consonants. The first sound in the English word *yard* [j] is a palatal consonant.

The velum is sometimes called the soft palate. Consonants which have the velum as their place of articulation are called **velar** consonants. The sound [k], as in *cat*, is produced with contact between the back of the tongue and the velum. [k] is a velar consonant. Velars include [k, g, ŋ].

The glottis is a structure located in the larynx or Adam's apple between the vocal folds (popularly called "vocal cords"). It has the ability to close off or restrict the flow of air exiting the lungs and passing through the larynx through constriction (or non-constriction) of the vocal folds. Consonant sounds which have the glottis as their place of articulation are called **glottal** consonants. Articulation in the glottis can be felt by focusing on the tight constriction in the larynx when pronouncing the interjection *oh-oh*. Before each vowel the glottis closes off the flow of air creating a subsequent burst. The consonant produced by this closure is called a glottal stop and is represented by the symbol [ʔ]. Note that in Standard English this sound has no orthographic representation, although in certain varieties of English, e.g., Cockney English, the <tt> in words like *better* is pronounced with a glottal stop. [h] as in the English word *hot* is often described as a glottal sound as well, as it will be here.

Manner of Articulation

Consonants can also be described by the manner of articulation, that is, whether they involve stopping the flow of air (stops), constricting the flow of air (fricatives), a combination of stopping and constricting the flow of air (affricates) or other means of manipulating the flow of air through the vocal tract, including the nasal cavity.

A **stop** involves stopping the flow of air. The bilabial sound [b], as in *about*, for example, is a stop. To produce that sound the lips are placed together tightly and the flow of air is briefly stopped. Stops in English include [p, b, t, d, k, g, ʔ].

Fricatives involve constriction of the flow of air. The labiodental sound [f], as in *fish*, for example, is produced by constricting the airflow between the lips and teeth. One way to distinguish between fricatives and stops is that fricatives, because they involve constriction, not stopping, can continue as long as the breath. The sound [f] can be articulated until all of the air flowing from the lungs is expelled. In contrast, the sound [b] cannot be continuous, because it requires that the flow of air be stopped. Fricatives include [f, v, θ, ð, s, z, ʃ, ʒ, h].

An **affricate** is a combination of a stop and a fricative. When making the sound [tʃ], as in *church*, first the flow of air is stopped at the alveolar ridge, and then it is allowed to continue across the palate in a fricative articulation. Affricates include [tʃ, dʒ]. Both [tʃ] and [dʒ] are alveo-palatal affricates.

An **approximant** is so called because in the production of these sounds, the articulators approach one another but with minimal constriction of air. These sounds can be contrasted with fricatives, but approximants involve a more open air flow than fricatives do. The sounds [w] and [j] are approximant sounds. They are sometimes referred to as glides.

The first sounds in the words *read* and *lemon* are called **liquids** (sometimes these are also classed as types of approximants.) The [ɹ] in *read* is a central liquid and it is made by bunching up the body of the tongue and constricting the larynx, while lifting the tip of the tongue. Some speakers curl the tongue to the palate in the pronunciation of the first sound in the word *read*, and in such cases the sound is said to have a retroflex place of articulation. We will use [ɹ] for both.

The [l] in *lemon* is a lateral liquid. Instead of allowing the flow of air to exit through the center of the mouth and over the tip of the tongue (as in [s]), lateral liquids close off the central air flow with the tip of the tongue and force the air flow to exit at the sides. By putting your hand in front of your mouth and articulating [s] and [l], you can feel the different routes of airflow.

Nasal consonants are made by raising the velum such that the flow of air through the mouth is closed off, thus forcing air through the nasal cavity. If you place a hand underneath your nostrils when pronouncing [m] for instance, you can feel the flow of air come out of the nose. Note that the nasal consonants in English are all stopped in the mouth but continuous in the nasal cavity. For example, when [m] is produced, both lips are pressed together and the flow of air is stopped through the mouth. The sound [m] can continue to be made until the airflow is exhausted because, although the sound is stopped in the mouth, it is continuous in the nasal passage. Nasals include [m,n,ŋ].

Voicing

Earlier we described the glottis as a structure in the larynx located between the vocal folds and involved in the articulation of the glottal stop and a glottal fricative. However, the state of the vocal folds within the glottis is quite important for another parameter of phonetic description, namely that of voicing.

Every human speech sound is classed as either voiced or voiceless. A voiced sound is produced by constriction of the vocal folds resulting in an audible vibration. In contrast, a voiceless sound does not involve such a constriction and no such vibration results. The distinction can be heard (or actually felt by placing your hand on your larynx) most easily in the production of fricatives in such pairs as [s] and [z]. Articulating the sound [s] results in no perceptible vibration in the larynx. When [z] is articulated, however, the vibration of the vocal folds is clearly perceptible.

At this point, it is now possible to describe each of the consonants of English by voice, place and manner. (+v indicates voiced; -v indicates voiceless.)

	Bilabial		Labio-dental		Inter-dental		Alveolar		Alveo-palatal		Palatal		Velar		Glottal	
	+V	-V	+V	-V	+V	-V	+V	-V	+V	-V	+V	-V	+V	-V	+V	-V
Stop	b	p					d	t					g	k		ʔ
Fricative			v	f	ð	θ	z	s	ʒ	ʃ						h
Affricate									dʒ	tʃ						
Nasal	m						n						ŋ			
Approximant	w										j					
Liquid: Central							ɹ									
Liquid: Lateral							l									

Summary of consonants: Place of articulation, manner of articulation, and voicing

Other Consonants Important in the History of English

The sounds described so far are those found in PDE. However, there are several more sounds that are important for a historical description of English. Among them are:

[x] voiceless, velar fricative	as in German *Buch* (book)
[ç] voiceless, palatal fricative	as in German *ich* (I) (or the first sound in *human* for many English speakers)
[r] voiced, alveolar trill	like the double <rr> in Spanish *perro* (dog)
[ɣ] voiced, velar, fricative	like the <g> in Spanish *lago* (lake)
[ʁ] voiced, uvular, trill	like the <r> German *richtig* (right)

A Note on [ɾ]

There is another sound that is important for discussing the sounds of English, particularly in Modern American English and that is the sound represented by the symbol [ɾ]. It is a voiced, alveolar, **tap** consonant and it occurs for the t-sound in the American English pronunciation of the words *better, ladder,* and *attic.* (A tap is a sound made by briefly hitting the region of articulation with the tongue. It is shorter in duration than a non-tap consonant.) Essentially, a t- or d-sound will be pronounced as a tap when the stress of the word falls on the syllable preceding the t- or d-sound. Notice that in a word like *attack*, the t-sound is [t] since the stress falls on the syllable after that t-sound. Again, [ɾ] is important for later varieties of English and will appear in subsequent chapters.

VOWELS

In phonetics, vowels contrast with consonants in that they are produced with little obstruction of the vocal tract. Distinct vowel articulations are made by changing the shape of the vocal tract.

Describing vowels according to their articulatory features is more difficult than describing consonants. One difficulty in describing vowel sounds is that while all speakers produce most consonants in roughly the same way, speakers show significant articulatory variation in the production of vowels for a number of reasons, such as the unique shape of an individual's mouth. The acoustic perception of vowels is of course rather more consistent; that is, listeners are fairly good at indicating which vowel they hear. Another difficulty in describing vowels is that while consonant articulations tend to be discreet, with one consonant articulation being at point A and another at point B, without possible gradation (what would be halfway between a [t] and an [s]?), vowel articulations are continuous and speakers can produce a large range of vowels between two points (although many of those vowel productions may never occur in that speaker's language).

The descriptors of vowels should thus be understood as (1) about the relative distance between vowels in the vocal tract and (2) more about acoustic perception than strictly articulatory production (although there is of course some correlation).

The American English vowels (along with a word to exemplify their pronunciation) are:

[i] b<u>ea</u>t   [u] b<u>oo</u>t
[ɪ] b<u>i</u>t   [ʊ] b<u>oo</u>k
[e] b<u>ai</u>t   [ə] <u>a</u>bout   [o] b<u>oa</u>t
[ɛ] b<u>e</u>t   [ʌ] b<u>u</u>tt   [ɔ] b<u>ou</u>ght
[æ] b<u>a</u>t   [ɑ] f<u>a</u>ther

Vowels are described according to

1. tongue height along a vertical axis,
2. horizontal location in the front, central or back regions of the vocal tract, and
3. sometimes a third or fourth descriptor such as lip rounding and/or
4. tenseness versus laxness.

In order to capture these vertical and horizontal descriptors, vowels are placed on a trapezoid which is only metaphorically representative of the oral space.

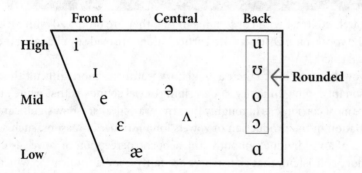

FIGURE 4.2   The Vowel Trapezoid.

From this chart, it is evident that [i] contrasts with [æ] in that [i] is a high vowel and [æ] is a low vowel; both are, however, front vowels. Also, [æ] contrasts with [ɑ] in that [æ] is a front vowel while [ɑ] is a back vowel; both are, however, low vowels, and so on.

Additionally note that the back vowels [u], [ʊ], [o], [ɔ] are described by a third term, namely the descriptor roundness. When these back vowels are articulated in English, they are produced with rounding of the lips. The symbol [y] also represents a rounded vowel, but in the high front region of the vowel space. (You pronounce it by articulating an [i] as in *beat* while rounding the lips.) As indicated above, it is the vowel sound in French *tu* or German *für*. This sound is also found in Old English (OE) (see Chapter 7).

One articulatory feature not shown on the chart is the tense-lax distinction. [i, u, e, o,] are tense vowels. [ɪ, ɛ, ʊ, ɔ, ʌ, ə] are lax vowels. The phonetic distinction between lax and tense vowels is complex and extends beyond mere tenseness and laxness. One important aspect of the distinction between tense and lax vowels is that it correlates with, among other things, vowel length. Tense vowels tend to be longer than lax vowels. In phonetic transcription, a long vowel is indicated by a colon, thus [i:] is long while [ɪ] is short. The issue of length can sometimes be confusing to English-speaking students who are new to phonetics because they likely learned in grammar school that the difference between the <u> in *tube* and the <u> in *tub* is a matter of length, with *tube* making the "long <u> sound" and *tub* making the "short <u> sound."

The difference between the vowels in *tube* and *tub* is not primarily one of length (although it is true that the vowel in *tube* is longer than that in *tub*). Instead the more salient difference between the two vowels is one of quality; that is, these two vowels are phonetically different vowels despite the fact that English orthography uses the same symbol <u> for both. The vowel in *tube* is [u:] while the vowel in *tub* is [ʌ].

The Complete Description for American Vowels

[i] b<u>ea</u>t high, front, tense		[u] b<u>oo</u>t high, back, tense, rounded
[ɪ] b<u>i</u>t high, front, lax		[ʊ] b<u>oo</u>k high, back, lax, rounded
[e] b<u>ai</u>t mid, front, tense	[ə] <u>a</u>bout mid, central, lax	[o] b<u>oa</u>t mid, back, tense, rounded
[ɛ] b<u>e</u>t mid, front, lax	[ʌ] b<u>u</u>tt mid, central, lax	[ɔ] b<u>ou</u>ght mid, back, lax, rounded
[æ] b<u>a</u>t low, front, lax		[ɑ] f<u>a</u>ther low, back

(Note that wherever "rounded" is not indicated, the vowel is assumed to be "unrounded.")

A Note on [ə] and [ʌ]
Both [ə] and [ʌ] are mid central vowels. Note however that [ə] never occurs in a stressed syllable.

A Note on [ɔ] and [ɑ]
Many varieties of American English do not have the sound [ɔ] in speech. While some speakers make a difference between *cot* [kɑt] and *caught* [kɔt] in regular speech, for others *cot* and *caught* are homophones both being pronounced as [kɑt]. For such speakers hearing the sound [ɔ] can be very difficult.

DIPHTHONGS

When two vowel sounds occur in a single syllable, the vowel sounds together are called a **diphthong**. English diphthongs include:

[oi]	b<u>oy</u>
[ai]	r<u>i</u>ght
[ɑu]	h<u>ou</u>se

In the production of diphthongs speakers are actually moving from one vowel space to another. Although the symbols given here would seem to indicate that for the vowel sound in *boy* a speaker starts at the same place of articulation for *boat* [o] and ends up at the place of articulation for *meet* [i], the acoustic effect depends more on the general path of movement rather than strict starting and ending points. Thus in reality the diphthong in the word *boy* starts out in the lower part of the mid back section of the vocal space and ends in the high front section. As a result of this range of possible positions, the representation of diphthongs can vary quite a bit in different textbooks.

A Note on [e] and [o] in English
A final point on diphthongs concerns the mid, tense vowels [e] and [o]. In most varieties of English, these vowels do not occur as a single vowel (called a **monophthong**). Instead they are produced as diphthongs. When an English speaker says *bait*, he/she is not saying [be:t] with a vowel like that in the Spanish word *grand<u>e</u>*. Instead the vowel in *bait* is [ei]; there is a slight movement from [e] towards the high front region of the vowel space. Similarly the [o] in *boat* is not a monophthong but really [ou]; that is, the vowel glides into the high back region of the vowel space. Whether or not these off-glides are noted in a given phonetic transcription has to do with how broad or narrow the transcription is.

STRESS

Since the vowel is the nucleus of the syllable, it is also the segment that carries stress. Stress is the point of a word in which greater articulatory exertion is made. Stress is indicated by a raised bar before the stressed syllable: *reason* is transcribed as [ˈɹizən]. Remember that [ə] never occurs in a stressed syllable.

SYLLABIC CONSONANTS

While vowels are the nucleus of a syllable, it is possible that some syllables might not have a vowel. In such cases, syllabic weight will fall on a liquid or a nasal. For instance, English speakers do not normally pronounce a vowel in the last syllable of the word *written* but instead elide the vowel sound and place the syllabic weight on the [n]. Those liquids are written with a line underneath to indicate syllabic weight; *written* is transcribed as [ɹɪtn̩].

PRACTICE WITH IPA: A NOTE ABOUT TRANSCRIPTION

Although phonetics is a field in which each sound is uniquely described and the phonetic alphabet is a system in which each sound is represented by one and only one symbol, the practice of transcription is not so clean-cut as one might expect. In other words, there is much variation in the practice of transcription. Variation may occur because we say things differently at different times, e.g., formal speaking, recitation speech, informal speech, etc. Therefore when one imagines how one says a word in preparation for transcription, depending on whether one is thinking of formal speech or informal speech, the phonetic quality of that word might vary.

Additional variation in transcription practice may occur because the differing levels of detail one wishes to examine. For instance, one may need (or simply wish) to capture each and every phonetic gesture in transcription. For instance the *t*- sounds in *take* and *stake* are phonetically quite distinct: the [t] in *take* is followed by a puff of air, or aspiration, while the [t] in *stake* occurs without such aspiration. You can feel the puff of air associated with aspiration by placing your hand in front of your mouth while pronouncing each word and contrasting the two t-sounds. In a narrower transcription, one might capture the aspirated [t] by placing a superscript [ʰ] after [t], e.g., [tʰ]. However, for a broad transcription, one may omit such details. In the exercise below a broader transcription is appropriate following the descriptions of English sounds given above. If one were to take more advanced coursework in linguistics, narrower transcription practices would be expected.

EXERCISE

4.1   Use IPA symbols to represent the sounds of the following words. The answer key follows the exercise.

Conventional Spelling   **IPA**
e.g., <cat>   [kæt]
1. <maze>
2. <mouse>
3. <mice>
4. <thigh>
5. <sign>
6. <quick>
7. <shake>
8. <churches>
9. <move>
10. <yeast>
11. <ought>
12. <look>
13. <feet>
14. <note>
15. <racket>
16. <rocket>
17. <gateway>
18. <poster>
19. <backache>
20. <pizza>
21. <oblige>
22. <candle>
23. <recipes>
24. <certain>
25. <peanuts>

CHAPTER FIVE

Germanic

Chapter 3 introduced the reconstruction of Proto-Indo-European (PIE). In this chapter, we will narrow our focus to the branch or family of PIE to which Present-Day English (PDE) belongs, Germanic.

MIGRATION OF THE INDO-EUROPEANS

Current scholarship posits a general period for Indo-European inhabitation of a common homeland from between the fifth and fourth millennia until about 2,500 BCE. Of course, these dates are very broad markers: no one would suggest that in the year 2,499 all common inhabitation of the Indo-European homeland ceased. But around 2,500 BCE sustained migration away from the Indo-European homeland had likely became significant enough that we can begin to talk about the development of branches or families of languages from Indo-European (IE).

Migration is an external motivation for language change. Migration puts speakers of one language in contact with speakers of other languages, for one thing, and language contact can motivate language change on many levels. Migration also isolates groups of speakers from other groups of speakers of the same language, and the languages spoken by these isolated groups will, over time, develop significant differences (consider, for example, the differences between British and American English, or the regional variations in American English in the present day).

The Indo-Europeans migrated throughout the Eurasian continent, from present-day India to Scandinavia. Records of Tocharian, an IE language, have been found as far east as China. After this period of migration and settlement, we can no longer talk about IE as a living language: rather, IE by that time would have developed into a number of new languages—languages that are clearly related to each other but also different enough from each other that speakers of some of these languages would not have understood speakers of others.

For a long time, scholars considered texts such as the Vedas, collections of hymns written in a form of Sanskrit, which can be dated as early as 1,500 BCE, to have been the oldest writings in languages descended from IE. However, later even older records of some ancient IE languages were discovered, such as the cuneiform writings in Hittite, dating from the sixteenth century BCE.

THE GERMANIC BRANCH OF INDO-EUROPEAN

The period during which Germanic developed is between 2,500 and 100 BCE. Again these are very rough dates. If we had to assign a date by which Germanic existed as a language distinct from IE, we could reasonably argue for a date of around 500 BCE. But it is essential to realize that this date cannot be precise: we can propose a rough period based on linguistic and historical reconstruction, but we cannot provide an exact date for the appearance of these early languages. During the period between about 2,500 and 100 BCE, Germanic-speaking peoples settled throughout much of what is now Europe north and west of the Danube, and east into present-day Russia. Significant to the history of the English language, during this period, the Germanic tribes did not extend their settlement to the island that would eventually become England. Large-scale Germanic settlement of the territory that would become England is not dated until the fifth century CE (see Chapter 7).

Germanic peoples did not leave much in the way of early written records of their language and culture. Although a set of symbols called **runes** was employed throughout the Germanic world, it is likely that the material into which these symbols was most often carved was a soft material like wood or bark which does not survive long under most conditions. Runic inscriptions do survive from as early as the second century CE, and quite a number of later inscriptions on wood, bone (even a human skull), and stone survive. But for the purposes of studying Germanic as a language, these inscriptions are too late: they record languages that have developed *from* Germanic. For our description of Germanic as a language, we are dependent on comparative reconstruction (see Chapter 3 and below in this chapter).

However, Germanic peoples did come into contact with other cultures, like that of the Romans, which kept records in writing. Some of those writings survive to the present day. The Romans not only fought Germanic tribes as they expanded and later defended the Roman Empire (beginning in the second century BCE, and continuing until the fall of Rome in the fifth century CE), but also eventually employed a large number of Germanic tribesmen within the Roman army. In fact, the Romans provide us with a number of descriptions of early Germanic peoples.

The Roman historian Tacitus, for example, writing around the end of the first century CE, describes the Germanic tribes: "All have fierce blue eyes, red hair, huge frames, fit only for a sudden exertion. They are less able to bear laborious work. Heat and thirst they cannot in the least endure; to cold and hunger their climate and their soil inure them."[1] One obvious problem with the descriptions that Tacitus provides is that these descriptions clearly come from a Roman perspective, and often these descriptions serve less to describe the Germanic peoples than to validate or critique Roman traditions and practices.

The descriptions Tacitus provides, however, continue to this day to influence descriptions of Germanic cultures. For example, Tacitus writes about the centrality of warfare and the bonds between warriors:

> When they go into battle, it is a disgrace for the chief to be surpassed in valour, a disgrace for his followers not to equal the valour of the chief. And it is an infamy and a reproach for life to have survived the chief, and returned from the field. To defend, to protect him, to ascribe one's own brave deeds to his renown, is the height of loyalty. The chief fights for victory; his vassals fight for their chief.... Feasts and entertainments, which, though inelegant, are plentifully furnished, are their only pay. The means of this bounty come from war and rapine. Nor are they as easily persuaded to plough the earth and to wait for the year's produce as to challenge an enemy and earn the honour of wounds. Nay, they actually think it tame and stupid to acquire by the sweat of toil what they might win by their blood.[2]

This description is still recognizable in many contemporary popular depictions of early Germanic peoples (as, for example, in films like *The Thirteenth Warrior* or the 2004 *King Arthur*).

Tacitus's descriptions, however culturally biased, are partially confirmed by the archeological evidence. For example, we can deduce from the remains and grave goods at burial sites that Germanic peoples farmed to some degree and hunted, and that Germanic culture centered on a male warrior elite, as Tacitus claims; and that Germanic peoples lived in smaller settlements and worshipped a number of gods.

By the time Tacitus wrote, at the end of the first century CE, the Germanic peoples he described identified themselves not as Germanic peoples as a whole, but as members of specific Germanic tribes. In the centuries to follow, the languages of these different tribes would develop into clearly separate languages. It is traditional to classify these languages as belonging to the North Germanic, East Germanic, and West Germanic groups.

---

1 Tacitus, *The Agricola and Germania*, trans. A.J. Church and W.J. Brodribb (London: Macmillan, 1877), 3.
2 Tacitus, *The Agricola and Germania*, 10.

NORTH, EAST, AND WEST GERMANIC

In the diagram of IE languages, included in Chapter 3 and reproduced below, the line of development follows from PIE to Germanic, and then to North, East and West Germanic.

There are no longer any living East Germanic languages. But an East Germanic language, Gothic, survives in the written record in a Biblical translation from the fourth century.

North Germanic languages include Old Norse and the present-day Scandinavian languages, Swedish, Norwegian, Icelandic, Danish, and Faroese. (But not Finnish—see Chapter 3.) Old Norse had a very significant influence on the development of English, as we will discuss in later chapters.

English is a West Germanic language, like German, Dutch, Frisian, and Yiddish. Note, however, that West Germanic has High and **Low West Germanic** groups. The terms "High" and "Low" are not about cultural valuation. "High" Germanic languages are grouped together on the basis of similar changes in the sound system of the language; these languages tended to be spoken in the southern and mountainous regions of the West Germanic linguistic territory. German and Yiddish are **High West Germanic** languages. English, Frisian, and Dutch are Low, West Germanic languages. The Low West Germanic languages may also be classified into two groups: the Anglo-Frisian group comprised of English and Frisian, and the Old Dutch group. For our exposition in this book, we will group English, Frisian and Dutch together as Low varieties.

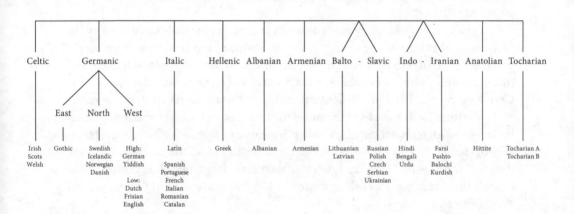

FIGURE 5.1   The Indo-European languages.

INTRODUCTION TO GERMANIC

Chapter 3 introduced the comparative method for reconstructing proto-languages. In that method, historical linguists compare the structures of related languages and then make hypotheses about the original form of the parent language. In order to carry out comparative reconstruction, however, linguists have to have some notion already that the languages to be compared are *in fact* related. But how is relatedness established?

The answer, at least in part, is found in Sir William Jones's famous 1786 proclamation, which was presented in Chapter 3. In that statement, Jones declared that Greek, Latin, and Sanskrit showed greater similarities in lexicon and grammar "than could possibly have been produced by accident."[3] Historical linguistic comparison begins, then, from the observation that the lexical and grammatical forms in the languages correspond in some systematic *and explainable* way.

It is also important to note that languages are related to one another by degree in the sense that they may be more related or less related. Referring back to the Indo-European family tree, it can be seen that English and Dutch are quite closely related; in the genetic model they might even be referred to as sister languages. English and Pashto, however, are more distantly related. Obviously then, the comparative method works not only to establish historical relatedness but also to make finer groupings of related languages.

Within the large related set of languages known as IE, Germanic is a higher-level group comprising the North, East, and West Germanic subgroups. As a subgroup distinct from other subgroups, such as Italic, Celtic, or Indic, the languages that make up the Germanic group show a number of similar, and somewhat distinct, structural details. In the remaining section of this chapter, we will review five distinctive features of Germanic.

FIVE DISTINCTIVE FEATURES OF GERMANIC

GRIMM'S LAW

Language is always changing, but most of that change is imperceptible to us during our lifetime. We certainly notice when a group of people have an accent different from our own (remembering of course that, to them, *we* have the accent!), but unless we are able to carry out some historical investigation, we don't know whether it is our or the others' pronunciation that is the original one (or if neither is the original). All we know is that another group "talks differently." For example, Americans notice

---

3   Philip Baldi, *An Introduction to the Indo-European Languages* (Carbondale, IL: Southern Illinois UP, 1983), 3.

that speakers of Southern UK Englishes, such as London English, pronounce /r/[4] differently from the way most Americans do, but without historical investigation we would not know whether the London English or American English "r" is the more "original" pronunciation.

Well before 1,000 BCE, speakers of dialects that would become the Germanic languages were already speaking their varieties of Indo-European with different accents/dialects from other varieties of Indo-European. Such small, slightly perceptible differences continued to occur until Germanic began to diverge from other varieties of IE, becoming a separate language and branch within the IE family, again probably by around 500 BCE.

Much later, in the early nineteenth century, a philologist (i.e., a scholar of historical languages and cultures) named Jakob Grimm made a series of observations about Germanic languages that enabled scholars to account for the systematic way in which the sounds of Germanic languages differed from the sounds of other Indo-European languages. Jakob Grimm, along with his brother Wilhelm, would later become famous for a collection of Germanic fairy tales, but he is important in the study of the history of the English language because he noted a set of regular correspondences between certain consonants in Germanic languages and consonants in other non-Germanic, Indo-European languages. There is some controversy as to how much of the discovery was in fact Grimm's. As we noted in Chapter 3, history has a tendency to associate big ideas with single figures, and consequently the set of Germanic sound changes discussed here have come to be known as **Grimm's Law**.

The essence of Grimm's Law is that certain consonants in Indo-European changed in Germanic. The change, also known as the **First Germanic Sound Shift**, affected specific groups of consonants at a time. The first set of changes is summarized as:

Proto-Indo-European		Germanic
p	>	f
t	>	θ
k	>	h

These changes should be read as "a voiceless, bilabial stop in IE became a voiceless labio-dental fricative in Germanic" and so on. The exercises at the end of this chapter ask you to write out the other two changes of this step in the same way.

The effect of this first set of changes is that a word with a /p/ in a non-Germanic, IE language will very often have a cognate in the Germanic languages with an /f/ in the same place; a non-Germanic /t/ will be /θ/ in Germanic, and a /k/ will be /h/. Although the operation of Grimm's Law is fairly straightforward, sometimes the consonants underwent further changes in various Germanic languages, so the cor-

---

4   The slanted brackets are a way of referring to a sound as a mental category, which will be explained further in Chapter 6.

respondence is not always immediately evident. The following are some examples of the change in Germanic. While the English word in each case would be enough to illustrate the effect of Grimm's Law, the examples from other Germanic languages are offered in order to show the broader linguistic scope of the change.

Non-Germanic, Indo-European	Germanic
pitar (father, Sanskrit)	_fader_ (father, Gothic)
tres (three, Latin)	_þrír_ (three, Icelandic)
kardiá (heart, Greek)	_Herz_ (heart, German)

The letter <þ> in the Icelandic word for _three_ is called "thorn." Its phonetic realization is [θ], the sound signaled in English with the letters <th>. Students of the history of English must become acquainted with <þ> because it was a frequently used letter in Old English (and other Germanic languages like Gothic). It has its origins in the runic alphabet.

The next set of changes affected voiced stops which became voiceless stops in Germanic:

Proto-Indo-European		Germanic
b	>	p
d	>	t
g	>	k

Examples:

Non-Germanic, Indo-European	Germanic
balá (swamp, Lithuanian)	_pool_ (English)
diente (tooth, Spanish)	_tunþu_ (tooth, Gothic)
góny (knee, Greek)	_cneo_ (knee, Old English)

In Old English (OE) the <c> was pronounced in the word _kneo_. In PDE, we spell _knee_ with an initial <k>, although that sound was lost in the word at some point in the history of English. We now sometimes think of the <k> as a "silent" letter.

The third set of correspondences shows an IE aspirated voiced stop becoming an unaspirated voiced stop. The /h/ after the consonant represents aspiration in the IE sounds.

Proto-Indo-European		Germanic
bh	>	b
dh	>	d
gh	>	g

Examples of this change are very hard to find in the daughter languages of IE because the aspirated voiced stop changed in most other IE languages too, although not necessarily into /b/, /d/, and /g/. However, Sanskrit sometimes preserved the original IE aspirated stop.

bhárami (I bear, Sanskrit)	*bairan* (to bear, Gothic)
dhrsnóti (he dares, Sanskrit)	*dare* (English)
*ghans (kind of aquatic bird, Indo-European)	*gans* (goose, Dutch)

Again, the asterisk at the beginning of the PIE word **ghans* means that the form is not attested but reconstructed.

In conclusion it should be noted that at the time Grimm formulated these sound changes, scholars, including Grimm himself, had already noted apparent irregularities. For example, one of the shifts predicted in Grimm's Law is /t/ → /θ/, but in the word for *father*, the IE /t/ did not become Germanic /θ/, but became instead /ð/ in Germanic, as in Gothic *fader*. (The letter <d> in Gothic when it occurs between two vowels represents the sound [ð].) Over the years, the apparent irregularities were explained by various scholars in various ways. The "exception" in Gothic *fader* was explained by **Karl Verner**[5] who showed that a voiceless stop between vowels became a voiced fricative in Germanic when the stress did not precede the stop. That is, Verner demonstrated that Grimm's Law operated predictably when the stress in the word followed the sound in question. But it did not operate in the same way if stress preceded the sound in question. The Proto-Indo-European word for father was reconstructed as **pitár*, with the stress on the last syllable, *after* the voiceless stop; therefore, Grimm's Law did not operate on that sound according to the rules explained above. Note, of course, that the /p/ sound in the word **pitár* is the first sound in the word, and consequently it shifts predictably, according to Grimm's Law, to /f/ in Germanic.

FIXED INITIAL STRESS ON THE ROOT

Stress patterns in IE may follow one of two very general types. Some languages have fixed stress systems in which the stress always falls on the same syllable of every word. Others allow stress on different syllables of a word depending on how many affixes are added to the word. These are called *variable stress* languages. For example, Spanish shows variable stress in the same word depending on the endings that are added to the word. Thus in Spanish the first-person singular form of the verb *hablar* in the present tense, *hablo* (I speak), has stress on the *hab-* syllable. However, the first-person plural form, *hablamos* (we speak), shows stress on the *-la-* syllable.

5   Karl A. Verner (1877). "Eine Ausnahme der ersten Lautverschiebung." *Zeitschrift für vergleichende Sprachforschung auf dem Gebiete der Indogermanischen Sprachen* 23.2: 97–130.

Germanic languages tend toward a fixed stress system, in which the stress falls on the first syllable of the root.

he̠stur (horses, Icelandic)   *o̠mvende* (convert, Norwegian)
Re̠gen (rain, German)   *le̠bedik* (lively, Yiddish)
bie̠zem (broom, Frisian)   *ho̠uses* (English)

English has been influenced by many other languages in its history and has borrowed many words from non-Germanic languages, especially French, Latin, and Greek. Therefore Modern English (ModE) has many examples of words that do not follow the pattern of fixed initial stress. Instead those borrowed words may show the stress pattern of the language they were borrowed from, or new stress patterns may have been created after borrowing into English:

cata̠strophe
produ̠ction
laissez-fa̠ire

TWO-TENSE SYSTEM

Chapter 3 briefly introduced the verb in IE and provided a verb synopsis from Ancient Greek. The verbal system of Ancient Greek was rather complex in terms of verbal affixes and the verb took many different forms depending on its tense, aspect, and mood. Students who have studied other non-Germanic IE languages are familiar with that complexity as well. For example in Spanish, the present tense has one set of endings (habl*o*, habl*as*, habl*a*...); the imperfect another set (habl*aba*, habl*abas*, habl*aba*...); the preterit another (habl*é*, habl*aste*, habl*ó*...); the future another (hablar*é*, hablar*ás*, hablar*á*...); the conditional still another (hablar*ía*, hablar*ías*, hablar*ía*...).

A comparison of the Germanic languages (especially the older varieties of them) suggests that Proto-Germanic expressed only two tenses through verbal affixes, the simple present and the simple past. Nor did it have elaborate aspectual forms as in Greek, Spanish, or any number of other IE languages. Even in the modern Germanic languages, verbal affixes express the simple present and simple past tense, as is seen in the following examples for the words *opens* and *opened* in three modern Germanic languages.

English	Swedish	German
opens	öppnar	öffnet
opened	öppnade	öffnete

The formal simplicity of tense and aspect in Germanic should not be taken to mean that there have not developed grammatical means of expressing future or specific aspectual categories. However, future and many aspect distinctions are expressed periphrastically instead of synthetically. In fact the development of periphrastic expressions for tense/aspect (as suggested in Chapter 2) has been extensive in English (and other Germanic languages). Here are only some of the periphrases that have developed to express tense/aspect meanings in the history of English.

Periphrasis	Tense/Aspect Meaning
will + verb	future
shall + verb	future
be going to + verb	future
is + -ing	present progressive
was + -ing	past progressive
have + -en	present perfect
had + -en	past perfect
keep on + -ing	iterative
used to + verb	past habitual

Obviously the development of these periphrases is an important part of the way that English has changed over the years.

STRONG AND WEAK ADJECTIVES

Students who have studied an Indo-European language other than English will remember that in almost all Indo-European languages adjectives agree with the nouns they modify. In Spanish for example, to say *a red dog* you would say *un perro rojo* (literally "a dog red" because adjectives normally follow the noun in Spanish). The word *rojo* ends in -*o*, signaling that it is singular and masculine. The gender and number of the adjective are governed by the noun it modifies, in this case *perro*, which is singular and masculine. However, if a person wants to say *a red house*, they would say *una casa roja*. Now the ending of the adjective has changed to -*a*, singular and feminine, because the noun it modifies, *casa*, is singular and feminine. If a person wanted to say *red houses*, then the adjective would be *rojas* because it would have to agree with the noun *casas*, which is now feminine and plural, *casas rojas*. We can sum up this situation in Spanish by saying that the adjective agrees with the noun in gender and number.

ModE has almost completely lost agreement of this sort. Agreement can be seen, however, by looking at the choice between *this* and *these* in the expressions *this house* and *these houses*. *This* is used because *house* is singular and *these* is used when the noun is plural, as it is in *houses*. Other than among demonstratives, ModE shows no agreement within the noun phrase (see Chapter 2).

However, older English and the modern Germanic languages do have agreement within the noun phrase. In this respect, they are more like Spanish. Thus, as is true in most IE languages, including all older Germanic languages, adjectives can take several different forms depending on the gender and number of the noun. Additionally, Germanic languages inherited a system of case from IE. In some modern Germanic languages, like German, and in all older varieties of Germanic languages, nouns agree not only in gender and number, but also in case. As we discussed in Chapter 3, case can be thought of as a grammatical system in which a noun changes its form based on whether it is the subject, direct object, indirect object, etc.

The agreement system in Germanic shows still one more feature: **strong** and **weak adjective** forms. Again, remember that many modern Germanic languages have lost this distinction, as has English. In this context, the terms strong and weak do not refer to any sense of the adjective's muscularity or power. The terms strong and weak adjectives refer to two different sets of adjectival forms that are used in specific syntactic environments. In general, a weak adjective form was used when the noun phrase was definite such that the adjective forms came to be used after the definite article, a possessive or a demonstrative, but not an indefinite article. The strong forms were in indefinite contexts, and thus were used when there was no determiner and eventually with the developing indefinite article. Compare these two German sentences:

Der grosse Hund liegt auf dem Boden. (The big dog lies on the floor.)
Ein grosser Hund liegt auf dem Boden. (A big dog lies on the floor.)

In both sentences the adjective *gross-* is masculine, singular, and nominative, because in both cases it modifies a singular, masculine noun that is acting as the subject of the sentence. However in the first sentence, the adjective is *grosse* and in the second it is *grosser*. The difference is that in the first sentence the noun phrase *der grosse Hund* begins with a determiner, the definite article *der*, and in that syntactic environment the weak form of the adjective is selected. However in the second sentence the noun phrase begins with an indefinite article, and in that syntactic environment, the strong form of the adjective is selected.

When a person learns German, he or she has to learn two different sets of endings for adjectives and then use them in the appropriate syntactic environment. While many modern Germanic languages no longer have the strong and weak adjective distinction, or only show traces of it, that system of adjectives was a prominent feature of all older Germanic languages, including Old English. Thus, we will return to that distinction in the next chapter.

STRONG AND WEAK VERBS

Germanic languages show a split system for marking simple past tense on verbs. In that system verbs are classed as **strong verbs** or **weak verbs** depending on a "dental suffix." These verbs include English examples like *walked, hurried, fretted*; the dental suffix attached to weak verbs in English is what English speakers probably think of as the regular *-ed* past tense suffix. However, while literate English speakers have been taught to think of that regular past tense marker in terms of its written form *-ed*, the regular past tense ending actually subsumes three different pronunciations in speech. For verbs that end in a voiced sound other than [d], the *-ed* will sound like [d]: *hurry* [hʌɹi] → *hurried* [hʌɹid], *call* [kɑl]→ *called* [kɑld], etc. For verbs that end in a voiceless sound other than [t], the *-ed*, however, sounds like [t]: *park* [pɑɹk] → *parked* [pɑɹkt], *miss* [mɪs]→ *missed* [mɪst]. In fact, some verbs actually have the past tense suffix written as <t>, *kept, dreamt*, etc. Finally for verbs that end in [d] or [t], the *-ed* will sound like [əd]: *hoard* [hoɹd] → *hoarded* [hoɹdəd], *rot* [ɹɑt]→ *rotted* [ɹɑɾəd].

It might also seem odd that *-ed* and its various pronunciations, all of which involve [t] or [d], should be called a dental suffix, since in Chapter 4 [t] and [d] are classified as alveolar consonants. In older phonetic classifications all sounds made at the alveolar ridge or the teeth were classed as "dental" and in historical or cross-Germanic studies the term remains. However, it is only in this instance that [t] and [d] should be thought of as dental.

The past tense formation strategy for strong verbs involves ablaut. Ablaut is a system of vowel gradations. Most English speakers learned ablaut as a concern of irregular verbs: *speak* → *spoke, drink* → *drank, meet* → *met*, etc. At this point it should be noted that "irregularity" is often not so irregular when one considers the historical development of the forms in question. Although in ModE, there may seem no reason for the <i> in *drink* to change to <a> in the simple past, there is a historical explanation for it. In fact, ablaut of this kind was much more regular in OE; it was part of a more comprehensible pattern that will be presented in Chapter 7.

While the examples of *talked* and *drank* show the weak/strong distinction in English, here in order to illustrate the feature within the broader context of Germanic we offer other examples of the third person singular of the simple present and the simple past from other Germanic languages.

	German	Gothic	Swedish
Weak	*werkt–werkte* (works–worked)	*sōkeiþ–sōkjada* (seeks–sought)	*frågar–frågade* (asks–asked)
Strong	*singt–sang* (sings–sang)	*bindeþ–band* (binds–bound)	*sjunger–sjöng* (sings–sang)

CONCLUSION

English is an Indo-European language. More specifically, it is a Germanic Indo-European language. It shares a range of features with other Indo-European languages, but historically and structurally, it is most closely related to other Germanic languages, with which it shares distinctive features such as a system of strong and weak verbs, a two-tense system, a system of strong and weak adjectives, fixed initial stress on the root, and a consonant system which differs from those of other Indo-European languages in ways that can be explained by Grimm's Law. Germanic is a reconstructed language, but textual evidence of the North, East, and West Germanic languages which develop from Germanic does survive. In Chapter 7, we will begin our study of the Low West Germanic language Old English.

EXERCISES

5.1 What are the rough dates for the period during which the Indo-Europeans likely inhabited a common homeland?

5.2 What are the rough dates for the period during which Germanic develops?

5.3 English is

   a. West Germanic
   b. East Germanic
   c. North Germanic

5.4 English is most closely related to

   a. Present-day German: both are High West Germanic languages
   b. Present-day Yiddish: both are Low East Germanic languages
   c. Present-day Dutch: both are Low West Germanic languages
   d. Present-day Swedish: both are High North Germanic languages
   e. Present-day Finnish: both are High West Germanic languages

Each of the following items demonstrates a feature of Germanic languages. Name that feature.

For example: Latin <u>p</u>ater   English <u>f</u>ather
              Latin <u>p</u>es, <u>p</u>edis   English <u>f</u>oot

These pairs demonstrate one phase of the consonant shift described by Grimm's Law (and thus one way in which the consonants of Germanic languages differ predictably from those of other Indo-European languages).

5.5 English   I praise. I prais<u>ed</u>. <u>I will praise</u>.
     Latin   Laud<u>ō</u>. Laudā<u>vī</u>. Laudā<u>bō</u>

     Old English Ić lufode <u>þone</u> god<u>an</u> mann.
                  I loved the good man.

                  Ić lufode   god<u>ne</u> mann.
                  I loved (a) good man.

     English   I wal<u>k</u>. I wal<u>ked</u>.
                  I study. I stud<u>ied</u>.
                  I drive. I dr<u>o</u>ve.
                  I sing. I s<u>a</u>ng.

     Old English *her*ie, *her*ian
     Latin   laud*ō*, laud*ā*re
                  (above, the italics indicate the place of stress in the word)

5.6 **The first step of Grimm's Law can be represented as**

Indo-European		**Germanic**
p	>	f
t	>	θ
k	>	h

The first of the changes listed above, IE p → Germanic f, should be read as "a voiceless bilabial stop in IE became, in Germanic, a voiceless labio-dental fricative."

Provide the description for the remaining changes in this step,

t   > θ
k   > h

A _____ _____ _____ in IE

became a _____ _____ _____
in Germanic.

A _____ _____ _____ in IE
became a _____ _____ _____
in Germanic.

5.7 Given the following PIE roots, supply the initial consonant sound you would expect in a Germanic language. Be sure to use IPA!

PIE	Germanic
*pisk-	_____
*trei-	_____
*dent-	_____
*gen-	_____
*kerd-	_____

5.8 Which of the following are retentions of features of IE in Germanic, and which are innovations? That is, which of the following descriptions of Germanic are also true of IE (retentions), and which are new features, features of Germanic which are *not* inherited from IE (innovations)?

a. a system of case which includes different inflections to mark the subject, the object, and the possessive
b. a two-tense system
c. a system of grammatical (not natural) gender
d. both strong and weak verbs, i.e., both the dental preterite and ablaut
e. a system of strong and weak adjectives

CHAPTER SIX

Four Important Terms and Concepts

Orthography, phonology, morphology, and syntax are important terms and concepts for the historical study of language. We are therefore pausing in this very short chapter to provide definitions and further exemplification of these essential terms and concepts. In all following chapters, we will assume that readers have a thorough understanding of what these terms mean. Orthographic forms are indicated with angled brackets, <>. Phonological forms are indicated with slanted brackets, //. Specific and more detailed sounds, i.e., phones, are indicated in square bracket [ ].

Orthography refers to the system for representing a language in *writing*. We sometimes use the term "conventional spelling" for orthography. It is essential to understand that orthography is about writing. It is not about sound or sound systems. The letter <s> must not be thought of as being equivalent to the sound [s]. As Chapter 4 explains, one of the reasons we need a system like IPA, with a one-to-one correspondence between sounds and symbols for representing those sounds, is that conventional spelling systems are not adequate for representing all of the sounds of a language. We have many more sounds in English than we have letters of the alphabet. And our set of orthographic symbols both includes multiple representatives for a single sound and represents multiple sounds with a single symbol. For example, the sound [f] can be represented as in *fish*, or *tough*, or *phenomenon*. The letter <s> represents several sounds, as in *soup, pleasure, cheese*. And conventional spelling includes a number of letters that do not represent sounds, such as the <k> in *knee*.

The orthography of English has changed in the course of its nearly 1,500 years of history. The word for ship, for example, was represented in the orthography of Old English as *scip*. The Old English (OE) word was pronounced with the same initial sound, [ʃ], as in Present-Day English (PDE). In this instance, we can see a difference in the orthography of the OE and PDE English words *scip* and *ship* even though the initial sound has remained the same.

Phonology, in contrast to orthography, refers to the sound system of a language. As a system, phonology is characterized by regular patterning. The basic unit of phonology is the **phoneme**, which we will define as an abstract mental category of a sound. In actual speech, that abstract mental category may manifest itself in slightly different sounds, however. The exact sound depends on the phonetic environment in which the phoneme is produced. The various manifestations in speech are referred to as **allophones** of the phoneme.

For example, speakers of English have stored in their minds a phoneme /p/. However, that /p/ manifests itself as [pʰ] (aspirated "p") or [p] (unaspirated "p") depending on where it occurs in the word that is spoken. If /p/ is to occur at the beginning of a word or before a stressed vowel it will be [pʰ], as in *peanut* [pʰinət]. When /p/ occurs before an unstressed vowel, it is [p], as in *repossess* [ripəzɛs]. The pattern of [pʰ] or [p] according to the above rule is completely regular and the statement of the distribution just given constitutes a *phonological rule*.

Another way of looking at a phoneme is that it is a collection of similar sounds: /p/ is the set containing [pʰ], [p], etc. (Note there are some other allophones, or variations of the sound /p/ that we haven't discussed.) The fact that a phoneme has different allophones is precisely why phonology is important in learning the history of a language, because sometimes phonemic–allophonic relationships can shift, as they do, for instance, when former allophones become separate phonemes. While such a change may not seem all that important on the surface, consider the fact that in some sense the development of phoneme status (phonemicization) raises the status of a sound into its own mental category, making speakers of a language aware of the sound on a new level. Therefore the sound may come to mark distinction, i.e., be able to make a difference in the meaning of a word. This awareness may then result in changes to the orthography of the language as well.

For example, the voiced fricatives [v], [ð] and [z] in Old English were merely allophones of the phonemes /f/, /θ/, and /s/. In addition, /f/ had at least two allophones—the voiced [v] and the voiceless [f]. As allophones, their distribution could be captured by a phonological rule: [v] appeared between two voiced sounds (most often between two vowels) and [f] appeared everywhere else. (Chapter 7 treats the OE fricatives in more detail). Thus the OE word *ofer* (over) was [ovɛr] because the /f/ occurred between vowels, i.e., two voiced sounds, and the OE word *for* (for) was [for] because /f/ was not between two voiced sounds.

So it is most likely that OE speakers didn't notice the difference between [f] and [v] any more than PDE speakers notice the difference between [pʰ] and [p]. However, toward the end of the OE period, [v] split off from [f] and became a phoneme in its own right, due to a number of internal and external pressures (see Chapter 8). With its new phonemic status, /v/ became distinctive; that is, it could signal the difference between words like *fat* and *vat*. One important effect of the emergence of phonemic status for [v] is that it prompts changes in conventional spelling; the letter <v> was never used for [v] in OE but was regularized in English orthography beginning in Middle English (ME) (along with <z>).

Morphology has to do with the composition of words and their meaningful parts. The smallest part of a word with meaning is called a **morpheme**. The word *cat* consists of only one morpheme, *cat*. We cannot divide the word into any smaller units that have meaning. But morphemes can certainly occur in combination, as, for example in compound words like *catfish*. And there are several different kinds of morphemes. In the word *cats*, for example, two morphemes can be identified. One, *cat*, is referential: it refers to something in the world outside of language. The other morpheme, *-s*, has a different kind of meaning: it tells us *cats* is plural. Another difference between these two morphemes is that one can occur independently: *cat* can occur as a freestanding word. But *-s* can occur only in combination with another morpheme: it is an affix.

We can divide morphemes into two broad categories, free and bound. **Free morphemes** can occur independently. They can be lexical or referential, like *cat*, or they can be grammatical, like the *is* in *is writing*. **Bound morphemes** like *-s* must occur in combination with a free morpheme. Bound morphemes can be inflectional, like *-s*, or derivational, like the suffix *-ly*. **Inflectional morphemes** carry grammatical meaning. Inflectional morphemes in PDE include the *-ing* of the present participle (as in *writing*), the *-s* of the third-person singular present indicative (as in *she writes*), the *-s* of the possessive (as in the *book's authors*), and the *-er* of the comparative (as in *smaller*).

Derivational morphemes can change the meaning of a word or can change the part of speech for a word. For example, *un-* changes the meaning of the word to which it is prefixed (*fashionable* → *unfashionable*) and *-ly* often changes a word from an adjective to an adverb (*sweet* → *sweetly*).

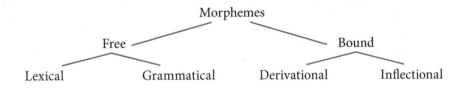

FIGURE 6.1   Classification of morphemes.

It is also possible for some roots of words to be bound and therefore not to appear as free morphemes. *-ceive* as in *deceive, conceive, perceive*, etc., is clearly a separate morpheme from the prefixes *de-, con-,* and *per-*, but it cannot stand alone as a word. Such morphemes are called bound roots (and cf. *-fer* in *confer, defer, refer,* and *-cede* in *concede, recede, precede,* etc.). Also, there are segments of words that have morpheme status, but whose meaning is not obvious. Consider for instance the *cran-* in *cranberry*. Since *berry* is so clearly a morpheme, *cran-* achieves morpheme status. Unlike the *black-* in *blackberry*, *cran-* does not occur as a free morpheme with a meaning anything like its meaning in *cranberry*. *Cran-* has as its likely source a word related to the English word *crane*.[1] *Cran-* is interesting because it has come to be used somewhat productively as an element in certain blended words, like *cranapple*. Such morphemes are called cranberry morphemes (and cf. *mul-* of *mulberry,* or *boysen-* of *boysenberry*.) While cranberry morphemes might seem meaningless from a synchronic standpoint, they are historically motivated. For instance, the *cob-* in *cobweb,* comes from the Middle English word *coppe* meaning *spider*.[2]

Syntax has to do with the meaningful arrangement of words into phrases and clauses. In PDE, the noun phrase can consist of a determiner followed by an adjective followed by a noun. But a noun phrase cannot be ordered as *adjective + noun + determiner. Matters like this one having to do with the meaningful ordering of words in phrases are matters of syntax. We can of course also consider syntax on the level of clauses and sentences.

As we have seen a few times already, one of the important developments in the history of English has been the addition of several verbal periphrases. Those developments fall under the topic of syntax. In Chapter 5, we showed that a two-tense verbal system was definitional of Germanic languages. The two tenses involved were the simple present and the simple past, both of which were expressed with inflectional suffixes. In other words, the forms were synthetic; that is, the grammatical information (tense) was expressed through bound morphology in a single-word form. However, in that chapter we also pointed out that many periphrastic verb forms for expressing various time and aspectual meanings have developed in the history of English (and continue to develop today). Those periphrastic forms are analytic (in contrast to synthetic) in that the grammatical information is expressed in a multi-word phrase. In the case of verbs, analytic (or periphrastic) forms will involve auxiliary verbs. Grammatical concepts expressed through analytic forms are a matter of syntax.

---

1   *OED Online,* s.v. *cranberry*.
2   *OED Online,* s.v. *cobweb*.

CHAPTER SEVEN

Old English

THE EARLY EXTERNAL HISTORY

The geographical territory that would eventually become England was not settled by Germanic peoples before about the fifth century CE. Rather, the people who lived in that territory were, for the most part, speakers of a number of Celtic languages. The Romans named the island **Britannia** after the **Britons**, one of these Celtic-speaking peoples.

The Britons, like the Germanic tribes on the continent, did not have a tradition of writing that might have made their history in their own terms available to us. They enter into our historical records largely through their contact with the Roman Empire. The Romans, under Julius Caesar, made military contact with the Britons in 55 and 54 BCE. In these early military contacts, the Romans were concerned less with conquest of the island than with acquiring tribute and preventing the Britons from allying with other Celtic tribes on the continent. But in 43 CE, under the rule the emperor Claudius, the Romans successfully imposed Roman rule on the Britons. For approximately the next 350 years, Britannia would be part of the Roman Empire.

ROMAN BRITAIN

During the 350 years during which Britannia was part of the Roman Empire, the Romans and Roman Britons built Roman-style villas, Roman roads, even Roman baths. The Romans also imported other aspects of Roman life, among them Roman literacy, so that for example, letters written by soldiers in Roman Britain survive and provide insight into what life was like in that colonial outpost. When the Romans accepted Christianity, Christianity also came to Roman Britain.

Although the Roman Empire was enormously powerful, it is also important to remember that Roman Britain was very far away from the political center of Rome (see Figure 7.1). And from the beginnings of Roman occupation, Britannia experienced both revolt from within the colony and attacks from without. Perhaps the most famous of the revolts from within is Boudicca's Revolt, in 60 or 61 CE, in which the Britons fought the Romans in a number of battles. In one of these battles, Londinium (Roman London) was burned to the ground. Evidence of the attacks from without is clear from the building of Hadrian's Wall in the early second century CE, a defensive structure stretching nearly from coast to coast. Much of Hadrian's Wall, which once marked the northernmost extent of Roman rule in Britannia, still stands.

FIGURE 7.1   Map of the Roman Empire.

Beginning in the fourth century CE, the Roman Empire itself was increasingly under attack in outposts like Roman Britain but more importantly, for the Romans, throughout the Empire. The Germanic tribes in this period posed significant threats to the Empire. The Visigoths and the Vandals, for example, not only attacked the peripheral colonies but penetrated into the very center of Rome, sacking the city of Rome itself in 410 and 455.

The Roman Empire, faced with these ongoing and serious threats as well as with a number of internal problems, withdrew its troops from colonial outposts like Roman Britain. The withdrawal of Roman troops from Britain, dated at around 410, is important to the history of the English language because it helped to create the political and economic conditions which made possible the large-scale migration and settlement of Germanic peoples in what had been Roman Britain.

The Romans had maintained a substantial military presence in Britain, with as many as 50,000 troops stationed there at some periods. As James Campbell writes, "This is a larger force than any medieval king of England ever managed to keep in the field, nor could any medieval king of England have maintained a standing force a tenth of that size."[1] The withdrawal of those troops would likely have caused a crisis under any circumstances. But in the middle of the fifth century, Roman Britain, now lacking the protection of the Roman army, was also besieged by a number of different peoples, among them, from the north and west, the Picts and the Scots, and from the east, tribes from the north Germanic plains including, notably, Germanic peoples: Angles, Saxons, Frisians, and Jutes.

THE ADVENT OF THE ANGLES, SAXONS, AND JUTES

The British historian Gildas, writing in the sixth century, describes the period during which the Britons were under attack by the Picts and Scots. He recounts an appeal to the Romans for aid, which did not come: "The barbarians drive us to the sea; the sea throws us back on the barbarians: thus two modes of death await us, we are either slain or drowned."[2] But in Gildas's account, the most terrible period for the Britons was that of the arrival of the Angles, Saxons, and Jutes.

As Gildas describes it, and as the later Anglo-Saxon historian **Bede** describes it two centuries later (731 CE), the Britons, driven to desperation by the attacks from the Picts and Scots, finally appeal not to the Romans, who had refused multiple earlier appeals, but to Germanic mercenaries. In 449 CE, according to Bede, at the invitation of the British king Vortigern, the Angles and Saxons came to Britain; they were granted land on the condition that they provided military aid to the Britons. Bede writes, "It was not long before such hordes of these alien peoples vied together to crowd into the island that the natives who had invited them began to live in terror.... In short, the fires kindled by the pagans proved to be God's just punishment on the sins of the nation...."[3]

It is unlikely that the settlement of these Germanic tribes was simply an invasion and slaughter, as Bede and Gildas describe it; it is more likely that it involved a large-scale migration to a territory where there was already a population of Germanic

---

1   James Campbell, Eric John, and Patrick Wormald, *The Anglo-Saxons* (New York: Penguin, 1991), 13–14.

2   Gildas, *De Excidio Britanniae*, in *Six Old English Chronicles*, trans. J.A. Giles (London: Henry G. Bohn, 1848), 308.

3   Bede the Venerable, *History of the English Church and People*, trans. Leo Sherley-Price, rev. R.E. Latham (New York: Penguin, 1987) 56–60.

settlers. And it is clear that the outcome was that the formerly Romanized Celtic-speaking Britons, as more or less unified political entities, were pushed out of the lands in the south and east, and into territories in the north and west, like Wales. It is also clear that within a century after the advent of these tribes from the North Germanic plains, a number of kingdoms ruled by people we can now call Anglo-Saxons dominated the island.

We can get some indication of what social relations were like between the Britons and the Anglo-Saxons by looking at words in English and in certain Celtic languages. By the time we have written records of the language of the Anglo-Saxons, their word *wealh* meant a Briton, or Welsh person, but also *stranger, foreigner* and even *slave*. The fact that the name of a conquered people came to have such clearly pejorative meanings reflects the attitude of the conquerors toward these people. Similarly, among Celtic speakers, even today, the word for Saxon preserves some indication of these relations: in Scottish *sassenach* or Welsh *saesneg* is synonymous with *foreigner* or *enemy*.

The Anglo-Saxons did absorb some words from the Britons, place names like *Thames* or *Kent*, and words for geological features like *torr* (a high, rocky peak), a common element in place names like *Torcross*. But the borrowing was quite limited and concentrated on native place names or words for geographical features unfamiliar to the Anglo-Saxons, former inhabitants of the flat northern Continental lowlands. In some ways, these patterns of borrowing are not unlike the borrowing that occurred in the American colonies when speakers of English borrowed native names for places like *Waukegan* from Native American languages. Patterns of borrowings such as these, being so largely tied to physicality (as opposed to more deeply cultural kinds of borrowing), being chiefly lexical (as opposed to grammatical), and numbering only about a dozen words in total, suggest strongly that Celtic-speaking peoples had little cultural influence among their conquerors. However, these patterns of borrowings alone cannot support a view of extended and long-term violence against Celtic speakers or of a wholesale emigration of Celtic speakers away from Anglo-Saxon territories.

We must emphasize that we discuss Anglo-Saxon dominance in terms of political entities: there must have been a considerable and sustained presence of the Britons in what would become Anglo-Saxon territories even long after Anglo-Saxon settlement, as archeological and now DNA evidence suggest. And subsequent Anglo-Saxon descriptions of the island maintain that such diversity continues well into the period of Anglo-Saxon dominance. The Anglo-Saxon Chronicle, one of the earliest histories written in a vernacular language, in this case Old English (OE), and dating from the end of the ninth century, for example, reiterates Bede's earlier description as it begins, "The island Britain is 800 miles long, and 200 miles broad. And there are in the island five languages; English, Welsh [or British], Scottish, Pictish, and

Latin."[4] Even more recently, linguists have begun to question the earlier dismissal of the influence of Celtic languages as limited to proper nouns and just a few lexical items. Filppula et al., for example, argue that certain unique grammatical features of English that set it apart from other Germanic languages, such as the use of the auxiliary *do* in questions (*Do you know the time?*), are due to the lasting linguistic influences of Celtic languages.

One reason for the representation of the advent of the Angles and Saxons as a violent and destructive invasion has to do with the nature of the sources which record that advent. Gildas was Celtic and a Christian monk. Bede, writing his *History of the English Church and People* in the early part of the eighth century, was also a Christian monk, and he wrote with a particular ideological investment. The Celtic Britons were Romanized and in many cases Christian. The Germanic tribes who came to dominate the Britons were neither Christian nor literate in the way that the Romans were. They did not leave a written history of these events in their own terms or from their own perspectives. For the Christian historians of the early Middle Ages, Germanic dominance over the native Christian people of the former Roman Britain was seen as, at best, punishment for the sins of those people.

CONVERSION OF THE ANGLO-SAXONS

Because these Germanic peoples did not leave written records, we have almost no record of their language during the early period of settlement. But in 596/597, Pope Gregory the Great instigated a plan to convert the Anglo-Saxon settlers to Christianity, and sent a group of monks under the leadership of Augustine to undertake the conversion. Within several generations of Augustine's mission, much of what would later become Anglo-Saxon England was converted to Christianity. Within a century and a half, it would become a center for Christian learning in Medieval Europe.

The conversion to Christianity is essential to the early history of the English language because with Christianity in the European Middle Ages comes literacy and written records. Before the conversion to Christianity, very few inscriptions survive, and these are brief, for example a single word carved in runic letters on a deer's anklebone, discovered at Caistor-by-Norwich, Norfolk. It is only after the conversion to Christianity that the Anglo-Saxons used writing extensively to transmit and preserve cultural materials, and hence only from after the conversion to Christianity that a significant number of written records of the language of the Anglo-Saxons survive.

Because the language of the Church during the Middle Ages was Latin, most of the written records that survive from this early period are not in English, but in

---

4 Text from Laud Misc. 636, fol 1r, Bodleian Library, Oxford. Translation is our own. Students interested in reading the Chronicle can find an online translation of the Anglo-Saxon Chronicle at the Online Medieval and Classical Library: http://omacl.org/Anglo/part1.html.

Latin. However, because Latin was a foreign language to the Anglo-Saxons, some of these Latin texts are glossed with OE words and phrases. The **Lindisfarne Gospels**, for example, were produced in the north of what is now England in the late seventh or early eighth century (see Figure 2). The manuscript is in Latin, but a later scribe wrote Old English words over and beside the Latin text, probably to make that text accessible to readers with less than fluent Latin (or at the very least more accessible to himself!). **Glossing**, the practice of annotating texts, provides us with many clues about OE, even when OE as a language is literally marginal to the Latin texts.

FIGURE 7.2   The Lindisfarne Gospels: Gospel of St Matthew the Evangelist, initial page. Lindisfarne, late 7th or early 8th century. British Library Cotton MS Nero D.IV.

BORROWINGS FROM LATIN

The visual image of the gloss also provides an apt metaphor for the relationship of Latin and English as languages off the page. Within religious domains, the Latin language held cultural and consequently linguistic dominance, and it is therefore no surprise that we find from this period a number of Latin borrowings into Old English. Many of these borrowings are closely associated with the Church. These borrowings include words like *angel, mass, priest*, and *nun*, words clearly associated with the introduction of Christianity. But Christianity, as we have already noted, also brought with it literacy. Borrowings like *school, gloss*, and *verse* were also introduced into Old English from Latin during this period. In addition, a number of words entered into English from Latin that reflected daily interactions in communities in which Latin was used and Old English was spoken, words like *oyster* and *sock*. The total number of Latin words borrowed into Old English during the early period following conversion to Christianity is around 450 words.[5]

One reason why we see fewer Latin borrowings than we might expect in this early period has to do with an Anglo-Saxon tendency to use native words for concepts that had analogues in Anglo-Saxon culture. The Old English word for *God*, for example, was *god*. The Anglo-Saxons did not borrow the Latin word *deus*. Rather, they used the native word in the new Christian context. Similarly, they used the native word *godspell* (literally "good news," *gospel* in Present-Day English [PDE]) instead of the Latin (from the Greek) *evangelium*.

EARLY ANGLO-SAXON/SCANDINAVIAN RELATIONS

The early history of Anglo-Saxon England was significantly affected by the conversion to Christianity: Christianity brought a number of cultural changes, including literacy. Anglo-Saxon England was also dramatically changed by another set of influences, this time at first violent conflict, and then settlement and cultural and linguistic exchange with another Germanic people, the Scandinavians. Although Anglo-Saxon sources often refer to these people as "Danes," the invaders and settlers were from a variety of places in Scandinavia: Present day Norway, Sweden, and Denmark. And, it should be mentioned, the boundaries and power relations among those peoples and places shifted throughout the period.

In 793, the northern monastery of Lindisfarne was attacked and plundered by Scandinavian raiders. While this attack was not the first Scandinavian attack on Anglo-Saxon England, it is often cited as the start of the **Viking Age**, a period lasting until the end of the eleventh century, during which Scandinavians raided, explored, conquered, and settled in territories ranging from England to Russia and

---

5   Albert C. Baugh and Thomas Cable, *A History of the English Language* (5th edition) (Upper Saddle River, NJ: Prentice Hall, 2002), 91.

even North America. Because they are so very significant to the history of the English language, we will return to the history of Anglo-Saxon/Scandinavian relations later in this chapter. We introduce them here for two reasons. The first is that these attacks broke up the early Anglo-Saxon kingdoms and made a fairly unified English kingdom possible: these attacks both created the political circumstances for a fairly unified English kingdom to arise, and contributed to the development of an idea of "Englishness" which could provide some ideological unity to that political entity in terms of cultural and linguistic identity. It is only after more than a century of Anglo-Saxon/Scandinavian conflict and Scandinavian settlement in England that an Anglo-Saxon king would claim to be not the king of a small regional kingdom, but the king of the English as a unified people. In fact, before the Scandinavian attacks, Anglo-Saxon England is best described as a number of small kingdoms, called the **Anglo-Saxon Heptarchy**.

FIGURE 7.3   The Anglo-Saxon Heptarchy. From *A Literary and Historical Atlas of Europe* by J.G. Bartholomew, 1910.

In the second half of the ninth century (865), the Scandinavian attacks on Anglo-Saxon territories became a full-scale military invasion, led by the famous sons of Ragnar Lodbrok. One by one, the kingdoms of the Heptarchy fell. The only kingdom to remain by 878 was the southern kingdom of **Wessex**. In 878, the king of Wessex, **Alfred the Great** (ruled 871–99), successfully defended Wessex and defeated the Scandinavian armies, led by Guthrum, at the Battle of Edington. After the Treaty of Wedmore, Alfred established a permanent settlement for Scandinavians to the north and east of Wessex. This settlement, called the **Danelaw**, allowed Scandinavians to live under Scandinavian law within territory that had once been part of the Heptarchy (see Figure 7.4). Alfred's successors chipped away at this territory, but of course they did not return it to its former rulers. Rather, Alfred's successors annexed that territory into Wessex. As generations of this "reclamation" accrued, Wessex, in a sense, eventually expanded until Alfred's successors could claim that they controlled a unified kingdom, albeit one with expanding and contracting borders, which we can identify as Anglo-Saxon England.

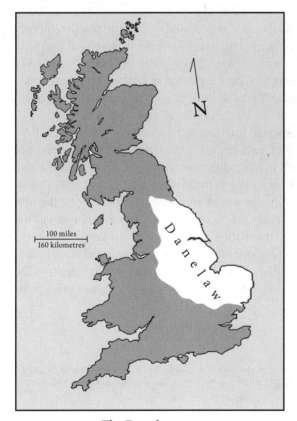

FIGURE 7.4   The Danelaw.

Thus, on one hand, Anglo-Saxon/Scandinavian relations are essential to the history of English because as a result of the conquest, settlement, and then reclamation, the small kingdoms of the Heptarchy were broken, and a single Anglo-Saxon kingdom came to dominate the territory.

Another reason why these relations are so important to the history of the English language has to do with another way in which Alfred the Great responded to the Scandinavian attacks. In his "Preface to Pastoral Care," Alfred wrote to a number of Church leaders about his sense of the damage caused by the period of Scandinavian attacks, damage to the churches, but also to the tradition of literacy in Latin which had, earlier in the eighth and ninth centuries, been so celebrated. He argued,

> When I remembered all this, then I remembered also how I saw, before it all was plundered and burned, how the churches throughout the English nation stood full of treasures and books, and also many servants of God, and how very little profit they knew from them, because they understood nothing in them, nor could they, because they were not written in their own language.[6]

Alfred argued that even before the physical damage caused by the conflict, literacy had been in decline in the Anglo-Saxon kingdoms. In order to develop it again, he proposed that boys who could be spared from their work in the fields should go to school, and that at school, students should be taught first *in English*. Alfred's ultimate goal was ostensibly to encourage students to learn to read in Latin. But he argued that learning a foreign language while learning to read and write was just too difficult, and for that reason he advocated learning to read and write in English first. Alfred also argued that a number of texts central to Christian teaching and practice should be translated into English so that education within the Church might also be developed. While we can only speculate as to whether Alfred planned that raising the stature of English as a language would affect sociopolitical unity, the new role of English in Anglo-Saxon literacy practices did have that effect. In part as the likely result of Alfred's programs of translation and education, literary production in English blossomed. English in fact has one of the strongest and earliest traditions of writing in the vernacular of all Medieval European languages. We have texts in OE to read as we study the history of English in no small part as a result of this investment in translation into OE.

---

6   Editions of the "Preface to Pastoral Care" are widely available. We have used the one from F.G. Cassidy and Richard N. Ringler, Bright's *Old English Grammar and Reader* (Fort Worth, TX: Harcourt Brace Jovanovich, 1971). The translation is our own.

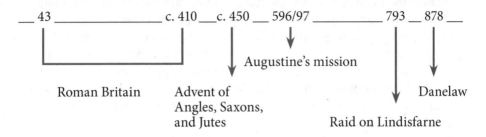

FIGURE 7.5   Timeline for the early external history of English.

OLD ENGLISH ORTHOGRAPHY AND PHONOLOGY

ORTHOGRAPHY

The first time readers encounter a text in OE, they are often surprised to find that it looks so unlike what they would have expected in an "English" text. They often do not even recognize the language as a variety of English.

Part of the initial strangeness of an OE text for present-day readers is that the language has changed, and has changed dramatically. However, the strangeness of the OE text at first glance may have less to do with the language than with the system for representing that language in writing, that is, the orthography of OE.

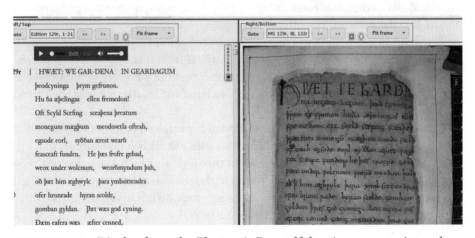

FIGURE 7.6   Display from the *Electronic Beowulf* showing manuscript and edition. Edited by Kevin Kiernan and programmed by Ionut Emil Jacob.

Figure 7.6 is an image from the *Electronic Beowulf*, a resource which makes it possible for scholars to view the famous—and fragile—late tenth-/early eleventh-century manuscript of the poem *Beowulf* in an electronic facsimile. The image shows the opening lines of *Beowulf* as it appears both in its manuscript and in a modern edition.

If we compare the modern edition and the manuscript, we will note immediately that although most of the letters in the OE text are letters that are still part of the orthography of English, the OE text contains some letter forms that the PDE alphabet does not include.

One of these letter forms appears in the first line of the manuscript text. It is the second letter of the first word of the text, and the first letter of the second. This letter, which looks like a pointy <p> is a letter from the English runic alphabet, and is called **wynn**. It represents the sound [w]. It is a modern convention not to use this letter in editions of OE, but it is used in Anglo-Saxon texts consistently. Modern editions of OE texts use the letter <w> where manuscripts in OE use wynn. As soon as one understands that the letter wynn represents the sound [w], it is not difficult to recognize that the second word of the manuscript text is *we*, the first-person plural pronoun.

There are three other letters in the OE alphabet that do not occur in the PDE alphabet. These three letters, <þ>, < ð >, and <æ>, are reproduced in modern editions of OE texts.

The first and second words in the second line of the modern edition reproduced in Figure 7.6 are *þeodcyninga* and *þrymm*. The first letter, <þ>, is, like wynn, a letter from the runic alphabet. It represented two sounds, both of which are represented in present-day orthography with <th>. In IPA these two sounds are represented as [θ] and [ð]. The name of this letter is **thorn**.

The second word in the third line of the modern edition reproduced in Figure 7.6 is *ða*. The letter <ð> is now called **eth**. In its capital form it is <Ð>. It represents *the same two sounds* represented by <þ>. Remember that the OE letter we now call eth is not the same as the IPA symbol [ð]. Eth as a letter in OE, like many other letters, could represent more than one sound.

Finally, the second word in the third line of the modern edition in Figure 7.6 is *æðelingas*. The first letter of that word, <æ>, is called **ash**. This symbol occurs in Latin texts, but it takes its name from a symbol in the runic alphabet. The letter <æ> represents the first sound in PDE *at*, the sound represented, conveniently, in IPA as [æ].

Once these symbols are familiar, readers generally do not have trouble recognizing words in OE that have very similar forms in PDE texts.

EXERCISE

7.1 Spell the following OE words in the alphabet of PDE. Once you have done so, you should be able to recognize those words. Answers can be found at the end of the book.

1. ðis _____
2. æt _____
3. þæt _____
4. pæð _____

OE orthography includes two **digraphs**. A digraph is a combination of two letters used to represent a single sound. <ch> is a digraph in PDE. The two letters together represent the sound [tʃ]. The digraphs in OE are different from those of PDE, but they represent sounds that are still part of English.

The digraph <sc> represented the sound [ʃ]. The word *ship* in PDE is a word that survives from OE, in which it would have sounded much as it does in PDE. But it would have been spelled <scip> in OE.

The digraph <cg> represented the sound [dʒ]. The PDE word *edge* is a word that survives from OE. In OE the word, pronounced much as it is in PDE, was spelled <ecg>. Note that the sound [dʒ] never occurs as the first sound of a word in OE.

One other combination of letters occurs in OE that does not occur in PDE. This combination, we should note, is not a digraph. OE uses the combination <cw> for the sounds [kw], whereas PDE uses <qu>. Hence, OE *cwic* is spelled in PDE <quick>.

EXERCISE

7.2 Write the following OE words in PDE. Once you have done so, you should be able to recognize those words. Answers can be found at the end of the book.

1. scield _____
2. fisc _____
3. wecg _____
4. micg _____

The discussion above is about ways in which the orthographic system of OE differed from that of PDE. In this discussion of the letters wynn, thorn, eth, and ash, and of the digraphs <sc> and <cg>, we have been concerned not with differences in the sound system, or differences in the sounds that make up that system. We have been strictly concerned with differences in the set of symbols used in writing the language. There are, however, a number of other differences in the orthography of OE that more closely intersect with differences in the phonology of OE. We will discuss the phonology in the latter portion of this section of the chapter, but readers should keep in mind that the following discussion of orthographic matters will be closely tied to the subsequent discussion of the phonology.

As we will discuss later in this section, the letters <g> and <c> each represented at least two different sounds. The letter <g> represented the sounds [g], [ɣ], and [j]. The letter <c> represented the sounds [k] and [tʃ]. As a general rule, we can say that <g> represented the sound [j] when it occurred before or between front vowels, or at the end of a syllable following a front vowel. In other environments, the letter <g> represented the sound [g] or [ɣ]. Similarly, <c> represented the sound [tʃ] when it occurred before or between front vowels, or at the end of a syllable following a front vowel. In other environments, the letter <c> represented the sound [k]. Note that while the letter <k> does occur in OE texts to represent the sound [k], it is not common. Modern editors of introductory texts follow a convention for distinguishing when these letters represented different sounds, however, and in this book, we will follow this convention. In this convention, the symbol <ġ> is used when the letter represents the sound [j] and the symbol <ċ> is used when the letter represents the sound [tʃ].

EXERCISE

7.3   Write the following OE words in PDE spelling. Once you have done so, you should be able to recognize those words. Answers can be found at the end of the book.

1. god   _____
2. græs   _____
3. græġ   _____
4. ġear   _____
5. ċild   _____
6. ċinn   _____
7. ċicen   _____
8. clæġ   _____

In OE, vowel length was distinctive. That is, vowels in OE differed by height, by frontedness, and by rounding, but also by the length of the vowel. The difference in OE between the word *god* with a long vowel and the word *god* with a short vowel was a meaningful difference. The word with the long vowel meant *good*. The word with the short vowel meant *god*. The vowel system will be explained in the phonology section below. Here, however, we note that while vowel length is not indicated in the orthography of most OE texts, many editors do represent vowel length in modern editions. When we are presenting forms in which vowel length is pertinent to our discussion, we will follow the convention of marking long vowels with a macron. For example, we will include the macron in *gōd* if we are contrasting it with the short vowel in *god*.

A useful fact about the history of orthography in English is that scribes after the OE period tended to double long vowels. Particularly in the case of long <o> and long <e>, later spellings of words which survive into Middle English (ME) and Modern English (ModE) tend to double the letter. Hence, OE *gōd* in ModE is spelled *good*.

Finally, the letter <y> did represent the high front rounded vowel [y] in OE. But that sound had merged with the high front vowel [i] in many dialects, and readers of OE texts can expect to find many words spelled both with <i> and with <y>.

EXERCISE

7.4   **Spell the following OE words in PDE. Once you have done so, you should be able to recognize those words.**

1. bōc   _____
2. cōc   _____
3. cwēn   _____
4. fēt   _____

Most consonants and vowels in OE, except those discussed above, have the phonetic value of their corresponding IPA symbol.

PHONOLOGY

Consonants

Old English had the following consonant phonemes (note that +v and –v under the place of articulation mean "voiced" and "voiceless" respectively).

	Bilabial	Labiodental	Interdental	Alveolar	Alveo-palatal	Palatal	Velar	Glottal
	+v | -v	+v | -v	+v | -v	+v | -v	+v | -v	+v | -v	+v | -v	+v | -v
stop	b | p			d | t			k | g	
fricative		| f	| θ	| s	| ʃ		| x	
affricate					dʒ | tʃ			
nasal	m |			n |				
approximant	w |			r |				

Vowels

OE had the following vowel phonemes (the colon in parentheses indicates that there were both long and short phonemes at that place of articulation).

i(:)   y (:)   u (:)
    e (:)   o (:)

       æ (:)   ɑ(:)

In addition to the single vowels given above, OE also had the following four diphthongs (as above, the colon in parentheses indicates that there were both long and short vowels for the first part of the diphthong).

e(:)o
æ (:)ɑ

The diphthongs in OE usually took the following form in orthography:

<eo> = e(:)o
<ea> = æ (:)ɑ

In PDE, vowels that occur in unstressed syllables have a strong tendency toward reduction and very often end up being pronounced as [ə]. For example, in the word *America*, primary stress falls on the second syllable with the full vowel sound [ɛ]. All other vowel sounds in *America* may be realized as [ə], although the third syllable can be [ɪ], [ɛ] or [ə] due to certain phonological rules that we won't go into now. Consider the unstressed syllable in the following words. An acute accent (´) indicates primary stress and a grave accent (`) indicates secondary stress; an unstressed syllable has neither:

télephòne [tɛləfon]
phótogràph [fotəgɹæf]
mésmerìze [mɛzməɹɑiz]

It is likely the case that by the end of the OE period, the same vowel reduction rule in unstressed syllables obtained. However, in many treatments of literary OE all vowels are pronounced.

EXERCISE

7.5   **Write the following OE words in phonetic transcription. (Note that the long mark, or macron, over the vowel indicates it is long. It should be written phonetically with a colon after it.) Answers can be found at the end of the book.**

eald   (old)   _____
ċild   (child)   _____
scīnan   (to shine)   _____
wecg   (mass of metal)   _____
cwēn   (queen)   _____

Some Allophonic Relationships: Voiced Fricatives

In Chapter 6, the allophonic distribution of [f]~[v], [θ]~[ð], and [s]~[z] was given. [f]~[v] were allophones of /f/; [θ]~[ð] were allphones of /θ/; and [s]~[z] were allophones of /s/. The phonological rule that explains their distribution is as follows:

/s/, /f/, /θ/ are voiced [z], [v], [ð] when they occur between voiced sounds (usually between two vowels).

ofer [over]
leðer [leðer]
dysiġ [dyzij]

/s/, /f/, /θ/ are voiceless [s], [f], [θ] everywhere else. Practically this means that the sounds will be realized as voiceless:
• at the beginning of words;
• at the end of words;
• next to voiceless sounds (including when [s, f, θ] are doubled).

flod [flod]
sæd [sæd]
oððe [oθθe]
æfter [æfter]
hūs [hu:s]

Chapter 6 also introduced the notion that towards the end of OE and in the early ME periods, [z], [v], [ð] split off from [s], [f], [θ] and became phonemes in their own right. We will return to this change in the next chapter.

EXERCISE

7.6   Write the following OE words in phonetic transcription. (Note that the long mark, or macron, over the vowel indicates it is long. It should be written phonetically with a colon after it.) Answers can be found at the end of the book.

scūfan	(to push)	_____
wīse	(manner)	_____
forþ	(forth)	_____
assa	(ass)	_____
eft	(afterwards)	_____

A Note on OE /x/

From the consonant chart above it can be seen that OE had the phoneme /x/, normally written as <h>. That phoneme could be realized as either [x] (voiceless, velar, fricative), [ç] (voiceless, alveopalatal, fricative), or [h] (voiceless, glottal, fricative). The phonological rule for describing the allophonic pattern for /h/ is as follows.

/x/ is realized as [h] at the beginning of a word before a vowel.

hūs [hu:s]
hand [hɑnd]

/x/ is realized as [x] after a back vowel or before another consonant.

seah [sæɑx]
hrefn [xrevn]
sōhte [so:xte]

/x/ is realized as [ç] after a high vowel.

> niht [niçt]
> riht [riçt]

A Note on OE /r/

The exact quality of /r/ in OE is unknown, and it probably varied quite a bit by geographical dialect. In some areas, it was likely an alveolar trill [r], as in Spanish [rr] pe*rr*o, or an alveolar tap [ɾ], like <r> in Spanish pe*r*o. In other areas, it may well have been a uvular [ʁ] or even a velar [x/ɣ] sound, as in French and many dialects of Modern German. In this treatment, we will follow the conventional wisdom that OE <r> was [r].

A Note on OE [ŋ]

In PDE, /n/ and /ŋ/ are fully phonemic, as proved by distinctive pairs, such as *seen* [sin] and *sing* [siŋ] in many dialects of American English.

In OE, however, [ŋ] only occurred before a [g] or a [k]. The [g] and [k] were *always* pronounced.

> hungor [huŋgor]
> singan [siŋgan]
> sang [saŋg]

In PDE orthography, [ŋ], spelled with an <n>, always appears next to a <g> or a <k>. In both OE and ModE, <nk> is pronounced [ŋk] as in PDE *sink* [sɪŋk]. However, <ng> in PDE may be [ŋg] as in finger [fɪŋgəɹ] or simply [ŋ] as in singer [sɪŋəɹ].

Phonological Processes

The phonological rules that have been presented so far involve a sound taking on qualities of surrounding sounds, except for the realization of /x/ as [h] at the beginning of the word. This is a very regular occurrence in all languages: sounds that reside next to each other tend to affect one another. Probably the most common effect of neighboring influence is **assimilation**.

Assimilation

Essentially assimilation can be defined as two sounds becoming more alike (cf. Latin *ad* [toward] + *similis* [similar] = "moving toward similarity"). Many of the phonological rules discussed so far are assimilatory in nature. For example, the phonological rule by which /s/, /f/, /θ/ are realized as voiced [z], [v], [ð] between voiced sounds is assimilation; underlying voiceless consonants become voiced when they occur between voiced sounds. Assimilation as it is seen to operate in phonological rules is obligatory; speakers *must* do it. If they do not, they break the rules of their language and in some sense are not speaking the language, or at the very least, speaking it in a very odd way. (Try to suppress aspirating [pʰ] at the beginning of words while talking to your family or friends. It will not be long before they notice, comment and even become angry with you!)

In some cases, assimilation is a variable process, meaning that a speaker may choose to assimilate sounds or not, although the speaker may not be completely conscious of that choice in some situations. For example in the sentence *I miss you*, there are two possible pronunciations, one with the [s] of *miss* assimilated to the [j] of *you* such that the [s] takes on the palatal quality of [j], [mɪʃju], and the other unassimilated [mɪsju]. This same palatalization in the *miss you* example has operated to change the pronunciation of some words completely. Can you ever say [tɪsju] for "tissue"? Most speakers of American English agree that [tɪsju] is not a word and only [tɪʃju] exists, although speakers of other Englishes may not agree.

The process of palatalization also operated on the sequence *sk just before the OE period, so that historical *sk after /i/ changed from [sk] to [ʃ] at the end of a word, and in some other environments as well, although it continued to be spelled <sc>. The remnants of the conditioning environment of that change are still evident in OE in that *fisc* and *disc* have [ʃ], while *ascað*, and *tusc* have [sk]. The phonetic sequence [sk] after /i/ at the end of a word was reintroduced into English from contact with the Scandinavians and their language, Norse, cf. *whisk* (< Old Norse *visk*).[7]

Deletion

Another highly frequent phonological process is deletion. **Deletion** is, as the name implies, the loss of some sound. For example in many West Germanic varieties (the Low varieties especially), /n/ is lost between a short vowel and voiceless fricative (and the vowel undergoes compensatory lengthening).[8] Thus Gothic *uns*–OE *ūs* (us), Gothic *munþs*–OE *mūþ* (mouth), Old High German *gans*–OE *gōs* (goose).

As we will see in upcoming chapters, deletion will occur frequently throughout the history of English. Sometimes the deletion is conditioned, as in the case of the loss of /n/ discussed in the preceding paragraph. Other times, however, loss can be unconditioned, that is, occur in single words. For example, the OE word *hlaford* becomes our ModE word *lord*. (See Chapter 8 on the deletion of /h/ before /l/.) However, [v] (remember from above that /f/ between vowels is [v]) is not always lost in words that contain that sound, even when it was in the same position between vowels, e.g., OE *scufan* > PDE *shove*.

---

7 Roger Lass, "Phonology and Morphology," in *The Cambridge History of the English Language: Volume II, 1066–1476*, ed. Norman Blake (Cambridge, Cambridge UP, 1992), 93.

8 Samuel Moore and Thomas A. Knott, *The Elements of Old English* (10th edition) (Ann Arbor, MI: The George Wahr Publishing Company, 1997), 123.

THE OLD ENGLISH VERBAL GROUP

MORPHOLOGY AND SYNTAX

An axiom that the reader of this text will come to know well is that the history of English can be summarized as moving incrementally from a more synthetic to a more analytic/periphrastic type of language. One consequence of this shift in type is that earlier varieties will show more grammatical work done in the morphological component of the language and later varieties will witness a shift of that grammatical work toward syntax. In PDE, very little grammatical work is done in the morphology any longer. Thus, the student of the history of English finds that the language becomes more "foreign" as he/she moves into the past. The psychological effect of such a correlation of temporal and structural distance is that PDE speakers think of older English as being harder. However, it is important to remember that notions of "difficulty" or "ease" in language learning are relative to the language one starts out from. Many other things being equal, it is easier for Spanish speakers to learn Italian than it is for them to learn Japanese. However, that is not to say that Japanese is absolutely harder than Italian.

Considered in this way, OE morphology is not necessarily harder, but it is more elaborate than the morphology in PDE. However, OE morphology underlies the same morphological system that we deal with in PDE, and many parts of the OE grammatical system are recognizable in PDE. For this reason, in this chapter, we will be referring to specific sections of earlier chapters, and especially Chapter 2, so that the continuities of grammatical structure can be stressed alongside the changes.

MORPHOLOGY AND SYNTAX IN THE VERB PHRASE

Strong–Weak Distinction

In Chapter 5, we saw that a typical feature of Germanic was the presence of two types of verbs, strong verbs and weak verbs. OE maintained that distinction. The difference between the two kinds of verbs is that strong verbs show past tense and past participle by means of ablaut, a gradation of vowels. Weak verbs on the other hand show past tense and past participle through suffixation of a dental preterit. In fact these two types persist into PDE, e.g., *sing–sang–sung* and *talk–talked–talked*. However, in the history of English certain other changes in the broad class of verbs have made it more useful to talk about regular verbs (verbs that add *-ed* to form the past and past participle) and irregular verbs (all verbs that aren't regular verbs). We will return to the regular/irregular distinction later in this book.

Tense and Mood

All OE verbs, whether strong or weak, showed variation in form according to tense and mood. Tense has been discussed at length in Chapter 5, Chapter 3, and Chapter 2. OE showed the typical Germanic system of distinguishing present and past tense. Again, it is important to remember that when we say that OE distinguished present and past tense, we mean that it did so grammatically. Certainly speakers/writers of OE could talk about other times and gradations of time; it's just that they might not have had grammatical means for doing so, as for example when we use the present tense in talking about future in *The train leaves tomorrow at noon*. In addition, OE verbs also showed several mood categories, among them indicative, subjunctive and imperative. Generally, the indicative mood was used when the assertion made in the verb phrase was thought to be factual or true and the subjunctive indicated that the assertion was hypothetical or conditional (although the actual use of the indicative and subjunctive moods is more complicated than this simple division). The imperative mood was used to deliver a command.

For comparison, here are the forms for *lufian*, a weak verb, and *bindan*, a strong verb.

	lufian (to love)	**bindan** (to bind)
Present indicative		
Sing. 1st person	lufi(ġ)e	binde
Sing. 2nd person	lufast	bindest, bintst
Sing. 3rd person	lufað	bindeð, bint
Pl. 1st, 2nd, 3rd	lufiað	bindað
Present subjunctive		
Sing.	lufi(ġ)e	binde
Pl.	lufien	binden
Preterite indicative		
Sing. 1st person	lufode	band
Sing. 2nd person	lufodest	bunde
Sing. 3rd person	lufode	band
Pl. 1st, 2nd, 3rd	lufodon	bundon
Preterite subjunctive		
Sing.	lufode	bunde
Pl.	lufoden	bunden

Imperative

Sing.	lufa	bind
Pl.	lufiað	bindað

Present participle

	lufiende	bindende

Past participle

	lufod	bunden

EXERCISE

7.7 Use the paradigms for *lufian* and *bindan* above to provide the verb forms in the following OE sentences. Answers can be found at the end of the book.

a. Þæt wīf _____ þone hund.
   The woman loved   the   dog.

b. Sē hunta _____ þone hund tō morgenne.
   The hunter (will) bind   the   dog   tomorrow.

c. "Iċ _____ þone hund," cwæð þæt wīf.
   "I love   that dog," said the woman.

d. "Þū _____ hund?" ascode sē hunta.
   "You love   (a) dog?" asked the hunter.

e. Þæt wīf _____ þone huntan.
   The woman bound   the   hunter.

Aspect

In Chapter 2, we saw that in addition to tense and mood, verbs also express aspect. While it is fair to say that all verbs express aspect, either because of the larger context/ situation or by default, some languages, such as Ancient Greek, as discussed in Chapter 2, have elaborate verb paradigms in which certain aspectual categories have unique inflectional forms. OE did not have morphological aspect; however, some aspectual categories were expressed or beginning to find expression in certain periphrastic verb forms. One of the most important of these in OE was the perfect construction.

The Perfect

In Chapter 2, the PDE perfect verb forms and meanings were discussed. That perfect construction has its roots in OE. Thus in OE, a perfect form often involved the auxiliary verb *habban* (to have) + the past participle form of the verb.

> *Ġesette   hæfde he hie   swa ġesæliġliċe...*
> Established had   he them so   happily...
> He had established them so happily...

> *ænne hæfde he swa swiđ   ġeworhte...*
> one   had   he so   strong made...
> He had made one so strong...

However, in addition to the auxiliary *habban*, the perfect sometimes used the auxiliary *beon/wesan* (to be) + the past participle.

> *Nu is   se dæġ cumen*
> Now is   the day come
> Now the day has come

The decision regarding the use of the *habban* or *beon* auxiliary is familiar to students of French, Italian, and German. *Beon* (to be) is selected when the verb in the past participle form is intransitive and denotes a change of state or location, like *become, grow, enter, come, go*. *Habban* (to have) is used elsewhere.

In later English, several more periphrases emerged, and will be treated in subsequent chapters.

THE OLD ENGLISH NOMINAL GROUP

OE PERSONAL PRONOUNS

Chapter 2 presented the system of the PDE pronouns. In that chapter, we saw that there were different forms of the personal pronoun when it occurred in certain syntactic environments. We saw that personal pronouns could be singular (*I, he, she*) or they could be plural (*we, they*). Singular and plural refer to the grammatical category of number. Personal pronouns could also be masculine (*he, him, his*), feminine (*she, her*), or neuter (*it, its*). Masculine, feminine, and neuter are terms within the grammatical category of gender. We also saw in Chapter 2 how personal pronouns could change form depending on whether they functioned as the subject (*I, he, she, we, they*), or as the object (*me, him, her, us, them*), or as possessors (*mine, his, hers, ours, theirs*). The grammatical system in which pronouns changed along with the syntactic category (i.e., subject, object, etc.) was called case. Because they are very familiar, we begin our study of the OE noun group with the personal pronouns.

As in PDE, the OE personal pronoun system showed forms that expressed number, case and gender. Here are the forms of the first-, second- and third-person pronouns. Note that this chart simplifies the forms somewhat: a number of forms varied across dialects and time. Accusative forms like *mec*, *þēc*, *ēowic*, and *ūsic*, for example, are not represented here, nor are some variants like *heom* for *him*. The specifics of number, case, and gender are discussed afterwards.

	1st person (I and we)	2nd person (you)	3rd person Masc. (he)	Neut. (it)	Fem. (she)
Sing.					
N	iċ	þū	hē	hit	hēo
G	mīn	þīn	his	his	hire
D	mē	þē	him	him	hire
A	mē	þē	hine	hit	hīe

	1st person	2nd person	Plural, all genders (they)
Pl.			
N	wē	ġē	hīe, hī
G	ūre	ēower	hira, hiera
D	ūs	ēow	him
A	ūs	ēow	hīe, hī

Number in the OE Personal Pronoun System: Singular, Plural, and Dual

The paradigms for the personal pronouns above provide the singular and plural forms for the pronouns; the distinction between singular and plural is the same as it is in PDE. In addition, OE signaled an additional number category: the dual. The dual was used to signal two, and exactly two, in number. Dual categories are not all that uncommon in languages. The OE dual was developed directly from IE; most of the older IE languages had a dual. In OE, the dual survived in the first and second persons.

	1st person sing.	dual	pl.	2nd person sing.	dual	pl.
Nom.	ic	wit	wē	þu	ġit	ġē
Gen.	mīn	uncer	ūre	þīn	incer	ēower
Dat.	mē	unc	ūs	þē	inc	ēow
Acc.	mē	unc	ūs	þē	inc	ēow

The dual pronouns in OE were admittedly rare in use: how often after all does one refer to exactly two persons? However, the rarity of the dual in OE does not merely reflect their inutility in (and eventual disappearance from) the English language but also makes their use a moment for special reflection. For instance, when the dual is encountered in OE literature, it is likely that the unique bond between the two referents in question is being foregrounded. In the OE poem "The Dream of the Rood" the Christian figures of Christ and the Holy Cross are depicted as sharing the Germanic warrior bond: Christ, the lord, and the Cross, a thane. As the Cross tells the story of Christ's crucifixion, he casts them together as combatants in battle and he uses the dual forms *wit* and *unc*. Even in the context in which the poem was written, the use of the dual would likely have seemed deliberate and powerful—an apt choice for the presentation of a narrative with such cultural significance.

Case in the OE Personal Pronoun System: Nominative, Genitive, Dative, and Accusative

In Chapter 2, the case categories for pronouns were listed as subjective, objective, and possessive. While those three categories fit the PDE system, we use a different set of terms for description of OE: **nominative**, **accusative**, **dative**, and **genitive**. The terms, however, can largely be matched up in that nominative = subjective and the genitive = possessive. In other words the nominative is used when the pronoun is the subject and the genitive shows possession.

PDE <u>We</u> are students.
OE   <u>Wē</u> sind leorningcnihtas

PDE This is <u>our</u> book.
OE   þis is <u>ūre</u> bōc.

The objective case in PDE is actually a collapsing together of the accusative and dative cases. Note that in PDE, we do not formally distinguish whether the pronoun is the direct object, the indirect object or the object of a preposition.

Jason saw <u>me</u> in the grocery store. (*me* = direct object)
Jason gave <u>me</u> a turnip. (*me* = indirect object)
Jason came with <u>me</u> to the post office. (*me* = object of a preposition)

But in Old English, the direct object and the indirect object had distinct cases often with distinct forms: the direct object was signaled by the accusative case:

Sē cniht   lufode <u>hine</u>.
The youth loved   him.

And the indirect object was indicated by the dative case:

Sē cniht   ġeaf <u>him</u> þā bōc.
The youth gave him the book

(You can see from the above OE forms that the accusative and dative case forms are already the same for many pronouns, e.g., *me*, showing that the collapse into the more general objective case was already well under way.) When the pronoun was the object of a preposition, it normally took the dative case, although under certain conditions and with certain prepositions, the accusative was also used for the object of preposition function.

þæt wīf   nam scipu from <u>him</u>.
That woman took ships from him.

Gender in the OE Personal Pronoun System: PDE Natural Gender versus OE Grammatiçal Gender

Like PDE, OE shows gender in the third-person singular personal pronoun forms: masculine (*hē, his, him, hine*), feminine (*hēo, hire, hire, hīe,*), and neuter (*hit, his, him, hit*). However, there is a crucial difference between the PDE and the OE systems. While the present-day system of gender is a so-called natural one, in which entities constructed as biologically male are masculine, female as feminine, and neither as neuter, OE nouns, even inanimate nouns, belonged to masculine, feminine, and neuter categories in ways that are not always predictable based on meaning. Thus in OE the word for *moon* is *mona* and it is masculine. The word for *sun* is *sunne* and it is feminine. Therefore when a pronoun is selected to refer to *mona* or *sunne*, the masculine and feminine forms are used in keeping with the gender of the nouns.

Sē mona scān.   <u>Hē</u> (masculine, singular, nominative) wæs wlitiġ.
The moon shone. It   was beautiful.

Sēo sunne scān.   <u>Hēo</u> (feminine, singular, nominative) wæs wlitiġu.
The sun shone.   It   was beautiful.

It can sometimes be difficult for a PDE speaker to accept the fact that Anglo-Saxons were not imbuing *mona* and *sunne* with masculine or feminine characteristics by using *he* and *hēo* to refer to them; *mona* and *sunne* were no more biologically sexed to an Anglo-Saxon speaking OE than they are to us today.

THE NOUN PHRASE AND AGREEMENT OF NUMBER, CASE, AND GENDER

Chapter 2 discussed the notion of the noun phrase. It will be remembered that in many languages, the headword of the NP, the noun, determines the morphological shape of the other elements of the noun phrase, the determiner, and the adjective.

As we have just seen above, the personal pronoun had distinct forms for number, case, and gender and it is exactly in these three categories that that noun and the other elements of the noun phrase must agree in OE. While PDE speakers still inflect nouns for number—that is, singular or plural—they do not mark nouns for case and only rarely do they mark them for gender.

Furthermore, as you will see in the forms of the noun given in the next section, nouns in OE also changed their form depending on case. The cases of the nouns are the same as those given for pronouns above: nominative, accusative, dative, genitive. The typical syntactic functions for these cases are the same as they were for the pronouns: nominative = subject, accusative = direct object, dative = indirect object and objects of most prepositions, and genitive = possession.

OE Nouns: Number, Case, and Gender
OE nouns could be masculine, feminine, or neuter:

	Masc.	Neut.	Fem.
	(stone)	(word)	(teaching)
Sing. Nom.	stān	word	lār
Sing. Gen.	stānes	wordes	lāre
Sing. Dat.	stāne	worde	lāre
Sing. Acc.	stān	word	lāre
Pl. Nom.	stānas	word	lāra, -e
Pl. Gen.	stāna	worda	lāra, -ena
Pl. Dat.	stānum	wordum	lārum
Pl. Acc.	stānas	word	lāra, -e

Determiners
Since elements within the OE noun phrase agreed in number, case, and gender, it follows that determiners in OE will have many different forms in order to agree with the noun.

For our discussion of the class of determiner in OE, we will focus on forms of the demonstrative (the distal demonstrative, see pp. 27 and 40) which in OE had begun to take on the function of a definite article. Thus the forms appearing in the chart below may be translated as *that/those*, or *the*, depending on the context.

Forms of the demonstrative/definite article, *se*, Þæt, *sēo* (that/the)

	Masc.	**Neut.**	**Fem.**
Sing. Nom.	sē	Þæt	sēo
Sing. Gen.	Þæs	Þæs	Þǣre
Sing. Dat.	Þǣm, þām	Þǣm, þām	Þǣre
Sing. Acc.	Þone	Þæt	Þā
Pl. Nom.	Þā	Þā	Þā
Pl. Gen.	Þāra	Þāra	Þāra
Pl. Dat.	Þǣm, þām	Þǣm, þām	Þǣm, þām
Pl. Acc.	Þā	Þā	Þā

Let's pause for a moment and consider how agreement works between the noun and the determiner. Let's say for instance that one uses the noun *stāne*. By looking at the noun paradigms above, we can determine that it is masculine, dative, and singular. Therefore, in order to select a determiner that agrees, we need to look at the place in the paradigm that intersects masculine, dative, and singular. That form would be *Þǣm*.

EXERCISE

7.8 **Given your understanding of the concept of agreement, and of case, gender, and number, and the above paradigms for the masculine, neuter, and feminine nouns as well as the demonstrative, translate the underlined phrases into OE. Answers can be found at the end of the book.**

 a. Those words were enormous.

   _____

 b. The student lifted the book from the stone.

   _____

 c. That teaching was profound.

   _____

 d. The woman knew the stones' properties.

   _____

Adjective

Adjective agreement within the noun phrase in OE is complicated by the system of strong and weak adjective declensions. In Chapter 5, the system of strong and weak adjective declensions was introduced as one of the features of Germanic. In that section, we saw that weak adjective forms were used when the noun phrase began with a determiner and strong forms were required when there was no determiner. This is the general rule in Old English as well. Strong and weak adjective declensions show variation according to number, case, and gender, as did the determiner class discussed in the last section.

Strong forms of *gōd* (good)

	Masc.	Neut.	Fem.
Sing. Nom.	gōd	gōd	gōd
Sing. Gen.	gōdes	gōdes	gōdre
Sing. Dat.	gōdum	gōdum	gōdre
Sing. Acc.	gōdne	gōd	gōde
Pl. Nom.	gōde	gōd	gōda, gōde
Pl. Gen.	gōdra	gōdra	gōdra
Pl. Dat.	gōdum	gōdum	gōdum
Pl. Acc.	gōde	gōd	gōda, gōde

Weak forms of *gōd* (good)

	Masc.	Neut.	Fem.
Sing. Nom.	gōda	gōde	gōde
Sing. Gen.	gōdan	gōdan	gōdan
Sing. Dat.	gōdan	gōdan	gōdan
Sing. Acc.	gōdan	gōde	gōdan
Pl. Nom.	gōdan	gōdan	gōdan
Pl. Gen.	gōdra, -ena	gōdra, -ena	gōdra, -ena
Pl. Dat.	gōdum	gōdum	gōdum
Pl. Acc.	gōdan	gōdan	gōdan

One source of potential confusion for PDE learners of OE is the fact that there was no indefinite article. The PDE *a ~ an* grammaticalized out of the OE numeral *an*, meaning *one*. Already in OE the numeral *an* begins to appear in contexts that are clear precursors to indefinite article use. For example:

Ðær   wearð Alexander þurhscoten mid anre flan
There was   Alexander pierced   with an   arrow.[9]

---

9 Orosius 3 9.143.22, quoted in Elisabeth Clos Traugott, "Syntax," in *The Cambridge History of the English Language: Volume I, The Beginnings to 1066*, ed. Richard Hogg (Cambridge, Cambridge UP, 1992), 176.

EXERCISE

7.9   Using the strong and weak adjective paradigms above, provide the correct form of *gōd* in the following sentences. Answers can be found at the end of the book.

Sē _____ leorningcniht (m. sg. nom.) hæfde bōc.
The good   student   had   (a) book.

_____ bēċ   (f. pl. nom.) sindon for eallum.
Good   books   are   for all.

Hēo ġeaf þæm _____ hunde (m. sg. dat.) bān.
She gave the good   dog   (a) bone.

Ðæs _____ wīfes (n. sg. gen.) hund wæs hungriġ.
The good   woman's   dog was hungry.

Other Noun Classes

Weak Nouns

The examples of nouns provided above are all strong noun declensions. In addition to strong nouns, however, OE English also had a robust set of nouns classified as weak nouns that took a different system of declension endings. Like strong nouns, weak nouns could be masculine, feminine, or neuter.

	Masc. (name)	Neut. (eye)	Fem. (tongue)
Sing. Nom.	nama	ēage	tunge
Sing. Gen.	naman	ēagan	tungan
Sing. Dat.	naman	ēagan	tungan
Sing. Acc.	naman	ēage	tungan
Pl. Nom.	naman	ēagan	tungan
Pl. Gen.	namena	ēagena	tungena
Pl. Dat.	namum	ēagum	tungum
Pl. Acc.	naman	ēagan	tungan

Minor Noun Classes

In addition to the strong and weak type of nouns presented so far, OE also had a number of minor classes of nouns. One of these involves nouns affected by **i-mutation**. I-mutation occurred in Pre-Old English during which time nouns such as **fōt* (foot) made their plural with the suffix that had once been **-iz*, yielding **fōtiz*. The **-i-* of the suffix, however, came to have an effect on the vowel of the stem, causing it to move to a front vowel position. In this way the mid back vowel *-o-* became the mid front vowel *-e-*. After the suffix was lost, the singular and plural were distinguished by a different vowel in the stem, *fōt* (singular) ~ *fēt* (plural).

I-Mutation Plurals

	Masc.	Fem.
	(man, person)	(book)
Sing. Nom.	mann	bōc
Sing. Gen.	mannes	bēc, bōce
Sing. Dat.	menn	bēc, bōce
Sing. Acc.	mann	bōc
Pl. Nom.	menn	bēc
Pl. Gen.	manna	bōca
Pl. Dat.	mannum	bōcum
Pl. Acc.	menn	bēc

"Irregular" Nouns in PDE

In PDE, the overwhelming majority of nouns are made plural by suffixing *-s* or *-es*. That plural suffix derived from the nominative and accusative plural forms of the strong masculine noun type (nouns like *stān*) exemplified above. However, there are some nouns in PDE that we consider irregular because they do not form their plural with *-s/-es*, e.g., *oxen* and *feet*. Those plurals are the retained forms of the weak and i-mutation nouns discussed above.

Another irregular plural noun type that also has its roots in OE noun forms is the zero-plural type, e.g., *sheep* (singular) ~ *sheep* (plural). Strong neuter nouns with a long vowel did not change their form in the singular and plural. See the forms of *word* above. This type of noun is the ancestor of zero-plural nouns like *deer* and *sheep*. One of the exciting things about learning the history of English is that a person can discover why irregularities exist in the grammar. In a historical context, these apparent irregularities often make perfect sense.

EXERCISE

7.10 Use the paradigms provided above to translate the following sentences into OE. Answers can be found at the end of the book.

 a. The good man loved that book.
 b. Those good men bound that book.
 c. Love (sing.) the man's words!
 d. Those men love those teachings.
 e. We two love you two.
 f. They bind men to those stones.
 g. She loves words.
 h. You (sing.) love good words.
 i. You (pl.) loved (a) good name.
 j. The good woman loved the man's eyes.

The word for *woman* is *wīf*. *Wīf* is a strong neuter noun, like *word*.

OLD ENGLISH SYNTAX

As will have become clear through study of the OE noun and verb groups, much of the work of grammar during that period of English was done in the morphological component of the language. The question remains: What was the role of syntax in OE?

OE syntax was often ignored by earlier scholars, who tended to focus on morphology, and has only quite recently been treated as the important topic that it is; happily, any modern treatment of OE grammar can no longer ignore syntax.

Some matters of syntax have already been addressed in the sections on the noun and verb groups, such as agreement within the noun phrase or the periphrastic verb forms, like the perfect. In this section we present some points on OE syntax that have not yet been addressed.

WORD-ORDER PATTERNING AND THE MYTH OF FREE WORD ORDER IN OE

It has sometimes been stated that languages that show major syntactic functions through morphological endings, that is case-languages like OE, have "free" word order. However, that is not really accurate. While often enough case languages will allow for a certain level of syntactic variability, meaning for example that the subject or objects can move around the verb for certain meanings or stylistic choices, there are bound to be dominant patterns.

It is true that in PDE, word order has come to take on a much greater grammatical significance; in part the more rigid syntax in PDE is the result of the fact that we no longer signal major syntactic functions of nouns through case endings. Indeed, in PDE, if a noun phrase is moved from the position before the verb, it will very often no longer be taken as the subject. So if the noun phrase *the giraffe* is changed to any other position in the simple sentence

The giraffe saw the lion.

the result is either a changed syntactic function for *the giraffe*, as in

The lion saw the giraffe (here *the giraffe* is the direct object, not the subject)

or a garbled, Yoda-like syntax that is difficult to process:

The lion the giraffe saw.

One fact about OE word order, and see also "The position of the verb" below, was that the verb tended to occur in certain positions, either as the second element of the clause or in the final position of the clause. It did not, however, regularly appear as the first element of the clause. However, in Bede's account of Cædmon, a shepherd into whom God instills the gift of song, we find just such an unusual word order in the OE story. In the passage following the details of who Cædmon is, the author wants to return to the event part of his story, the part in which Cædmon starts to sing spontaneously. Whereas the word order prior to the shift back to the event had been in regular OE order (e.g., verb final, verb in second position), the shift in narrative starts out:

Wæs he se   mon in weorldhade geseted
Was he the man in secular life placed
That man was placed in secular life.

Notice how the sentence begins with a verb, again an order not typical of the OE clause. One possible reason for the unusual word order may have been to signal that very topic shift we have been referring to, a shift away from the description of Cædmon the man and back to the event of his divine inspiration.[10]

Again, word order patterns in OE may not have been the same as they are in PDE, but they exist nonetheless. Claims of "free" word order are problematic because they

---

10 Traugott, "Syntax," 279.

are empirically untrue and, even more perniciously, they gloss over an important area of description and study of the OE language.

THE POSITION OF THE VERB

One area of considerable interest in OE syntax is the position of the verb. Linguists have identified two major types of languages with regard to the position of the verb: those in which the verb occurs before the object (VO languages) and those in which the verb occurs after the object (OV languages). English, Spanish, Swahili, and many others are VO-type languages, while Japanese, Korean and Old English are of the OV-type. English has shifted from being an OV to a VO language in its history.

Even in OE we find evidence that the shift was under way. In many types of subordinate clauses, the verb appeared predominantly in the final position, as it does in the second clause below:

Hæfde iċ þā þæs cyninges wīċ...ġescēawod
Had   I then the king's camp...looked on,
I had then looked on the king's camp

þe hē mid his fierde in ġeferen hæfde.
which he with his army into travelled had.
which he had travelled into with his army

However, in main clauses, the verb has already come to be established as the second element of the clause, often referred to as the V2 position. Often the first element of the clause was a subject:

Se ærendraca cōm tō Ēadmund cyninge...
The messgenger came to Edmund King...
The messenger came to King Edmund...

But when another expression like an adverbial, particularly *þā* (*when* or *then*) began the sentence, the verb still appeared as the second element; in those instances the subject appeared after the verb.

þā cōmon wē tō sumre byriġ.
Then came we   to a certain town.
Then we came to a certain town.

These facts about the order of the verb in OE are interesting for several reasons. First we can note that the verb-final rule for subordinate clauses and the V2 rule for main clauses are similar in Standard Modern German and Dutch.

Second, the force of the V2 pattern is still found in several sentence types in PDE in which the verb appears in the second position and the subject is placed after the verb. The usual pattern is subject then verb in PDE; recognition of the V2 pattern in OE motivates this seemingly exceptional pattern of PDE syntax:

Never had he heard such blatant misuse of the word "reticent."
Out of the bushes leapt the ferocious tiger.

Another syntactic environment in PDE in which V2 positioning is still evident involves sentences that begin with the adverbs *here* or *there*:

Here comes Mark.

In the sentence, *Mark* is the subject, but it follows the verb since the adverb *here* occupies the pre-verbal position.

Finally, the shift from an OV to a VO type of language also motivates, on some level, a few other curious aspects of English syntax. For example, OV languages tend to have case markers, as did OE, but they also tend to have **postpositions**. A postposition is essentially like a preposition, but as the name implies a postposition appears after the noun, not before, as does a preposition. An example of a postposition can be seen in Japanese, a language indicated above as being of the OV type.

Kare-wa Tokyo-kara   Osaka-ni ikimashita.
He   Tokyo-from Osaka-to went
He went to Osaka from Tokyo.

The proclivity towards postpositions in OV languages then accounts for the sometimes archaic sounding adverbials that persist in PDE, such as *herein, therefore, therefrom*, etc.

Furthermore OV languages tend to show possessor + noun order while VO languages tend towards noun + possessor order. So again, the shift from OV to VO order in English correlates with the presence of two possessive constructions in English. The first is the older OV pattern where the possessor precedes the noun: *the dog's bone*. That older pattern coexists alongside the newer patterns *the bone of the dog*, in which the possessor follows the noun in a prepositional phrase.

Thus the shift from OV to VO may not only explain certain variable patterns but also appears to correlate with certain other syntactic changes that are important for a history of English.

PARATAXIS

In Chapter 2, we presented the simple, compound, and complex sentence types. To review, a simple sentence is an independent clause standing alone:

Dogs pant to cool off.

A compound sentence comprises two or more independent clauses joined by coordinate conjunctions:

Dogs pant to cool off but turtles take expensive trips to the sea.

A complex sentence involves an independent clause and one or more subordinate clauses:

Dogs that spend their days in the hot sun pant to cool off.

Linguists commonly refer to a more nuanced set of distinctions of clause combining strategies: **parataxis**, **hypotaxis**, and **subordination**.

In parataxis, the placement of clauses is such that each has parallel independent status. Parataxis can involve compound sentences in which independent clauses are linked by conjunctions (known as syndetic parataxis) or it can be simple juxtaposition of independent clauses (known as asyndetic parataxis). The most famous example of asyndetic parataxis is probably Caesar's self-congratulatory statement:

I came. I saw. I conquered.

One should never underestimate the rhetorical power of parataxis. Caesar was no schlub when it came to writing in his native Latin (in which the above example is actually *Veni. Vidi. Vici.*). The juxtaposition of the three independent clauses represents in a very straightforward way the actual sequence of the events and makes the "I" who is narrating seem determined and very purposeful—a desirable attribute for the politician-leader to assert. In fact, to add in other grammatical items as a means of tying these clauses together would weaken that rhetorical thrust: *Before I conquered, I first came and subsequently saw.*

Hypotaxis involves the placement of clauses such that one is dependent on the other but still somewhat independent of it grammatically, i.e., not part of the independent clause grammar (contrast subordination below).

Hypotaxis includes so-called adverb clauses:

After we heard the story, we started to believe him.

Certainly we would have to say that *after we heard his story* is dependent; it cannot stand alone in PDE as a complete sentence. However, none of the elements in the *after we heard his story* clause play any role in the main clause. This is quite different from subordination, the next category of clause combining.

In subordination the placement of clauses is such that one is subsumed within the grammar of the other. Defined as such, examples of subordination in this scheme include relative clauses, also known as adjective clauses, which modify nouns within the independent clause:

The committee considered the proposal that the citizens drafted.

The best example of subordination, however, would include noun clauses, which involve a situation in which the entire subordinate clause performs a core syntactic function in the independent clause.

We found that the price of gas soared after the summer.

In this case, *that the price of gas soared after the summer* is the direct object of the independent or main verb. In fact, we could even begin to speak of interdependence, since if you remove the noun clause in this example, you are left without a complete clause at all.

OE shows a preference for paratactic and hypotactic clause combining. An example of parataxis:

Sum swīþe ġelǣred munuc cōm suþan... and se munuc   hātte Abbo.
One very learned   monk came south   and he monk was called Abbo.
A certain very learned monk came from the south... and the monk was named Abbo.

One very frequent hypotactic structure in OE is the *þā... þā* construction. Note that in this construction the word *þā* is not the form of the demonstrative we have encountered: this is a different word. You may have noticed above that we provided both the meaning *then* and the meaning *when* for the word *þā*. In the very common *þā... þā* construction two clauses beginning with *þā* are joined. One of these clauses will be subordinate, and the *þā* will be translated in PDE as *when*. One of the clauses will be independent, and its *þā* will be translated as *then*.

þā on þone þriddan dæġ, þā hīe þā dūne ġesawon,
Then on the third day, when they saw the mountain,

...þā cwæþ Abrahām tō þæm twæm cnapum þus.
...then spoke Abraham to the two boys thus.

One way to distinguish the subordinate from the independent clause in this construction is that in the independent clause, the subject most often follows the verb since the verb will retain its V2 position following þā. In the subordinate clause (the *when* clause), however, the verb will show a tendency to appear in final position.

Subordination of the type we are very accustomed to in PDE is much rarer but does occur in OE.

Ġeongum mannum ġedafenaþ þæt hīe leornien sumne wisdom,
That they should learn some wisdom befits young men,

and þæm ealdum ġedafenaþ þæt hīe tǣcen sum ġerād hiera ġeonglingum,
and that they should teach some council befits old men,

for þæm þe þurh lāre biþ se ġelēafa ġehealden.
because through learning the faith is preserved.

One explanation for the infrequency of subordination in OE is that English as a language had only relatively recently begun to appear in written form, and throughout the OE period always occupied a literary second seat to Latin. Latin, in contradistinction, had a number of elaborate subordinating strategies and it is very obvious that writers in the OE period struggled with translating those strategies. In the later ME period and especially in the Early Modern period, as English comes to be more widely appreciated as a viable language for literary expression per se, subordinating strategies are more fully worked out. We will return to the emergence of those strategies in subsequent chapters.

However, one should not make the assumption that the predominance of parataxis in OE is an indication that it was a primitive language. As we have already said above, parataxis, and hypotaxis for that matter, can be very effective from a rhetorical standpoint. And as we will see, even during the period of English when many more subordinating strategies were in use, authors such as the translators of the King James Bible would exploit the rhetorical strategies of parataxis and hypotaxis. In fact, it is wholly possible to defend the stylistic and rhetorical efficacy of parataxis for reasons of clarity and straightforwardness.

OLD ENGLISH AND OLD NORSE

SCANDINAVIANS IN ENGLAND

Significant numbers of Scandinavians settled in England beginning in the late ninth century, following the establishment of the Danelaw after 878, a region in the north-eastern part of England in which Scandinavians could live under Scandinavian law.

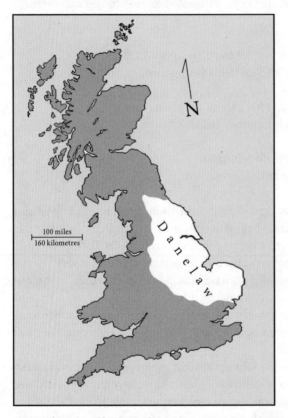

FIGURE 7.7 The Danelaw.

As we discussed briefly earlier, Alfred the Great's successors would "reclaim" most of the Danelaw, although not in the sense that it returned to its previous kingdoms, so that by 927 Æthelstan could be considered the king not only of Wessex, but of Anglo-Saxon England. Of course, the borders of this kingdom shifted considerably, and pockets of Scandinavian control, like the Scandinavian kingdom of York, remained for periods of time. But by the mid-tenth century, most of the territory of England was under Anglo-Saxon rule.

The Anglo-Saxons did reclaim political control of much of the former Danelaw; however, the territories settled by Scandinavians after 878 remained heavily influenced by that settlement. The distribution of Scandinavian place-names in that territory to this day reflects the patterns of that long-term settlement. Similarly, the number of family names which suggest Scandinavian lineage reflect a pattern of long-term settlement and intermarriage in the territories covered by the Danelaw. Figure 7.8 shows a representation of place names with clear Scandinavian sources, names which include elements like *thorp* (from the Norse word for *hamlet*) or *by* (from the Norse word for *village*). Figure 7.9 shows a distribution for the origin of family names ending in *-son*, reflecting a likely Scandinavian lineage.

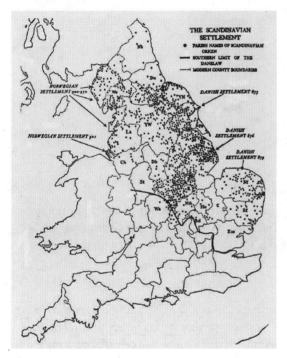

FIGURE 7.8   Map of Scandinavian settlement of England, by A.H. Smith, 1956. Copyright © The English Place-Name Society. Used with permission.

Settlement in the Danelaw allowed for prolonged contact between speakers of Old Norse and speakers of OE. There was certainly intermarriage between Anglo-Saxons and Scandinavian settlers. And the fact that for at least the early period of settlement, speakers of Norse had a degree of political control meant that Old Norse as a language had a level of prestige among some sectors of the population. These are external conditions that are very likely to motivate language change.

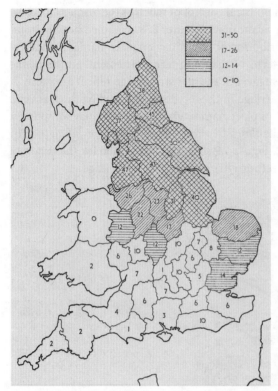

FIGURE 7.9   **Distribution of English family names ending in** *–son*. **From** *The Viking Legacy: The Scandinavian Influence on the English and Gaelic Languages* by John Geipel (Newton Abbott: David & Charles, 1971). Reprinted with the permission of the Estate of John Geipel.

But there are a number of additional factors at play as well. Anglo-Saxon and Scandinavian cultures shared a body of Germanic mythology and other cultural materials. Scandinavian social structure, like Anglo-Saxon society, still centered on a male warrior elite; and literary texts in both Old Norse and OE privileged heroic bonds among members of that warrior elite. Although Christianity was widespread in England well before the ninth century, Anglo-Saxon paganism is preserved in the literature, as well as in cultural celebrations, and even in the names for days of the week, some of which are derived from the Germanic pantheon: Wednesday, from Woden's day, Tuesday, from Tiw's day, Thursday from Thor's day, Friday from Frea's day. While the Scandinavians are often represented in Anglo-Saxon sources as "heathen," their mythology, however disavowed by Anglo-Saxon Christian writers, was also familiar to the Anglo-Saxons.

Furthermore, as we discussed in Chapter 5, OE is a Low West Germanic language, and Old Norse is a North Germanic language. But both Old English and Old Norse are Germanic languages. They are clearly different languages. But they were also similar enough that it is likely that speakers of these languages, like speakers of Spanish and Italian, could probably with some effort have understood one another in many encounters. Anglo-Saxons would have found the Scandinavian settlers to be foreign in many ways, but they would also have found them to be familiar, both culturally and linguistically.

Any time that speakers of different languages come into contact and attempt to communicate, those speakers will need to make certain decisions regarding language choices. They may choose a language that is native to neither group, a so-called lingua franca, or they may settle for one or the other of the languages of the speakers. Normally, if one group's language is chosen over the other it is because of cultural or political dominance, and as we have seen above, and will certainly see below, the tides of cultural and political dominance between the Anglo-Saxons and the Scandinavians shifted throughout the entire OE period.

The fact is that there was probably a range of communication strategies between the Anglo-Saxons and the Scandinavians depending on any number of factors: larger concentration of speakers (i.e., geography), topic, period of settlement, etc. We would also have to acknowledge the evidence in the history of English that suggests that the communication strategies involved two-way accommodation: in other words, the varieties of Germanic spoken by the Anglo-Saxons and the Scandinavians were so similar that speakers of both could accommodate one another in ways that allowed interchange of linguistic features. As we will see a bit later, just such a view of linguistic interchange is well justified by the appearance of certain grammatical forms in English, the source of which could only be the varieties of Norse spoken by the Scandinavians.

In the early part of the eleventh century, yet another wave of Scandinavian attacks on England strongly reinforced those sociopolitical conditions that allowed for the linguistic influence of the Norse language onto English.

ENGLAND AS PART OF A SCANDINAVIAN EMPIRE

Beginning in the last decades of the tenth century, Scandinavian attacks again became serious threats to the Anglo-Saxons. It is important to remember that although the conflicts between the Scandinavian Great Army and the Anglo-Saxons were resolved after the establishment of the Danelaw, other conflicts arose during the late ninth and early tenth centuries, often involving attacks launched from Scandinavian strongholds and settlements elsewhere. In 892, for example, another large Scandinavian army travelled across the Channel and attacked the south of England.[11] Similarly,

---

11 Simon Keynes, "The Vikings in England, c. 790–1016," in *The Oxford Illustrated History of the Vikings*, ed. Peter Sawyer (Oxford: Oxford UP, 1997).

the Old English poem "The Battle of Brunanburh" records a battle in 937 between an army of Scandinavians from Ireland and an Anglo-Saxon army. But these attacks met with effective resistance. The Scandinavian armies of 892 dispersed by 896. The Battle of Brunanburh is an English victory: the poem on this battle concludes, "The Northmen departed on their nailed ships."[12]

The new phase of Scandinavian attacks at the end of the tenth century is made more serious because by that time England was a fairly large territory, and, given the relative stability of the preceding century, it was also a relatively prosperous country. Alfred the Great had to defend Wessex, but Æthelred the Unready (ruled 979–1016) had to defend England, a territory several times the size of Wessex. Furthermore, the attacks at the end of the tenth century were not independent ventures, but were explicitly associated with the ruling powers in Scandinavia, in particular, with the Danish king, Swein Forkbeard (ruled 987–1014). Swein himself was likely present at the spectacular English defeat at Maldon in 991, as well as in the raids of 994, 1003–04, and, of course, as we will discuss below, in 1013–14.[13]

Æthelred attempted to defend his kingdom through a number of strategies, the most notable among them for our study being through a marriage alliance with Emma of Normandy, and through the payment of tribute.

The first strategy we have listed involved securing an alliance on the continent. This strategy would have enormous consequences for the history of England, albeit consequences unimagined at the time.

Explaining this alliance requires a little bit of backtracking. Scandinavians during the Viking Age roamed throughout Europe, and reached as far as Russia, Constantinople (modern-day Istanbul, Turkey), and even North America. In some places, conflicts with the Scandinavians were resolved, as they were in England, with the establishment of a territory for Scandinavian settlement and rule within another country. In the case of England, the Danelaw was established after 878 as a permanent settlement of Scandinavians within territory that had been part of the Heptarchy. In the case of France, **Normandy** was established around 911 as a settlement of "Northmen" within French territory.

In 1002, Æthelred married **Emma of Normandy**, the sister of Richard II, the Duke of Normandy. In doing so, he attempted to secure from the Normans protection against the Danes, or at least the promise that the Normans would not provide aid to the Danes. This marriage established a link between the English royal family and the Dukes of Normandy. We will return to the significance of this link as it puts into motion the kinds of abrupt political and social changes that will mark the beginnings of the Middle English period.

---

12 "The Battle of Brunanburh," in *A Choice of Anglo-Saxon Verse*, ed. and trans. Richard Hamer (Atlantic Highlands, Humanities P, 1981), line 53. Translation ours.

13 Philip Pulsiano, ed., *Medieval Scandinavia: An Encyclopedia* (New York: Garland, 1993), 627.

The second strategy, the payment of tribute, was a common one. The invading army would be paid off with gold and treasure. During Æthelred's reign the tax to fund payments of tribute to the Scandinavians was called the Danegeld. The obvious problem, in retrospect, with the payment of the tribute was that although it did work in the short term, and Scandinavian armies did withdraw upon receipt of the payment, it also enabled those same armies to go home and raise even more powerful armies to return and demand even larger payments. Even a quick overview of the escalating demands for tribute, and the willingness to make those payments, makes this problem evident: payments rose from 10,000 pounds of tribute in 991 to 48,000 pounds in 1012.[14] Needless to say, in addition to being a manifestly ineffective long-term strategy, Æthelred's imposition of the Danegeld on the English also eroded support for his already unpopular reign considerably.

In 1013–14, Swein Forkbeard successfully defeated Æthelred in battle, drove Æthelred into exile, and became, briefly, the king of England. Swein died shortly thereafter, however. In 1015 Swein's son Cnut invaded England, and in 1016, after the deaths of both Æthelred and his son Edmund Ironside, **Cnut** became the king of England.

Significantly, Cnut was not just the king of England. He was also the king of Denmark, and by the end of his reign he controlled a Scandinavian empire that included England, Denmark, and parts of Norway. During the reign of Cnut (ruled 1016–35) and his sons (Harold Harefoot [ruled 1035–40] and Harthacnut [ruled 1040–42]), England was part of a Scandinavian empire, and it would remain so until 1042, when the Wessex line was restored under Edward the Confessor (ruled 1042–66).

It is important to take a moment to consider that at this point in English history, a Dane and his line would be the rulers of England. This is hardly a scenario in which we can place the Scandinavians on one side and the Anglo-Saxons on another of some distinct sociopolitical divide. The two political (and cultural) spheres overlapped and influenced one another, likely much more than written histories of the peoples would suggest. As we have already mentioned, a significant piece of evidence for the sustained and abiding level of contact between the two peoples is linguistic and involves profound influence of Norse on English.

INFLUENCE OF NORSE ON ENGLISH

While it is true that Latin had an influence on English, during the Old English period that influence is for the most part limited to lexical borrowings of the sort we discussed in section one of this chapter, borrowings which number less than 500 items even by the end of the OE period.[15]

---

14   Keynes, "The Vikings in England," 76.
15   Baugh and Cable, *A History of the English Language*, 91.

Borrowings of lexical items from Old Norse even by the most conservative estimates more than double those from Latin during this period. Moreover, the lexical borrowings are significantly different in kind from those from Latin.

Latin borrowings, as discussed above (p. 119), included words for concepts associated with Christianity, and with those aspects of life associated in the Middle Ages with Christianity, among them literacy and education. These were words like *angel, martyr, grammatical*, and *master*. Lexical borrowings from Norse, however, included words for common everyday items and relationships, and often duplicated words that already existed in OE. These borrowings include words like *skin, sky, egg, gift*, and *give*. The Anglo-Saxons certainly had skin, looked at the sky, ate eggs and gave gifts long before the Scandinavian settlements. Furthermore, they had words for these things in English, often words very close in form to those borrowed from Norse. For example, the Old English word for *egg* was *æġ*, and the word for *gift* was *ġiefu*. As we hinted above, the borrowings of the Norse forms reflect not only the close and prolonged contact between speakers of both languages, but also the fact that the languages were already closely related such that speakers of the two varieties could have easily accommodated each other with sometimes very few structural or phonetic adjustments.

This pattern of lexical borrowing alone merits close attention to Old Norse and to Anglo-Scandinavian relations during the OE period. But very significantly, the influence of Old Norse on English extends beyond matters of lexicon into the grammar of English. Readers will recall the discussion of borrowing in Chapter 3 and the fact that while lexical borrowing occurs with relative ease, the borrowing of grammatical material is rarer.

We have already seen how phonetically similar certain lexical items were in Norse and English; of course, this is because the two languages were rather closely related. As related languages, they also shared extensive similarities in their grammatical structures (e.g., pronoun and verbal paradigms), although the specific forms within those paradigms sometimes differed more than the overall system itself. In two often-discussed areas of English grammar, it is clear that the source for the PDE forms is Norse, and not OE.

First, in OE the third-person plural forms of the personal pronoun all began with /h/. Those forms are repeated below. The initial interdental fricative for the PDE forms (i.e., *they, them, their*) has its source in the Norse third-person personal pronouns, all of which began with just such an interdental fricative, although originally the fricative may have been voiceless. That a new pronoun entered English from Norse is clear evidence of a profound level of contact.

It should be mentioned that some historians of English have suggested that the motivation for the borrowing of the *th-* forms of the pronoun into English had to do with the fact that the third-person plural forms beginning with *h-* were too similar to the third-person singular forms, which also began with *h-* (*he* = he, *heo* = she, etc.).

However, that position is weakened when we consider that in spoken English we tolerate considerable phonetic similarity between third-person singular and plural reference in the object case: "Get him" versus "Get 'em." In fact, it is possible that the *'em* variation of the third person plural object form is not merely *them* with the <th> dropped, but a continuation of the OE object form *hem*.

In another example of Norse grammatical influence we find that half of the forms used for the verb *be* have their source in Norse. The OE present plural forms of the verb *be* were quite similar to those in other Low West Germanic languages, *sind* or *sindon*. However, in later English those forms were replaced by *are*. The paradigm of the verb *be* then reflects in a fairly iconic way the sociopolitical melding of the Scandinavians and Anglo-Saxons as well the effects of that blending on the linguistic structure of English.

Old English **Plural, all genders**	**Old Norse** **Masc.**	**Fem.**	**Neut.**
Nom. hīe, hī	þeir	þær	þau
Gen. hira, hiera	þeira	þeira	þeira
Dat. him	þeim	þeim	þeim
Acc. hīe, hī	þā	þær	þau

Old English **Present indicative**	**Old Norse**		
Sing. 1st	eom	em	
Sing. 2nd	eart	ert	
Sing. 3rd	is	er	
Pl. 1st	sind, sindon	erum	
Pl. 2nd	sind, sindon	eruð	
Pl. 3rd	sind, sindon	eru	

A NOTE ON GENEALOGY THAT WILL BECOME MORE SIGNIFICANT LATER

While in this study we do not focus on individual leadership as much as on larger cultural movement, readers may wish to consider the following lines of descent and the international relationships and alliances that these lines both reflect and create.

It is a fascinating fact, and a significant one in English history, for example, that Æthelred married Emma of Normandy in 1002. It is also significant that Cnut *also* married Emma, in 1017. Cnut would be succeeded first by his son with his first wife, and next by his son with Emma. The next king of England, Edward the Confessor, was Emma's son by Æthelred. When William the Conqueror claimed the throne of

England in 1066, his blood relationship to Emma was compelling indeed. And the link that the marriages to Emma provided between the English royal family and the Dukes of Normandy would lay the foundation for a profound shift from international connections between England and Scandinavia, to one between England and France.

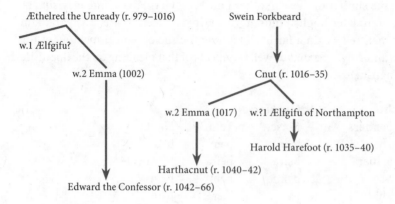

FIGURE 7.10   Kings of England 979–1066.

OLD ENGLISH LITERATURE

ORAL POETRY AND TEXTUAL CULTURE

The tenth-century OE poem "Deor" opens with an allusion to the story of Weland the Smith, a character from Germanic mythology. Weland, a craftsman able to create wonderful artifacts, is captured and enslaved so that he will work for his captor. To keep him from escaping, his captor, Niðhad, cuts his hamstrings. Weland eventually takes a terrible revenge: he rapes Niðhad's daughter and kills his sons; he makes gems out of the sons' eyeballs and cups from their skulls. He then makes himself a pair of artificial wings and escapes. The refrain of the poem,

> *þæs ofereode, þisses swa mæg*
> That passed,   so   can this

frames the story of Weland as well as each the following stanzas of the poem, all of which contain allusions to other mythic and historical tragedies.

The poem concludes with the narrator's own story. The narrator explains,

þæt ić be mē sylfum   secgan wille,
þæt ić hwīle wæs   Heodeninga scop,
dryhtne dyre.

I wish to say about myself
that for a while I was the poet of the Heodenings,
dear to the lord.

The tragedy he bemoans is that while he was once a poet dear to his lord, he has since been replaced by another poet. He has lost his job. The last line of the poem is the refrain, "That passed, so can this."

Contemporary readers are often shocked by this final stanza. There are few instances in which losing one's job can be seen as equivalent to having one's skull made into a cup. One common way of reading the conclusion to the poem is that the comparison to the mythological and historical tragedies that precede it puts the poet's loss into perspective: if those tragedies can pass, so can this much more trivial problem.

Another interpretation requires attention to the OE. The word for *poet* in the OE is *scop*. The *scop* is an oral poet in the early Germanic world. "Deor," by evoking the figure of the *scop*, reminds us that many cultures which do not extensively use writing systems preserve and transmit their histories through memory, and that the *scop* carried that body of cultural knowledge. The narrator of "Deor" thus very craftily suggests to us that the stories like those he carries of Weland and Niđhad will be lost when he is no longer there to tell them. And in fact, while the story of Weland has been preserved, other allusions in the poem refer to stories and histories that have not survived.

Although we read "Deor" to this day only because it was written down, the poem nonetheless provides an insight into one of the fundamental ways in which the literary experience of the Anglo-Saxons differed from our own: even while OE literature, like the poem "Deor," was being written down, for the Anglo-Saxons there was also an immediate context in which literature was primarily oral, not written, and this oral literature functioned as the means by which essential cultural knowledge was remembered and transmitted.

THE MANUSCRIPT

OE literature thus not surprisingly records anxieties about the transition to literacy. One of a set of one hundred literary riddles, Exeter Book Riddle 26, for example, recounts the processes by which a book is made. As it does so it also makes clear that this creation fundamentally involves violence.

The poem, narrated by the book itself as a "speaking object," begins,

Mec feonda sum	feore besnyþede,
woruldstrenga binom,	wætte siþþan,
dyfde on wætre,	dyde eft þonan,
sette on sunnan,	þære ic swiþe beleas
herum þam þe ic hæfde.	Heard mec siþþan
snað seaxes ecg....	

A certain enemy deprived me of life,
took my strength in the world, wetted me afterwards,
dipped me in water, afterwards took me out,
set me in the sun, where I lost
the hairs that I had. The hard edge of a knife
scraped me....[16]

The riddle details the process through which the physical book is made. Books in Anglo-Saxon England were not made of paper. They were written on animal skins. The first action the speaker describes is the killing of an animal: "a certain enemy deprived me of life." Of course, the first step to making a medieval book is killing the animal to be used for its skin. But the riddle very intriguingly identifies itself both as the living animal killed for its skin, and as the transformed substance, the **vellum** or **parchment** on which the book is written.

The killing of the animal may certainly be taken as the literal killing of an animal necessary for the production of vellum. However, one might also consider that the transition to literacy itself may also have been understood to involve a kind of violence to the native tradition of oral poetry, the tradition that "Deor" represents as so central to the transmission of cultural knowledge. (In fact, "Deor" may represent the native tradition of oral poetry as already lost at the time of the poem's written transmission.)

The riddle continues,

fingras feoldan	on mec fugles wyn
geond speddropum	spyrede geneahhe,
ofer brunne brerd,	beamtelge swealg,
streames dæle,	stop eft on mec,
siþade sweartlast.	

---

16 "Riddle 26," in *The Exeter Book*, ed. George Philip Krapp and Elliott Van Kirk Dobbie (New York, Columbia UP, 1936), lines 1–6. Translation is our own.

fingers folded me, and on me the joy of a bird
sprinkled me with lucky droppings
over the brown surface, swallowed the ink
a share of the stream, afterwards on me traveled
the dark trail.

Another way in which medieval books differed from books in the present day is that they were manuscripts, written by hand. The riddle here narrates the process by which the scribe writes the text by hand.

In subsequent lines, the book in this riddle is bound with a cover, and bejeweled: it is no ordinary book, in other words, but *the* Book, i.e., the Bible, in the Christian context in which the poem was written. Riddle 26 thus illustrates yet another important difference between the literature of the present day and Old English literature. The OE literature that has survived in writing was produced in a Christian context. Readers will recall from the first section of this chapter that literacy came to Europe in the Middle Ages through Christianity, and the Church remained the center of education and textual production. While not all OE literary texts are explicitly Christian, they were all produced in a Christian context. Riddle 26 promises that the Book offers a transformation for the better: "if the children of men wish to use me, they will be healthier, and more victorious, with bolder hearts,... they will have more friends... who will increase their glory and happiness...."[17] The power of the poem, however, in part results from its insistence not only on this transformative potential, but also on the idea that while a certain kind of life is gained, another is lost in the transition to a textual culture.

ANGLO-SAXON CULTURAL VALUES AND ANGLO-SAXON CHRISTIAN LITERATURE

We have emphasized that OE literature was produced in a Christian context. But it would be a mistake to assume that Anglo-Saxons encountered Christianity in exactly the terms that present-day Christians do.

We have already discussed the importance of the eighth-century Venerable Bede. Bede's *History of the English Church and People*, completed around 731, provides much invaluable information on early Anglo-Saxon history. Bede's history also contains some of the most famous moments in OE literature. Significantly, Bede himself wrote in the language of the Church, Latin, not in OE. However, Bede's *History* was translated into Old English, and multiple copies of both the Latin and the OE texts survive.

Perhaps one of the most often quoted passages from Bede's *History* is the story of the conversion of the seventh-century King Edwin. In this story, Edwin is given advice on whether or not to convert to Christianity by his closest councilor, the (pagan) high priest Coifi. Coifi argues,

---

17 "Riddle 26," 18–24.

This is how the present life of man on earth, King, appears to me in comparison with that time which is unknown to us. You are sitting feasting with your ealdormen and thegns in winter time; the fire is burning on the hearth in the middle of the hall and all inside is warm, while outside the wintry storms of rain and snow are raging; and a sparrow flies swiftly through the hall. It enters in at one door and quickly flies out through the other. For the few moments it is inside, the storm and wintry tempest cannot touch it, but after the briefest moment of calm, it flits from your sight, out of the wintery storm and into it again. So this life of man appears but for a moment; what follows or indeed what went before, we know not at all....[18]

The argument Coifi makes is that life is short, and that it is preceded by the unknown and followed by the unknown, but that Christianity promises an answer to questions about what came before and what comes afterwards, and for that reason should be adopted. As he presents this story, Bede employs a central metaphor in Germanic culture and in OE poetry: the metaphor of life in the hall.

The hall in much OE literature is the center of secular life. More particularly, it is the center of the life of noble men, the warrior elite. The hall is where noble men celebrate the bonds of loyalty and service that hold them together. By evoking the metaphor of the hall, and by linking that metaphor to Christian conversion, Bede extends the community of the hall to a Christian history that then encompasses it. The metaphor also positions Bede's own project of writing the *History* in the eighth century. Bede is at once presenting a Christian history of the English to the English, and presenting the *idea* of a Christian history to the English in terms that appeal to the values of Anglo-Saxon secular society.

Even explicitly Christian texts that deal directly with central narratives of Christianity, like the temptation or the crucifixion, clearly reflect the cultural values of Anglo-Saxon society. Perhaps the most famous example of this is the OE poem, "The Dream of the Rood."

"The Dream of the Rood" is a dream vision in which the story of the crucifixion is narrated by a speaking object, the cross itself. The narration by the cross enables the poem to present the story of the crucifixion very differently from the way it is presented in the New Testament. The cross functions metaphorically in the poem as a loyal companion to a heroic warrior. In the poem, Christ is never passive, but rather strips himself and aggressively embraces the cross. The cross narrates,

Ongyrede Hine þa geong hæleð,	(þæt wæs God ælmihtig)
strang and stiðmod.	Gestah he on gealgan heanne,
modig on manigra gesyhðe,	þa he wolde mancyn lysan.

---

18 Bede the Venerable, "Ecclesiastical History of the English People," in *Beowulf,* ed. and trans. R.M. Liuzza (Peterborough, ON: Broadview P, 2000), 184.

The young hero—God almighty—stripped himself,
strong and resolute; he climbed on the high gallows,
courageous in the sight of many, when he wished to redeem mankind.[19]

Here the poem presents Christ as a "young hero." And importantly, a young hero accompanied by a loyal companion. OE heroic literature emphasizes the bonds between men, in particular the bonds between a lord and the warriors who fight with and for him. These bonds suggest a relationship among noble men very close to the relationship that Tacitus called the *comitatus* in his *Germania* (see Chapter 5). While *comitatus* is not an Old English term, scholars continue to refer to the bond between noble men celebrated in Old English heroic texts as the comitatus bond. "The Dream of the Rood," by representing the cross as a loyal warrior accompanying his lord on a heroic venture thus recasts the story of the crucifixion presented in the New Testament so that it evokes that privileged bond for its Anglo-Saxon audience.

OLD ENGLISH POETICS

Poetry in PDE traditions is still associated with rhyme, despite the fact that much, if not most poetry written in PDE does not rhyme. But rhyme would not become a regular feature of English poetry until the ME period: rhyme is not native to English poetry.

Old English poetry, as a rule, did not rhyme. Lines and half-lines in OE poetry are connected by **alliteration**, the repetition of initial word sounds. For example, in these lines from the famous epic *Beowulf* (late tenth/early eleventh century) which portray the monster Grendel seizing his sleeping victims, the repetition of initial sounds is clear. Here we have italicized and underlined the repeated sounds.

ac he ge*f*eng hraðe	*f*orman siðe
*S*læpende rinc,	*s*lat unwearnum,
*B*at *b*anlocan,	*b*lod edrum dranc,
*S*ynsnædum *s*wealh,	*s*ona hæfde
*U*nlyfigendes	*ea*l gefeormod,
*F*et and *f*olma.	

He seized at once at his first pass
a sleeping man, slit him open suddenly
bit the bone-locker, drank blood from his veins,
gobbled flesh in chunks, and soon had
completely devoured that dead man,
feet and fingertips.[20]

---

19   "Dream," in *The Vercelli Book*, ed. George Philip Krapp (New York: Columbia UP, 1932), lines 39–41.
20   R.D. Fulk, Robert E. Bjork, and John D. Niles, eds. *Klaeber's Beowulf and the Fight at Finnsburg* (Toronto: U of Toronto P, 2008), lines 740–45.

The extended space in the middle of each line of verse is called a **caesura**. The caesura divides each line of verse into two half-lines. The half-lines are connected by patterns of alliteration. The caesura is an important element in the scansion of OE poetry, but it should be noted that the representation of the caesura by extended space in the text is—like the division into poetic lines—a modern editorial convention rather than an OE one.

Anglo-Saxon scribes tended to write texts in OE from one side of the page to the next, with very little in the way of punctuation or capitalization, and without division into poetic lines. In fact, in some traditions, scribes did not include even spaces between words. In the image from the *Electronic Beowulf* below, the OE manuscript is juxtaposed with a modern edition. It is very clear that the manuscript does not break the text into poetic lines, and it does not include a representation of the caesura. The modern edition, however, carefully both breaks the text into lines and represents the caesura by an extended space between half-lines.

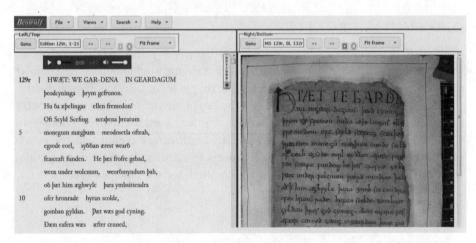

FIGURE 7.11   Display from the *Electronic Beowulf* showing manuscript and edition. Edited by Kevin Kiernan and programmed by Iunut Emil Jacob.

PARATAXIS AND APPOSITION

One of the most common rhetorical devices in OE literature is apposition. In Chapter 2, the appositive was defined as a noun phrase in any position expanded by a defining noun phrase following it. In the sentence *My sister, a physician, said not to worry* the noun phrase *a physician* is in apposition.

In *Beowulf*, for example, just at the moment when Beowulf is about to grasp Grendel's arm, the poem employs apposition:

Gemunde þa se goda,   mæg Higelaces,
afenspræce,   uplang astod
and him fæste wiðfeng;   fingras burston.

Remembered then the good man, the kinsman of Higelac,
his evening-speech, stood upright
and grasped him hard; fingers burst.[21]

The noun phrase *mæg Higelaces* (the kinsman of Higelac) is in apposition to *se goda* (the good man.) "The kinsman of Higelac" is a restating of "the good man," i.e., Beowulf here. Both noun phrases have the same referent, Beowulf, the hero of the poem. But note that the repetition is not simply a repetition. The poem in fact contrasts the fatherless monster, Grendel, with Beowulf, who is frequently identified by his kin-group relationships. The apposition thus reinforces the idea that being a "good man" and not a monster has much to do with being identified with a community, or being recognizable through kinship.

Apposition occurs so frequently in Old English literature that it has been called not merely a literary device but "a habit of mind."[22] Fred Robinson in his *Beowulf and the Appositive Style* extends a reading of apposition beyond the recursive noun phrases we have discussed to larger syntactic and even narrative units. Following Robinson, we can consider aspects of the language like the paratactic syntax of OE to have a literary function. Apposition, like parataxis, involves placing equivalent structures beside each other without explicit explanation of what the connection between the two structures might be. The apposition of "the good man" and "the kinsman of Higelac" in the passage above requires that the reader engage in the construction of the explanation of the connection between the two noun phrases. Similarly, parataxis juxtaposes clauses, but the logical relationship among those clauses remains implicit.

Very often in language, paratactically arranged clauses may signal some sort of cause and effect:

The wind blew fiercely. The statue fell over.

In this exchange we understand that it is because of the wind that the statue fell over.

Paratactically arranged clauses may also derive their meaning from that fact that the events are arranged in the same order that they happen in the real world, as did Caesar's famous *I came. I saw. I conquered* statement discussed earlier.

---

21 Fulk et al., *Klaeber's Beowulf and the Fight at Finnsburg*, lines 758–60.
22 Fred C. Robinson, *Beowulf and the Appositive Style* (Knoxville, TN: U of Tennessee P, 1985), 80.

We often mistakenly think that language meaning, especially in conjunction with grammatical structures, has an invariable interpretation. However, grammatical structures like parataxis are actually *semantically* loose and allow for multiple interpretations. In other words they are a dynamic site of meaning making wherein literary insight is not only invited but welcomed. The negotiable meaning afforded by loose syntactic arrangements does not, however, imply that in deriving a literary meaning, any analysis goes. Apposition and parataxis, by requiring that their listeners/readers actively provide the logical connections between their elements, also require that those readers inhabit a context in which those connections are implicitly shared knowledge. We understand the logical relationship of the clauses *I came. I saw. I conquered* because as inheritors of the Greco-Roman tradition, we share quite a bit of information about Julius Caesar and the Roman Empire. Perhaps with particular clarity in the case of these appositive and paratactic structures, meaning making for a text must involve careful linguistic, literary, and sociohistorical research concerning the creation of the text as well as its creators.

Around 950 manuscripts survive from the OE period. These manuscripts include texts in Latin as well as texts in OE. Among all of these manuscripts, only a handful of codices consist of poetry alone.[23] The vast majority of written texts from the OE period, then, are not poetic texts. Discussions of OE literature—including this one—tend to privilege poetic texts. But there are many kinds of literature that are not poetry in the OE corpus, and there are texts in many genres, some literary, some not, among them saints' lives, sermons, meditations and histories. And of course there are many other kinds of writing: laws, medical texts, maps of the world, astrological writings, treatises on the reckoning of time, catalogues of wonders and monstrosities, just to name a few. The corpus of OE writing in fact challenges us to consider what might be literary, or scientific, or historical, particularly from a present-day perspective.

---

23 Many thanks to Sharon Rowley, Christopher Newport University, for this reminder.

CHAPTER EIGHT

Middle English

THE NORMAN CONQUEST

FIGURE 8.1   Death of Harold from *The Bayeux Tapestry*, c. 1070. Bayeux Museum.

The **Norman Conquest** is often presented as the single most significant external event in the history of the English language. Even in broader historical treatments, the Norman Conquest is described as an event of unparalleled consequences for the English: "Probably no other conquest in European history has had such disastrous consequences for the defeated";[1] "Few countries have had so sharp a break in their

---

1   John Gillingham and Ralph A. Griffiths, *The Oxford History of Britain: The Middle Ages* (Oxford: Oxford UP, 1988), 2.

history as that which broke Harold in 1066."[2] 1066, the year of the Conquest, is called "the date that English people remember from history lessons at school long after they have forgotten all the others"[3] and even "one of the most important dates in the history of the Western world."[4]

There is no question that the Norman Conquest is of great significance to the history of England and of English. In this introduction, however, we will consider it in the context of some of the other very significant external events and influences on the language we have already discussed.

Readers will recall from Chapter 7 that Anglo-Saxon England was conquered twice in the eleventh century. Between 1016 and 1042, England was ruled by the Danish king Cnut and his sons Harold Harefoot and Harthacnut as part of a Scandinavian empire.

During this period of Scandinavian rule, the surviving Anglo-Saxon ruling family lived in exile, in Normandy. Æthelred the Unready had married Emma of Normandy in 1002. When Æthelred was driven into exile, he went to Normandy, and after his death, Æthelred's children remained in Normandy. Emma, who had been married to Æthelred, returned to England in 1017 when she married Cnut, and she maintained a very powerful presence in his court. Æthelred's son, Edward the Confessor, who would come to the English throne in 1042, spent most of his early life in Normandy. Thus, when the Normans conquered England, it cannot have been the case that their language and culture was not already at least familiar to the Anglo-Saxon court: there had been exchange, intermarriage, and diplomatic contacts between England and Normandy for over sixty years.

Nonetheless, the Norman Conquest does mark a dramatic turning point in very broad terms. From the eighth through the eleventh century, England was closely connected to the Scandinavian world. There was a significant settlement of Scandinavians in England; as Germanic peoples, the Anglo-Saxons shared a body of cultural affinities with the Danes, Swedes, and Norwegians; Old English and Norse languages were likely mutually intelligible; and finally England was actually part of a Scandinavian empire. After the Conquest, however, the focus of England's political and cultural connections shifted away from Scandinavia and toward the Continent, particularly to France. England was, in the years after the Conquest, part of a Norman empire. And in the centuries after the Conquest, English kings began to assert themselves as legitimate inheritors of the kingdom of France: post-Conquest English kings eventually acquired control of so much land in France and involved themselves so closely in French political life, in fact, that by the fourteenth century, they would themselves claim the title "King of France."

---

2   James Campbell, Eric John, and Patrick Wormald, *The Anglo-Saxons* (New York: Penguin, 1982), 240.

3   David Howarth, *1066: The Year of the Conquest* (New York: Penguin, 1977), 7.

4   Howarth, *1066*, cover.

EVENTS LEADING UP TO THE CONQUEST

After the rule of Cnut and his sons, in 1042 Edward the Confessor, the son of Æthelred and Emma, returned to England. Edward ruled from 1042 until 1066, when he died without an heir. Very shortly after his death, the English *witan*, official councilors, appointed **Harold Godwinson** king. Harold Godwinson was the son of the single most powerful nobleman in England. Earl Godwin and his five sons controlled more land in England than even Edward the Confessor did. Harold Godwinson's sister, Edith, had been the wife of Edward the Confessor. Additionally, Harold's claim to the throne was supported by a story that on his deathbed, Edward promised it to him.

But in Normandy, William, known as William the Bastard, also claimed the throne of England. William based his claim on his blood relation to Emma (the wife of both Cnut and Æthelred), as well as on a story involving a promise from Edward that William would inherit the throne and a promise from Harold Godwinson that Harold would not interfere with William's claim. William also secured the approval of the Pope. When Harold Godwinson was appointed king of England, William began to prepare his invasion of England.

The situation was made all the more dangerous for Harold Godwinson by the fact that there were also other challenges to his rule. The most significant of these challenges was the claim of the Norwegian king, Harald Hardrada. Harald Hardrada had a claim to the English throne based on a treaty between one of Cnut's son's, Harthacnut, and Magnus, the king of Norway.

In the early months of 1066, we can see England literally poised between a Scandinavian claim and a Continental one: in September, Harald Hardrada's army prepared for an attack on England from the north, and William's army prepared for an attack on England from the south.

Because the wind, in late September 1066, blew in a direction more favorable to the Norwegians than to the Normans, the Norwegians landed in England first. Harold Godwinson quickly gathered and led an Anglo-Saxon army north. The Anglo-Saxons defeated the Norwegians decisively at the **Battle of Stamford Bridge** on 25 September. This defeat is often taken as the event that marks the end of the Viking Age.

The Battle of Stamford Bridge did not secure Harold Godwinson's reign, however. On 28 September, just three days after the battle, William's army landed at Pevensey, in the south of England. Harold Godwinson gathered his army in the north and marched south to meet the Normans.

At the **Battle of Hastings**, on 14 October 1066, the Normans defeated the English. Harold Godwinson was killed, as was a significant portion of the English male ruling class. William the Bastard, now William the Conqueror, would go on to be crowned king of England on Christmas day in 1066.

IMMEDIATE CONSEQUENCES OF THE CONQUEST

William rewarded the noblemen in his army with land in England, effectively displacing the English from positions of power. Furthermore, William also installed Normans in positions within the English church. In the generations immediately following the conquest, most positions of power in England were held by Normans. This shift in the make-up of the ruling class in England is important to the history of the English language because Normans did not speak English: they spoke a dialect of French.

Of course, it is essential to remember that the total immigration of Normans following the Conquest is unlikely to have exceeded about 10 per cent of the total population. Most people in England continued to speak English, and in fact to speak only English. But after the Conquest, almost everyone *with political power* in England spoke a dialect of French, and some did not speak English at all.

LEXICAL BORROWINGS FROM FRENCH

The linguistic fallout from the societal hierarchy that emerged after the Norman Conquest is predictable. As we have seen, Norman French speakers controlled specific, and quite important, areas of activity, including a feudal economy, government, court life, warfare, law, church, and eventually other elements of "high" culture, among them fashion and art. Thus it is not surprising that it was in these areas that we find an influx of Norman French words into English in the two hundred years following the Battle of Hastings and the ascension of William to the English throne. In fact, many of the words we have used above have their roots in borrowings from French during the two centuries following the Conquest: *govern* and *court*, for example, are words introduced into English from French in the two centuries following the Conquest, and *war*, while it occurs in late Old English (OE), does not have the same meaning as it acquires when it is reinforced after the Conquest by its meaning in French.

In the years between 1250 and 1500, French continued to dominate high culture. And not surprisingly, those years witness a very dramatic influx of borrowings from French associated with those sociolinguistic domains. The borrowings in the first century after the Conquest number around 600; the total borrowings from French into English during the Middle English (ME) period, however, number around 10,000.

The following provides a list of examples of those borrowed words within these semantic fields.

Feudalism
Fief, vassal, liege, prince, duke, baron

Government
Crown, government, reign, realm, state, parliament

Court Life
Courteous, noble, refined, honor, heraldry

War
War, battle, arms, assault, siege, officer, lieutenant, sergeant, soldier, troops

Law
Justice, judge, plead, accuse, felony, penalty, marriage, petty (cf. French *petit* [small]), as in petty larceny

Church
Religion, service, trinity, savior, angel, clergy, parish, preach, pray, sermon

Fashion
Apparel, dress, costume, garment

Art
Beauty, color, art, design, figure, ornament

Education
Pupil, pencil (in the original French, a fine brush for writing)

Cuisine
Sauce, boil, pastry, soup, jelly

This list could be greatly expanded. When reckoning French borrowings into English, however, care must be taken not to over-ascribe all such borrowings to the effects of a Norman ruling class. The French language held a position of prestige for many years after the Norman Conquest, well through the later Medieval period, through the Early Modern English (EModE) period, and even into modern times in certain domains. However, while the Norman influence after 1066 was more localized, deriving from a rather specific set of historical effects and new power relations, the later prestige of the French language was based on a supra-regional variety of that language that held prestige on an international scale. Thus the much later borrowings of French words like *lingerie* (early nineteenth century) and *coq au vin* (mid-twentieth century), happen in a different language relationship and come from different dialects than those of the French borrowings of the early ME period.

Whether it involves Norman or later French, it is always of interest to note how the relationships between specific borrowed words and native words continue to communicate the kinds of social relationships, particularly in terms of prestige, that we have been talking about. For instance, we see the dynamics of that relationship between the native English *stool* alongside the French borrowing *chair*, or between the borrowed *mansion* and the native *house*. The prestige and power that accompanies French words has also resulted in an interesting lexical tic in English in that we have two etymologically different sets of words for many types of meat and the animals from which those meats are prepared, as we discussed in the Introduction (p. 17).

We emphasize, however, that while English was not the language of the first generation of the Norman rulers in England, it did remain the language of the vast majority of English people. English was not used as a *literary* language among the Norman ruling class, however, and for that reason, it may appear to us as if English is lost during the period after the Conquest. But that is not possible, as the subsequent "re-emergence" of English makes very clear. English continues as a language *spoken* by English people even when French replaces it as a language of prestige at court, in high culture and in written texts.

THE RE-EMERGENCE OF ENGLISH

During the thirteenth and fourteenth centuries, a number of external pressures contribute to the re-emergence of English. These pressures include:

- the separation of English and French territories;
- prolonged hostility between England and France (the Hundred Years' War);
- loss of French as a native language in England;
- shifts in the prestige of dialects of French;
- increase in geographic, economic, and social mobility for speakers of English.

William the Conqueror's successors expanded their control over territories in France. Most dramatically, Henry II (ruled 1154–89), after his 1152 marriage to Eleanor of Aquitaine, controlled lands in France that included not only Normandy, Maine, Anjou, and Brittany, but also the vast and wealthy territory of Aquitaine. English kings, by the end of the twelfth century, in addition to being the kings of England, controlled much of the territory of France.

But there was a complication. English kings held those territories as vassals of the kings of France. Vassalage was a feature of land tenure in much of medieval Europe. Noblemen held their land not as their own, but as tenants-in-chief of their overlords, and ultimately the king. They held their land on the condition of their service to the king and the king could revoke a holding if he judged that a vassal had not performed appropriate service. Kings of England held their wide tracts of lands in France—Normandy, Brittany, Aquitaine—as vassals of the kings of France. By the end of the twelfth century, however, the king of England could challenge the power of the king of France on a number of levels: the king of England was the king of an independent and wealthy country on its own, and the king of England had control of lands in France at least equaling, and perhaps exceeding those of the king of France.

FIGURE 8.2   **Representation of the ceremony of homage, in which a nobleman becomes the vassal of his overlord. The Royal Prosecutor, the Scribe and the Feudal Lord, from Capbreu de Clayra et de Millas, 1292.**

In 1204, a confrontation between King **John Lackland** (ruled 1199–1216) and Philip, the king of France, arose from exactly these tensions (among others). Philip summoned John to his court. John refused to go. Philip confiscated some of John's land on the grounds that John had not performed appropriate service as a vassal. In the ensuing military conflict, the English king, John Lackland, lost control of Normandy. In the subsequent years, Philip confiscated lands held by English barons, and English nobles increasingly divided their land among their heirs so that fewer nobles held both lands in England and lands in France.

The English continued both to hold land in France and to maintain the legitimacy of their claim to control those lands, however, and when in 1328 the French king Charles IV died without a clear male heir, Edward III, the king of England, would make a claim to the throne of France. The **Hundred Years' War**, waged for over a hundred years, ended in a victory for the French, and the political separation of

England and France. England lost all of its holdings in France (except for the port of Calais) by the end of the war.

The political separation of England and France beginning with the loss of Normandy and continuing over the period of the Hundred Years' War is important to the re-emergence of English because it is associated with a shift in cultural identification with respect to French and English as languages. French became during this period not only the language of high culture, but also the language of the principal opposing force in a war that lasted over a century. Pressure to identify as *English* and *not French* thus contributed to a turn towards English as the language of the English.

Other pressures operated at the same time. French by the fourteenth century was no longer the first language of the ruling class in England. In fact, as early as the mid-thirteenth century, texts appear for teaching French to upper-class children. If French was a language that must be taught with a textbook, it could not have been a language that children were learning at home as their first language. Although French remained a language of considerable prestige, it was no longer the native language of the ruling class in England as it had been immediately after the Conquest.

Furthermore, Norman French and Anglo-Norman French were by the early fourteenth century no longer dialects of prestige. To speak the sort of French spoken in Norman England, or even learned at later English schools, was to mark oneself as uneducated, or unsophisticated. The poet Geoffrey Chaucer, for example, famously pokes fun at the French of one of his characters:

And Frenssh she spak ful faire and fetisly,
After the scole of Stratford atte Bowe,
For Frenssh of Parys was to hire unknowe....

And she spoke French very handsomely and elegantly,
In the manner of the school of Stratford,
For the French of Paris was unknown to her....[5]

In addition to these pressures, which might have resulted in a turn towards increased use of English in high culture and in written texts, a number of other factors contribute to the rise in power of sectors of English society which had never identified themselves with the use of French: the peasant and middle classes. We note here, however, that the term "middle class" is not a medieval term. Medieval scholars themselves understood what we might now call class divisions in terms of "estates," and divided society into Those Who Fight (the ruling class), Those Who Pray (those associated with the Church), and Those Who Work (everyone else).

---

5 General Prologue, in *The Riverside Chaucer*, ed. Larry Dean Benson (Boston: Houghton Mifflin, 1987), lines 124–26. Present-Day English (PDE) ours.

In 1348, a catastrophic epidemic now called the **Black Plague** struck in England. Mortality rates from the first wave of the Black Plague in England reached to about a third of the total population. And the plague returned, though with diminishing force, at intervals throughout the next centuries: in 1361, 1368–69, 1371, 1375, 1390, 1405....

One of the consequences of the plague was a labor shortage, and with it unprecedented geographic, economic, and social mobility for the laboring classes. A clear indication of a new sense of power for these laboring classes is provided by the English **Peasants' Revolt** of 1381. In 1381, in reaction to a repeated pattern of taxation levied to fund the ongoing Hundred Years' War, English peasants and artisans revolted, marched to London, and demanded among other things the revocation of some kinds of serfdom. One of the slogans of the revolt was the couplet from John Ball, "When Adam dug and Eve spun, who was then a gentleman?" This couplet powerfully expresses a number of sentiments that marked the turbulent period after the plague: that the noble classes could no longer justify their privilege on the basis of anything they did as Those Who Fight; that in a perfect world, Those Who Work might also be lords. Although the revolt terrified the English ruling class, the revolt was not ultimately successful. However, the fact that such a revolt took place at all reveals that the laboring and artisan classes in England increasingly both recognized their class interests and were willing to act to resist economic and class oppression. The Peasants' Revolt is important to a history of English as a language because it marks the increasing social consciousness, and economic power, of that portion of the English population that never spoke French, and that identified English as its own language.

We say that English "re-emerged" in the fourteenth century in the confluence of these pressures, but with the reminder that English had never gone away: English re-emerged in written record but it had not ceased being spoken in the preceding centuries.

As will be clear in the following sections of this chapter, when English re-emerged it looked much more like Present-Day English (PDE) than OE had. Part of what makes the difference from OE appear so dramatic is that there are not many records of its gradual change. We tend to look at OE texts and contrast them to ME texts from about 400 years later. And because English was not used in many written contexts between the Conquest and the re-emergence, it was also not subject to the conservative effects of writing on language (a topic we will explore explicitly in the next chapter). But it is true that during the period between the end of the OE period and the re-emergence of English, English underwent a number of changes. While many of those changes were anticipated already in the OE period, the extent of those changes during the ME period was such that speakers of PDE will be able to read texts in ME with only minimal training: the changes in the 400 years between the OE text *Beowulf* and ME texts like the *Canterbury Tales* are such that it may appear that English changed significantly more in those 400 years than it has in the 650 years between the ME period and the present day.

ORTHOGRAPHY AND PHONOLOGY

ORTHOGRAPHY

When English "re-emerged" as a language in which a large number of texts were written, its orthography, not surprisingly, reflected the influence of conventions for writing in dialects of French as well as in a variety of handwriting styles.

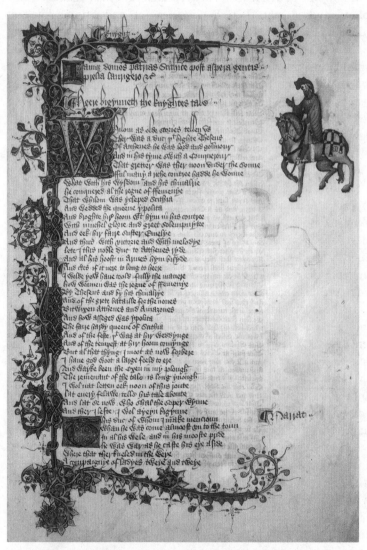

FIGURE 8.3   Ellesmere Manuscript EL 26 C9 f. 10r (detail).

After studying OE, students are often struck by the fact that the orthography of ME is quite similar to that of PDE. While orthography is not standardized until after the ME period, it is true that orthographic conventions are generally set in place during the ME period. The reason why ME spelling looks so familiar to readers of PDE is that spelling did not change much after the ME period. However, the sounds of the language have changed, some of them quite dramatically, as we will see.

The image above is from one of the most famous manuscripts of Chaucer's *Canterbury Tales*, the early-fifteenth-century Ellesmere manuscript, now housed at the Huntington Library in California. The passage represented is from the opening of the Knight's Tale: the first line in the excerpt above is "Heere bigynneth the knyghtes tale."

Chapter 7 introduced two symbols from the OE runic alphabet that were integrated into the orthography of OE, wynn, <ᚹ> and thorn, <þ>. Very obviously in the image shown above, by the end of the ME period, wynn had been replaced by <w>, as in the very large capital <w> at the top of the page. While the thorn persisted for some time, its use would be diminished during the ME period, as would that of the letter we now call eth, <ð>, which represented the same sounds. The introductory line in the passage in the image, for example, "Heere bigynneth the knyghtes tale," represents the sounds [ð, θ] not with <ð> or <þ> but with the digraph <th>.

Among purely orthographic differences between OE and ME, we can document the loss of the letters wynn, thorn, and eth and their replacement by <w> and <th> respectively.

ME introduces a number of digraphs in addition to <th>. The chart below represents those introductions and the letters or digraphs they replaced.

Old English	Middle English	IPA
ð	th	[ð, θ]
þ	th	[ð, θ]
ū	ou, ow	[u:]
ċ	ch	[tʃ]
sc	sh	[ʃ]
cg	gg, dg(e)	[dʒ]
h	gh	[x, ç]
hw	wh	[hw]

The dot in <ċ> is, as presented in the last chapter, a PDE editorial convention. The orthographic change from <hw> to <wh> accompanied a phonological change in some dialects of ME, as will be discussed in the next section.

EXERCISE

8.1 The following words were pronounced very similarly, if not identically, in OE and ME. The orthographic changes in ME make them much more easily recognizable in PDE, however. Answers appear at the end of the book.

For each of the following OE words, provide the ME spelling.

OE ðis   ME _____

OE scip   ME _____

OE ecg   ME _____

OE mūþ   ME _____

OE nū   ME _____

OE ċild   ME _____

OE miht   ME _____

In addition to these replacements, ME introduces <qu> to replace the combination <cw> in OE, [kw]. The spelling <gu> for [g] is also introduced, first in French borrowings like *guile* but eventually extending to native words as well.

The letter <c> in ME can be pronounced [s], an orthographic convention also introduced first from French borrowings, hence, from French, the words *city* and *place*. This spelling spread to some native words as well, such as *mice*.

The letter <k> was available in OE, and does occur in OE manuscripts. But its use is considerably extended in ME, especially before the letters <i, e, n>, and after vowels, sometimes spelled <ck> in the latter contexts.

ME often indicated vowel length by doubling the long vowels, particularly in the case of <e> and <o>. Remember that the macron over the vowel in Old English is largely a convention of PDE editing.

Old English	Middle English
ē	ee
ō	oo

EXERCISE

8.2   Provide the ME spelling of the following OE words. Answers appear at the end of the book.

OE ðē   ME _____
OE gōd   ME _____
OE fēt   ME _____
OE cwēn   ME _____
OE cniht . ME _____
OE gilt   ME _____

A number of changes in the orthography of ME coincide with changes in the phonology, and will be discussed below. Those changes include the following:

- the loss of the letter ash, <æ>;
- the introduction of the letter <v> for [v] and several vowel articulations of <u>. In many manuscript traditions, <v> and <u> could be used interchangeably;
- the increased use of the letter <z> for [z].

PHONOLOGY

In the preceding section, the changes were all orthographical in nature. That is, they are changes to the customary way that words were represented in terms of spelling. The very fact that changes can be made to the spelling without a corresponding change in the way the word is pronounced is a good example of the conventionalized and relatively more arbitrary way that spelling systems, like our alphabet, come to represent the sounds of a word. Still, since it is a goal of alphabet systems to represent the sounds of a word, it is not surprising that some sound changes will also affect spelling changes, and again, many of those sound changes (and the corresponding changes in spelling) bring the language closer to its modern-day appearance and thus make it more recognizable as English for the PDE-speaking student.

UNCONDITIONED SOUND CHANGES

In our discussion of sound change from OE to ME, we will first consider **unconditioned sound changes**, that is, those changes that occurred to a group of sounds regardless of where the sound happened to occur.

[æ] > [ɑ]

Apparently in all dialects, although at different rates and with a few distinct details, the short low, front, unrounded vowel [æ] moved down and back toward [ɑ]. With this change, the letter ash < æ> faded away from manuscript spelling, replaced by <a>, the letter we still find in the examples listed below.

Old English	Middle English
Þæt	that
æt	at
æppel	apple

[ɑ:] > [ɔ]

Accompanying this change, the letter <a> in these words come to be written frequently as <o>.

Old English	Middle English
ban	bon(e)
stan	ston(e)
na	no

The change did not affect northern dialects, and the older English forms can be seen even in the 1790 poem "Tam o' Shanter" by Scottish poet Robert Burns:

> By this time he was cross the ford,
> Where in the snaw the chapman smoor'd;
> And past the birks and meikle stane,
> Where drunken Charlie brak's neck-bane;

> By this time he was across the ford,
> where in the snow the peddler was smothered
> and past the birch trees and mighty stone
> where drunken Charlie broke his neck bone

[y] > [i]

Many varieties of OE had a high, front, rounded vowel [y], as in Modern French *tu* [ty] or Modern German *über* [ybə]. However, in ME, [y] unrounded to [i] in many varieties.

Old English	Middle English
fyr	fire
mys	mice
cynn	kin

CONDITIONED SOUND CHANGES

Other changes from OE to ME were **conditioned sound changes**, by which it is meant that the change did not affect every single instance of a given sound, but only the sound as it occurred in certain phonetic (and sometimes morphological) environments.

Word-final [m] > [n]

Even by the end of the OE period in some dialects, word-final [m] had begun to change to [n]. Subsequently [n] at the ends of words, particularly if it was part of an ending, began to disappear (see "Loss of Word-Final [n]" below).

The change was not so likely in monomorphemic words (i.e., those words in which the [m] was part of the stem and not an inflectional ending), e.g., OE *botm*: PDE *bottom*. Thus, the change from [m] to [n] was most likely in those cases where the [m] marked some inflectional category, such as the dative plural (see again Chapter 7). Obviously this change made the grammatical distinction in case in the plural less obvious and therefore contributed, rather directly, to the demise of the OE case system among nouns, a topic addressed in the next section.

Reduction and Loss of Unstressed Vowels in Word Final Syllables

In PDE, words with multiple syllables that end in a vowel, other than [i], tend to have a final schwa sound:

> mozzarella [mɑtsəɹɛlə]
> America [əmɛɹɪkə]

Even in some regional pronunciations of *window* as *windah* [wɪndə] and *Missouri* as *Missourah* [mɪzʊɹə], we hear the same tendency. What each of the words exemplified so far has in common is that the final vowel is unstressed. In fact, on consulting a phonetically reversed dictionary of English, a dictionary in which words are listed in reverse according to the sound—not letter—that they end in,[6] it becomes apparent that it is exceedingly rare for a word to end in a full vowel in English—at all. (The majority of words that do end in a vowel, end either with "silent e," which of course isn't a vowel at all in speech, or with an <a>, which as in the words above, represents the schwa sound.

In OE, however, if a word ended in a vowel, the vowel had its full pronunciation:

> *soðlice* [soðlitʃe] (truthfully)
> *earwunga* [æərwungɑ] (without cause)
> *ġiefu* [jievu] (gift)
> *bieldo* [bieldo] (boldness)

---

6 Gustav Muthmann, *Reverse English Dictionary: Based on Phonological and Morphological Principles* (New York: Mouton de Gruyter, 1999).

If we look back at the forms of the noun in OE in Chapter 7 (pp. 140, 143–44), it is clear that full vowels carried some weight in terms of distinguishing case. The falling together of those different vowel sounds will again have damaging effects on the OE case system, a point we return to in the next section.

Loss of Word-Final [n]

During ME, a final [n] was lost in many words, but the loss tended to affect inflectional endings on nouns and on verbs. For example, as presented in Chapter 7, the OE infinitive ended in [n], e.g., *macian* (to make). During the ME period, infinitives lose that final [n], e.g., *(to) make*. According to Roger Lass, whereas 100 per cent of the infinitives were marked with final [n] in 1140, only 2 per cent are marked with final [n] by 1480.[7]

Loss of Word-Initial /h/ before [l], [n] or [r]

In OE, /h/ (phonetically realized as [x]) occurred before [l], [n] and [r] in a number of words. That consonant cluster was simplified in ME through deletion of the /h/:

Old English	Middle English
hreddan [xreddan]	ridde(n) [ridə] (to rid)
hnutu [xnutu]	nut [nut]
hlyp [xlyp]	lep [lep] (leap)

In many varieties of ME, /h/ was also lost before [w]. However the spelling changed such that the <h> and <w> were reversed to <wh>, suggesting that at least at first the /h/ was still pronounced in some way:

Old English		Middle English
hwæt [xwæt]	>	what [wɑt]
hwilom [xwilom]	>	whilom [wiləm] (once)
hwæðer [xwæðer]	>	whether [wɛðer]

In some dialects, initial /h/ was preserved before [w], and can still be heard today. In fact while it has become a somewhat stereotyped feature of Texan speech in the US, the feature exists in a number of dialects in the US and UK. The feature was regularly taught as the correct pronunciation in American schools all over the US throughout the early part of the twentieth century.

Vowel Lengthening

a. The vowels [i] and [o] become long before [nd]: OE *windan* [i] > ME *wind* [iː], OE > *bindan* [i] > ME *bind* [iː].

---

7   Roger Lass, "Phonology and Morphology," in *The Cambridge History of the English Language: Volume II, 1066–1476*, edited by Norman Blake (Cambridge: Cambridge UP, 1992), 98.

b. The vowels [i] and [u] become long before [mb]: OE *klimban* [i] > ME *climb* [i:], OE *funden* [u] > ME *found* [u:] (note the spelling change of <u> to <ou>).

c. Any vowel before [ld] becomes long (but not before [ldr]): OE *ċild* [i] > ME *child* [i:] (note the spelling change <c> > <ch>). Note, however, that the lengthening does not affect the [i] in ME *children* [i].

Vowel Shortening

A long vowel in a syllable closed by a consonant cluster, including doubled consonants, became a short vowel. OE softe [o:] > ME softe [o] (soft). Note especially that this sound change affected the present tense and past tense forms of several verbs:

OE spelling	OE phonetics	ME spelling	ME phonetics
a. present			
hide	[hi:de]	hide	[hi:də]
past			
hidde	[hi:dde]	hidde	[hidə]
b. present			
cepe	[ke:pe]	kepe	[ke:pə]
past			
cepte	[ke:pte]	kepte	[kepte]

Phonemicization of Voiced Fricatives

In this section, we will review a set of sound changes (actually a single sound change that affected a class of sounds) that added phonemes to ME. Note that for this discussion you have to understand the difference between phonemes and allophones (review Chapter 6), particularly how [f], [s], [θ] on the one hand, and [v], [z], [ð] on the other were allophones of /f/, /s/, and /θ/ in OE (review Chapter 7).

The phones [v], [z], [ð], which had been allophones of /f/, /s/, and /θ/ in OE, became phonemes in their own right (/v/, /z/, /ð/). The phonemic status of /v/, /z/, /ð/ is made obvious in PDE through the following set of distinctive pairs:

fat–vat
sap–zap
ether–either

There are four factors working together that might account for the phonemicization of /v/, /z/, /ð/:

a. Loan words, mostly from French, established new minimal pairs:

fine–vine
few–view

b. There was increased dialect mixing, in which there were certain dialects, chiefly in the south of England, in which [s], [v], and [θ] were pronounced as voiced sounds, [v], [z], [ð]. In those dialects *fox* would have been pronounced [voks] (and it is from one of those dialects that we get our word *vixen*, i.e., a female fox). It is interesting to note that some speakers of PDE still show this dialect feature, saying "zink" for *sink*.

c. The effects of assimilation set up some minimal-pair contrasts between different word classes. In order to understand these effects, it is necessary to remember that essentially the OE rule by which /f/, /s/ and /θ/ were pronounced as [v], [z], [ð] was assimilation. Assimilation is when two sounds become pronounced more alike. Since the voiced sounds [v], [z], [ð] occurred when /f/, /s/, and /θ/ were next to voiced sounds, it is clear that [v], [z], [ð] resulted from the spread of voicing from adjacent sounds.

In ME we find that final fricatives among nouns tend to be voiceless following their pronunciation in the nominative (and often accusative) singular, in which the fricative is at the end of a word: *hus* (house) [hus]. But the verb that was derived from that noun would have been pronounced [huz-] because the fricative was rarely ever alone at the end of the word but more likely between two vowels, as in the infinitive form *husian* [huziɑn]. The effect was the establishment of noun–verb contrasts where the noun has a voiceless fricative and the verb has a voiced fricative at the end of the stem: noun = [hus]; verb = [huz-]. This contrast frequently appears even in ModE:

Noun	Verb
house [hɑus]	to house [hɑuz]
teeth [tiθ]	to teethe [tið]

EXERCISE

8.3 **Supply the IPA for the following noun/verb pairs. Answers appear at the end of the book.**

grief _____ to grieve _____
breath _____ to breathe _____
belief _____ to believe _____

d. In ME, the initial or final fricatives of many function words were voiced. Function words are those grammatical words like *was, is, this, that, the, of,* etc. Note that each of these words in OE would have had the voiceless allophones [f], [s], [θ] of the phonemes /f/, /s/, and /θ/, as the first or last segment of the word. In ME, however, these came to be pronounced [v], [z], [ð].

Two orthographic changes reflect the phonemicization of these voiced fricatives, the introduction of the letter <v> for [v] and the increased use of the letter <z> for [z].

EXERCISE

8.4 **Based on the information given in this section, fill in the OE and ME pronunciation in phonetics. While our focus is on the voicing of the fricatives, there may be some other sound changes that you will need to account for. Answers appear at the end of this section of the chapter.**

OE spelling	OE pronunciation	ME spelling	ME pronunciation
wæs	_____	was	_____
is	_____	is	_____
ðis	_____	this	_____
ðæt	_____	that	_____
of	_____	of	_____

THE NOMINAL GROUP

SOUND CHANGE AND THE MORPHOLOGICAL RESTRUC-TURING OF STRONG MASCULINE NOUNS

As we have already seen in the previous section, a number of sound changes during the ME period affected the ends of words especially. These sound changes were reductive in nature; full vowels became schwas and some final segments of words were lost. The operation of these changes at the end of words in English is motivated by the Germanic feature of fixed initial stress. That is, since major stress tended to occur early in words, the ends of words were left vulnerable to just the kinds of reductive changes under discussion.

In fact, similar kinds of reductive tendencies are found in English today. Consider, for example, the pronunciation of *elementary*. While it is certainly possible that one might pronounce the word as [ɛlɛmɛntərɪ], it is also equally, if not more likely, particularly in casual speech, that the word would be pronounced [ɛlɛmɛntrɪ], that is, with the deletion of the vowel sound in the fourth syllable. As another example, consider words that have an unstressed schwa followed by a nasal sound, e.g., *written*, *Clinton*, or *kitten*, particularly after /t/ or /d/. It is highly unusual to pronounce the final syllable with a vowel at all and the words end with a syllabic [n], written with a line underneath, [n̩]. In other words, speakers of most Englishes most of the time do not pronounce a vowel in the last syllable of those words, but merely give syllabic weight to the [n̩].

In order to see the effects of word-final reductive changes, let's consider what would have happened to a strong masculine noun in ME. The OE strong masculine noun *cniht* (young man) is given below, showing the OE form on the left and the eventual ME form on the right of the arrow.

		OE		**Late ME**
Sing.	**Nom.**	cniht	>	knight
	Gen.	cnihtes	>	knights
	Dat.	cnihte	>	knight
	Acc.	cniht	>	knight
Pl.	**Nom.**	cnihtas	>	knights
	Gen.	cnihta	>	knights
	Dat.	cnihtum	>	knights
	Acc.	cnihtas	>	knights

We can note that for this class of nouns nothing happens to the nominative and accusative singular forms. However, because of the reductive forces at play on word-final vowels, the -*e* of the dative singular was eventually lost, making it identical to the nominative and accusative singular forms. Word-final -*s* was not susceptible to loss. Therefore although the vowel in that final syllable was lost, the -*s* remained, and signaled possession. Note, however, that at the early stages of English, the possessive -*s* was not written orthographically with an apostrophe. That practice would not become common until the seventeenth century. The -*s* of the plural nominative and accusative, similar to the -*s* of the genitive singular, also remained, although again the vowels in those forms were deleted in accordance with the sound changes discussed earlier.

The dative plural form is of special interest. If it were the only sound change at play in the restructuring of ME nouns, we should expect the following: the vowel [u] reduced to [ə] and then deleted and the [m] changed to [n] and then deleted, leaving the form *knight*. However, we have the form *knights* (and similarly *knights* in the genitive plural). Thus in addition to the loss of some sounds, there is also the spread of other sounds around the strong masculine noun paradigm, specifically the plural and the possessive -*s*.

The question we now ask is: what is it about the noun paradigm that motivates the moving around of the plural and possessive -*s*? The answer to this question has already been suggested; the endings of words in OE were not just any old sounds, but were meaningful within the system of case. For example, the -*s* of the nominative and accusative plural was not merely an -*s* sound, as it arguably is in the PDE word *linguistics*. Rather, it meant "plural." So the sound losses that we have been talking about obliterated a number of grammatical meanings within the strong masculine noun paradigm (e.g., dative singular, dative plural, genitive plural) and weakened the entire system of case in the paradigm (which had depended on those very meaning distinctions) and thus created the impetus for morphological restructuring in the paradigm.

Theories abound as to the exact steps and motivations for this restructuring, but one likely scenario is that once the dative endings were lost, there was essentially no case outside the genitive left, since the accusative and nominative were already identical in strong masculine nouns. Thus distinction by case was no longer relevant, and greater prominence arose for distinctions that signaled number in the paradigm—singular and plural. The greater prominence in singular versus plural distinctions would leave the dative plural in a precarious situation if its form had been affected only by sound change, since such effects would yield *knight*. But a dative plural *knight* looks far too much like the singular form, a singular which is now identical in the nominative, accusative and dative grammatical forms—that's a pretty strong singular!

Consequently, pressures arose within the paradigm that caused realignment of meaningful endings. Plural was now the most meaningful distinction, and since plural was marked with -s for all of the nominative and accusative grammatical forms and since there was essentially no difference in nominative, accusative, and dative in the singular, the pressure was high for the dative plural to move in line with the nominative and accusative plurals; in other words, the dative collapsed in the plural (as it had in the singular) with the rest of the noun forms—except the genitive, which has its own story to tell.

The story of genitive -s will largely be told in the EModE period in the next chapter. For now, we note that the -s marking for possessive meaning was preserved from the OE genitive case in the strong masculine noun paradigm. Whether the -s of the genitive plural is the plural -s or the new possessive -s is unclear, although there is some evidence that it is primarily the plural. Consider for instance that some speakers of English will pronounce the plural possessive with two s's, as in *the cats'* [kætsəz] *food*, as if to suggest that the first [s] is the plural and the second a possessive marker. More evidence for this analysis will emerge in the EModE period.

ANALOGY: RESTRUCTURING ACROSS NOUN PARADIGMS

As we have just seen, the -s became meaningful for signaling plural in the strong masculine noun paradigm. However, it is clear that that same -s came to signal the plural for almost every noun in English, including those that were not historically members of the strong masculine group. Consider again the neuter and feminine strong paradigms from OE:

	Masc. (stone)	Neut. (word)	Fem. (teaching)
Sing. Nom.	stān	word	lār
Sing. Gen.	stānes	wordes	lāre
Sing. Dat.	stāne	worde	lāre
Sing. Acc.	stān	word	lāre
Pl. Nom.	stānas	word	lāra, -e
Pl. Gen.	stāna	worda	lāra, -ena
Pl. Dat.	stānum	wordum	lārum
Pl. Acc.	stānas	word	lāra, -e

As is evident, the plurals in these paradigms are not inflected with -s. How did the -s from the strong masculine paradigm spread to these other strong paradigms? The answer is analogical spread.

Language is a cognitive entity. While there is much debate as to the exact nature of the cognitive status of language, it is clear that at least in some respects language behaves like other cognitive routines, such as memory. In ways not unlike what one does when one has to remember what the product of 6 x 7 is, one has to remember what the plural of a noun is. Luckily most nouns are very regular in this respect and form their plurals with an -s. But what about those that don't? It can sometimes be more difficult to remember those plurals. Many people have trouble summoning the plural of *syllabus*, *fish*, *axis*, *corpus*, or *vertebra*.

Looking again at the various noun paradigms from OE, it is obvious that the concept of plural was signaled in a number of different ways. While it is wholly possible for languages to sustain such diffuse pluralization patterns, as does Modern German, the same kinds of restructuring pressures in the strong masculine paradigm were also affecting other noun paradigms. In those paradigms, the salient distinction shifted also to number, i.e., singular versus plural.

The eventual strategy for signaling singular and plural forms came to be modeled on the strong masculine pattern for all nouns. This may be partly due to sound change: many of the final sounds that had signaled distinctions in case in the strong neuter and feminine nouns were already non-existent or highly susceptible to loss, e.g., the -e for accusative, dative, and genitive singular in the strong feminine noun paradigm. Thus, it was a relatively simple matter for those paradigms to conform to the ø-plural pattern that we saw in the strong masculine noun paradigm.

However, to explain why the s-plural pattern arose in neuter and feminine nouns, we cannot invoke sound change, because the plural in neither of those paradigms involved -s. The -s that came to mark the plural of those nouns instead spread to those paradigms from the strong masculine type through a process known as **analogy**. Essentially, analogy is the process whereby forms pattern alike based on internal linguistic pressures. In the case of the strong noun paradigms, we note that strong masculine nouns accounted for some 35 per cent of all nouns in English, while strong feminine nouns and strong neuter nouns accounted for only 25 per cent each. Again, in this restructuring in which number is becoming the most important morphological distinction in the nominal group, the greater proportion of nouns had the -s plural, and was the most readily called up in the mind.

LOSS OF GRAMMATICAL GENDER

Obviously with the ø-singular/s-plural pattern spreading to other strong (and weak, see below) paradigms, noun classification according to grammatical gender becomes defunct. It will be remembered that grammatical gender is not about biological gender; recall that the OE word for woman, *wif*, was neuter. However, with the loss of grammatical gender, natural gender patterns, those based on biologically determined gender, take over. Thus, in ME we find the patterns that we still use today.

LOSS OF [N] IN WEAK NOUN PARADIGMS: REDUX

Histories of English frequently present the loss of the final [n] among the weak nouns as purely the result of a sound change; however, that may be misleading. It will be remembered that word-final [n] marked many of the case categories in the weak noun paradigms:

Weak Nouns

	Masc. (name)	Neut. (eye)	Fem. (tongue)
Sing. Nom.	nama	ēage	tunge
Sing. Gen.	naman	ēagan	tungan
Sing. Dat.	naman	ēagan	tungan
Sing. Acc.	naman	ēage	tungan
Pl. Nom.	naman	ēagan	tungan
Pl. Gen.	namena	ēagena	tungena
Pl. Dat.	namum	ēagum	tungum
Pl. Acc.	naman	ēagan	tungan

However, it is more likely that shift of most weak nouns to the common ø-singular/s-plural pattern was the result of analogy; that is, weak nouns began to pattern like strong nouns. Weak nouns accounted for only a small percentage of all nouns in OE. One important piece of evidence for the view that the loss of [n] among weak nouns was the product of analogy and not sound change is the fact that many stem-final -*n* words survived from OE, e.g., the word for seven, *seofan*. Additionally, some weak noun patterns persisted throughout the ME period, and at least two nouns continue to show the OE -*n* plural of weak nouns: *oxen* and *children*. Even in the EModE period, Shakespeare used the plural *shoon* for *shoes*.

Now, one might claim that the retention of the -*n* on these few words is explainable in terms of resistance to sound change, but when we consider the other kinds of words in which an irregular plural is retained, it becomes clear that the motivation for the retention of -*n* may be accounted for in morphological terms.

RETENTION OF IRREGULAR PLURALS: REVERSED MARKEDNESS

Here is a fairly complete list of nouns with irregular plurals that stem from patterns in OE, such as the strong neuter noun paradigm or the weak noun paradigms, and that persist into PDE. (Note the list won't contain later "irregular" plurals from Latin or Greek, e.g., *syllabus, syllabi*):

ø-plural

Sing.	Pl.
fish	fish
sheep	sheep
deer	deer

I-mutation plural

Sing.	Pl.
mouse	mice
louse	lice
tooth	teeth
man/woman	men/women
foot	feet
goose	geese

N-plural

Sing.	Pl.
ox	oxen
child	children

Is there a common property among these nouns in terms of their plural? It has been suggested that in discourse these nouns occur as frequently in the plural as in the singular.[8] In other words, it is extremely common to speak of these nouns in their paired or collective senses. In fact, ø-plural marking has extended to several words denoting game animals, e.g., *We went to Alaska and hunted bear.*

The fact that the *n*-plural is retained among those nouns for which plural is as likely to occur as the singular suggests that the loss of *-n* among nouns was sensitive to the semantics of the noun, particularly the plural, making it a morphological concern, not merely a sound change.

ADJECTIVES

Like nouns, adjectives underwent significant simplification during ME: in fact, adjectives lost all case and gender distinctions. Throughout the ME period, some remnants of the Germanic strong–weak distinction remain. For example, monosyllabic adjectives could show the following systematic distribution in late ME:

	Strong	Weak
Sing.	good	goode
Pl.	goode	goode

8　Peter Tiersma, "Local and General Markedness," *Language* 58 (1982): 832–49.

But even this pattern showed variation, and the possibility of supressing the <e> for stylistic purposes was available. It is fairly safe to say that the OE distinction of strong and weak adjective usage was defunct by the end of the ME period.

DETERMINERS

Definite Article
In the OE period the demonstrative and definite article functions overlapped, signaled by the same set of forms. In ME, the definite article and demonstrative functions split. The form *the* (early on spelled <ðe> or <þe>) came to serve as the general definite article form for all nouns.

Indefinite Article
OE had no indefinite article proper. However, beginning even in OE, the word for the number one, *ān*, came to signal indefinite status for a noun. In ME, the indefinite article became an established grammatical feature of the nominal system. It is also during this time that the familiar pattern for the indefinite article became established: <a> appeared before words beginning with a consonant sound and <an> appeared before words beginning with a vowel sound.

Demonstrative
The demonstrative also underwent reduction of case and gender distinctions in conjunction with those losses occurring on nouns. The system that developed in ME, and remains in PDE, distinguishes singular and plural and distal and proximal meanings.

	Proximal	Distal
Sing.	this	that
Pl.	these	those

The demonstrative forms have especially convoluted histories. While *this* and *that* developed fairly straightforwardly from the OE words *þis* and *þæt*, the plural of *þæt*, *þā*, developed by sound change into *tho*. In fact, *tho* was used throughout the ME period. However, the form *those* also developed with the analogical plural -*s* which, as we have discussed, spread to almost all nouns. If OE *þis* had developed naturally, its plural *þās* would have become homophonous with the new plural of the distal demonstrative, *those*. However, the vowel of the singular *þis* was extended to the plural and the form *these* developed with a nonhistorical vowel.

Personal Pronouns

You will remember that pronouns even into PDE continue to show case. The first-person pronoun, for instance, is *I* when it is the subject and *me* when it is the object: *I* love you ~ You love *me*. Thus we can say that the changes involving pronouns as we move into the ME period are not as disruptive to the case system of OE as the changes that happened among nouns. One change that does occur, however, is the collapse or conflation of the accusative and dative cases into a single case that we call simply the objective case. Consequently the nominative case has been recast as the subjective case. The following chart gives the OE accusative and dative forms and their ME reflexes.

		Old English		**Middle English**		
Sing.						
1st		**Acc.**	me	**Obj.**	me	
		Dat.	me			
2nd		**Acc.**	þe	**Obj.**	thee	(this was also spelled <þe> and
		Dat.	þe			<the> in ME)
3rd						
Masc.		**Acc.**	hine	**Obj.**	him	
		Dat.	him			
Fem.		**Acc.**	hie	**Obj.**	her	
		Dat.	hire			
Neut.		**Acc.**	hit	**Obj.**	it	(some dialects preserved *hit*, and
		Dat.	him			some still do today)
Plural						
1st		**Acc.**	us	**Obj.**	us	
		Dat.	us			
2nd		**Acc.**	eow	**Obj.**	you	(there was much spelling variation
		Dat.	eow			with this pronoun.)
3rd		**Acc.**	hie	**Obj.**	them	
		Dat.	him			

Note that when there is a distinction between the accusative and dative forms, it is the dative form that almost always survived as the ME objective form. The neuter *hit* is the exception to this tendency. If *him* had survived as the objective form of the neuter, we would have identical forms for the masculine and neuter objective forms; both would be *him*. So perhaps the accusative *(h)it* survived in order to preserve maximal morphological distinction between masculine, feminine, and neuter forms: *him*, *her*, and *it*.

Nearly all of the forms of the pronouns in ME can be explained as preservation of OE forms, although sometimes with sound changes (cf. Iċ [itʃ] > I [i]). The forms *they*, *them*, and *their*, however, cannot be explained by sound change. Instead, as discussed in Chapter 7, those <th> forms came into ME as *they*, *them*, and *their* (with variant spellings) from Norse, in which the forms were *þeir*, *þeim*, and *þeira*. There are a few interesting facts about this replacement.

First, the <th> forms would have been commonly spoken forms in the north and east of England where there was the greatest concentration of Norse-speaking settlers, i.e., the Danelaw area. From those northern and eastern areas, the forms would have become mixed with English forms during this period of increased geographic mobility and especially with increased immigration into London, the region that spoke the variety of English that would be central to the later development of standard English.

Second, while the <h> forms continued to be used throughout the ME period, those uses diminish in favor of the <th> forms. Chaucer for instance uses both <th> and <h> forms:

Nevere eft ne was ther angre <u>hem</u> betwene (The Franklin's Tale, line 1554)
And every wight that was about <u>them</u> tho (Troilus and Criseyde 2, line 215)

Third, *they* and *their* enter English at a faster rate than *them*. The OE plural *him* form is used until late in the ME period and even into the EModE period.[9] It seems likely that the *'em* used in PDE (*get 'em*) may be a retention of the OE plural *him* pronoun form (meaning *them*).

The development of the form *she* is an unsettled question among history of English scholars. Some have suggested that *she* is a natural sound change from [heo], i.e., a change in the first syllable of the OE third-person singular feminine pronoun from [he-] to [ʃe]. Others have traced the origins of *she* to the OE feminine demonstrative form *seo*, for which the development of /s/ to /ʃ/ seems very likely. Still others have sought the origin of *she* in Norse, although the transference would not be as direct as it was with the third-person plural forms. The Old Norse word for *she* was *honn* and it doesn't seem likely that *honn* somehow changed to *she*. What may have been the case, however, was that a Norse accented form of *heo* [hje(o)] developed by natural

9 Lass, "Phonology and Morpholoy," 120.

sound change into [ʃi]: compare the Norse *Hjetland > Shetland*. Since sound change is gradual and goes through extended periods of geographical and idiosyncratic variation, the Norse accent and subsequent sound change account would motivate the many ME spellings of the third-person singular feminine subject pronoun: *heo, sche, ho, he, zhe*, etc.

EXERCISE

8.5 Even though the ME pronouns come to look much more like present-day forms, they are pronounced quite differently. Provide the phonetic spellings for the ME pronoun forms listed:

ME form	IPA
I	_____
Me	_____
Min	_____
Thou	_____
Thee	_____
Thin	_____
He	_____
Hit	_____
She	_____
We	_____
Us	_____
Ye	_____

THE VERBAL GROUP

EXPANSION OF THE VERB PHRASE

The OE verb system was largely synthetic. Graphically we can illustrate the synthetic nature of the OE verb as:

Verb phrase

|

Verb

What this graphic captures is the fact that in OE, most sentences contained single verbs that were simple present or simple past. Note how the PDE translation also preserves the synthetic simple present and simple past in the following examples:

Ić cweðe nu.	I now say.
He mid Gode wunode.	He lived with God.

As we know, in PDE there are a number of verbal periphrases, and some verb phrases can consist of as many as four auxiliaries, although such verb phrases are rare. Three-auxiliary verb phrases, however, are fairly common, as in the example below.

The aircraft will have been flown for more than 50 years before it is retired.

The verb phrase in this sentence can be illustrated as:

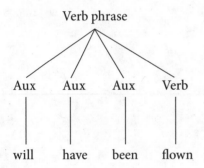

In the ME period we begin to witness the expansion of the verb phrase (e.g., the rise in frequency and types of periphrastic verb forms). The following auxiliary verbs can be observed in ME.

The passive auxiliary *be* (PDE: The book <u>is/was</u> stolen):

Now be ye caught!	Now you are caught!

The passive form with *be* was actually not new and had been fairly frequently used in OE.

The modal auxiliaries (PDE: *may, might, can, could, shall, should, will, would, must*). While these forms were used in OE, they often had full lexical meanings or only nascent modal meanings:

He cann sprecan Englisc   He knows how to speak English.

Modal meanings in OE were infrequent. However, in ME modal meanings increase.

He can speke English.   (now meaning *be able to*)

Have or *be* in the perfect (PDE: He <u>has seen</u> the facts [present perfect]/He <u>had left</u> before anyone could see him [past perfect]).

This form is attested for OE but in ME it becomes more frequent and more fixed within the verbal system.

As we discussed earlier, in OE and in ME there were two possible auxiliaries, the *have* auxiliary and the *be* auxiliary (as opposed to PDE in which only *have* is possible). In OE the rule for choosing between the *have* and *be* auxiliaries was to use *be* when the verb was intransitive (i.e., didn't have a direct object) and signaled change of location (like the verbs *come*, *go*, *leave*, *pass*, and so on; note that the same basic rule still applies to German, French, Italian, etc.). The *have* auxiliary was used with all other verbs. By and large this rule still operated in ME:

Sumer is icumen in   Summer has come in.
(ME lyrics)
(*is* is the auxiliary from the verb *to be* and *icumen* is the past participle of the verb *cuman* "to come")

Syn oother folk han seyd   Since other people have said
(Tale of Sir Thopas, line 1895)
(*han* is the auxiliary from the verb *to have* and *seyd* is the past participle)

However, increasingly a number of verbs that "should have" been used with the *be* auxiliary came to be used with the *have* auxiliary. In the following example, the auxiliary *be* would be expected with the past participle *falle*, since it indicates movement. (Also note how the expected -*n* for the past participle of *falle*, cf. *fallen*, was missing because of the tendency to lose final consonants) (see p. 184).

Or elles ye han falle in freletee   otherwise you (plural) have fallen
                                          into frailty
(Physician's Tale, line 78)

Be in the progressive (PDE: He *is taking* the bus).
In OE the present participle (PDE: *speaking*) had the suffix -*ende* (e.g., *sprecende* [speaking]). In ME, the familiar -*ing* replaces -*ende* in most dialects, although in

the north of England, -ende/-ande continued well into the ME period. In OE and early ME, we find instances of the auxiliary verb be + the present participle both with -ende and with -ing:

> is libbende
> is living (-inge, -ynge)

It is tempting to try to link this historical construction with the ModE progressive, since they look alike syntactically. But the problem with such a link is that the OE and ME instances often don't have a progressive meaning and instead are more interchangeable with other verb forms and tenses. While it is very regular for more specific meanings, like progressive, to become more general over time in a language, development in the opposite direction is less likely.

However, another form began to appear more frequently in ME (although it also has its origins in OE). We will call it the **locative construction**. It is made up of the verb be + a preposition (usually *on*) + the **gerund**.

> *and hii funde þane king; þar he was an hontyng* (note that *on* is spelled *an* in this example)
> and they found the king where he was (on) hunting (*Layamon*)

The gerund is a verb form that works like a noun. *Taking*, in *Taking a walk is good for your heart*, is a gerund because it is functioning as the subject of the sentence, and subjects are nouns (or pronouns). *Taking*, in *he is taking*, in contrast, is part of the verb phrase, and it is a present participle. When the OE participle *-ende* is replaced with *-ing* the present participle and the gerund become identical in form. We can say that *hunting* is a gerund in the example above because it is the object of the preposition *an* (on), and being an object of a preposition is a noun function.

Later we will discuss in more detail the relationship of the two constructions with the development of the progressive. For now we note the presence of both constructions as important pieces of the ME verb inventory.

THE PERIPHRASTIC INFINITIVE

Readers will remember that the infinitive in OE was synthetic, with the suffix -an.

> *sprecan* (to speak)

In ME, the infinitive was increasingly expressed periphrastically with *to*.

> *to speke* (to speak)

In some linguistic theories *to* is treated analogously to auxiliary verbs. We include it here as part of the general trend toward periphrasis.

STRONG VERBS BECOME WEAK VERBS

As you will remember from OE, there were two types of verbs: strong verbs and weak verbs. Even in OE there were proportionally more weak verbs than strong verbs. Additionally, as we saw in Chapter 7, there was not just one way to form the past tense among strong verbs; there were many. In contrast, forming the past tense for all weak verbs involved the suffixing of the so-called dental preterit. In other words, the past-tense strategy for weak verbs was more unified than that for strong verbs. Therefore, the past-tense strategy associated with weak verbs spread by analogy to strong verbs (compare the regular plural -*s* for nouns).

The following is a list of verbs which had been strong verbs in OE but which became weak in the twelfth century.[10]

Bow, brew, burn, climb, flee, flow, help, mourn, row, step, walk, weep

If we look up *flow* in the Oxford English Dictionary, we find:

pa. tènse OE fléow, *pl.* fleowon, ME fleaw, flew, *south.* vleau; weak forms: ME fléowede, *Orm.* flowedd, ME floȝed, flowede, 15 flowd, 15– flowed.

That is, we will find the strong past tense forms for the verb being gradually replaced by the suffixing of the dental preterit onto the stem of the verb. This trend will continue in the history of English and even continues today. The productivity of the weak suffix -*ed*, which we now think of as the regular past tense suffix, is today still spreading to historically strong verbs, e.g., present *slay*: past *slew ~ slayed, shine: shone ~ shined, dream: dreamt ~ dreamed*. We can also prove its productivity by considering what happens when a new verb enters the language, e.g., *texted, facebooked*, etc.

LOSS OF WORD-FINAL /n/

Earlier we saw that word-final /n/ was lost, but we saw too that the loss was not motivated purely by sound change on nouns; it was motivated also by analogy. It will also be recalled that /n/ was an inflection on several parts of the verb, most notably in the plural forms of the past tense, the infinitive and subjunctive forms.

In fact, in many varieties of ME, at least early on, verbal /n/ had taken on an even greater functional load since it spread by analogy to plural forms in the pres-

---

10 Albert C. Baugh and Thomas Cable, *A History of the English Language* (5th edition) (Upper Saddle River, NJ: Prentice Hall, 2002), 163–64.

ent tense. For many dialects throughout much of the ME period, verbal inflections remain. Thus in some respects the verb in ME tends to be very similar to the OE verb for *hear*:

	Sing.	Pl.
1st	here	hereth/heren
2nd	herest	hereth/heren
3rd	hereth	hereth/heren

However, by the end of the ME period, that word-final /n/ on verb forms dropped away, partly as a result of sound change, but also due to the systematic pressure of morphological restructuring. However, since the /n/ on nouns and the /n/ on verbs were lost at different rates and involved different kinds of pressures, we should think of them as interrelated but separate phenomena.

DIALECT VARIATION AND VERB FORMS

Finally, as we noted in Chapter 7, in the later part of the OE period, a literary standard based on the West Saxon dialect emerged. Just as with ModE, uniformity was only apparent. In fact there existed several dialects of OE. Dialect variation was not suppressed by the West Saxon standard, and many examples of that variation are available to us from the OE period. The survival of that variation is apparent insofar as after the reemergence of English in post-Conquest England, texts show much dialect variation, particularly because there was not yet a literary standard and no one center or area of text production. One dialect difference is that between -*s* and -*th* inflection on verbs in the present tense. In southern English (e.g., around London), the ME continuation of the OE -þ in the third-person singular, *he telleth* (note the change in spelling from þ→ *th*), is documented. In northern English, -*s* was the more regular ending for the third-person singular: *he telles*.

In fact, in the north, the -*s* could appear on all inflected forms of the verb:

I telles, he telles, we telles, they telles.

The competition between -*th* and -*s* for the third-person singular would continue into the EModE period, and eventually become resolved in favor of -*s*.

EXERCISES

The following are probably the most famous lines of poetry from the ME period: the opening lines of the *Canterbury Tales*.

Whan that Aprille with his shoures soote	When April with his showers sweet
The droghte of March hath perced to the roote,	The drought of March has pierced to the root,
And bathed every veyne in swich licour	And bathed every vein in such liquor
Of which vertu engendred is the flour;	Of which virtue engendered is the flower;
Whan Zephirus eek with his sweete breeth	When Zephirus (the west wind) also with his sweet breath
Inspired hath in every holt and heath	Breathed has into every grove and field
The tender croppes, and the yonge sonne	The tender crops, and the young sun
Hath in the Ram his half cours yronne,	Has in the Ram (Aries) his half course run,
And smale foweles maken melodye,	And small birds make melody,
That slepen al the nyght with open ye	That sleep all the night with open eyes
(So Priketh hem Nature in hir corages),	(So pricks them Nature in their hearts),
Thanne longen folk to goon on pilgrimages,	Then long people to go on pilgrimages
And palmeres for to seken strounge strondes,	And pilgrims to seek far-away shores,
To ferne hawles, kowthe in sondry londes;	To faraway shrines known in various lands
And specially from every shires ende	And especially from every shire's end
Of Engelond to Caunterbury they wende,	Of England to Canterbury they turned,
The hooly blissful martir for to seke,	The holy blissful martyr to seek,
That hem hath holpen whan that they were seeke.	That them has helped when they were sick.

8.6   Find at least three examples of the use of the perfect periphrasis with *have* + past participle.

8.7   Find at least two examples of the periphrastic infinitive.

8.8   Look closely at the following lines:

And smale foweles maken melodye,	And small birds make melody,
That slepen al the nyght with open ye	That sleep all the night with open eyes

What is the third-person plural present suffix on the verbs here? Given your knowledge of sound changes occurring in the ME period, as well as your knowledge of PDE, what will happen to that suffix (and note it is already happening in ME)?

8.9   What is the third-person singular present suffix in this passage? What suffix will replace that ending by the EModE period?

8.10 Consider the following lines from Chaucer's The Reeve's Tale. In this tale, Chaucer represents the speech of two young men from the north of England.

"Symond," quod John, "by God, nede has na peer." (line 4026)
 Symond, said John, by God, need has no equal

"By God, right by the hopur wil I stande,"
 By God, right by the hopper will I stand,
Quod John, "and se howgates the corn gas in." (lines 4036–37)
 Said John, and see how the corn goes in

What is the third-person singular present suffix in these passages?

A NOTE ABOUT SYNTAX IN MIDDLE ENGLISH

An obvious consequence of the loss of case distinction in the nominal group (excluding pronouns) is that syntactic functions were no longer expressed through case and were increasingly a matter of word order.

In OE, word order followed a number of common patterns. As we discussed in Chapter 7, while word order was not "free" in OE, case distinctions made possible significant flexibility in word order with pragmatically, rather than grammatically, different meanings, especially in poetry. When case distinction eroded in the ME period, word order became much more necessary for establishing grammatical meaning. Whereas in OE the sentence Se hunta lufode þone hund is grammatically identical to þone hund lufode se hunta, in ME, as in PDE, the syntactic functions of nouns are determined by word order; the syntactic functions of nouns in the sentence The hunter loved the dog cannot be grammatically identical to those in The dog loved the hunter.

LITERATURE IN THE MIDDLE ENGLISH PERIOD

Literature from the ME period (c. 1100–1500) is written in three different languages: French (Anglo-Norman as well as other dialects of French), Latin, and ME. In fact, one major author from the fourteenth century, **John Gower** (c. 1330–1408), wrote a long poem in each of the three languages of England during this period:

Mirour de l'Omme (in French), *Vox Clementis* (in Latin), and *Confessio Amantis* (in Middle English).

Given that the ruling class in England in this period is first Norman French, and then later maintains close ties to France both politically and culturally, it is hardly surprising that much of this literature shows the influence, in both form and content, of continental literatures, particularly of the literatures being written in France.

KING ARTHUR

The figure of King **Arthur** has come into the imagination of the present day as an icon both of the Middle Ages and of Englishness, so much so that the figure of Arthur has a kind of selling power and can appear as a brand name, as it does with King Arthur flour.

FIGURE 8.4   King Arthur Flour logo.

But in the earliest literature we have from England, literature from the Old English period, there is not one single mention of Arthur, at least not explicitly and certainly not by name. Gildas, the British historian we mentioned as one of Bede's sources, mentions a British victory over the Anglo-Saxons around the year 500, and he mentions a Romano-British leader. While the historical figure of Arthur may be associated with this figure, Gildas does not refer to him as Arthur. There is similarly a mention of a battle between the Britons and the Anglo-Saxons, but no mention of any Arthur in Bede's *History of the English Church and People*. The ninth-century Welsh historian Nennius has a paragraph or so on an Arthur, but this Arthur is not a king but a general, who kills 960 men in a single day. Although King Arthur, if he ever lived, would have lived during the time of the advent of the Angles and Saxons into the former Roman Britain, it is not until six hundred years later, *after the Norman Conquest*, that a clearly recognizable figure of Arthur enters into the literature of England.

One does not have to think hard about why no literature celebrating Arthur, King of the Britons, survives from the OE period. The Anglo-Saxons would have been those Germanic invaders whom the Britons fought against, and who eventually came to dominate the Britons politically. The Anglo-Saxons would not have celebrated the figure of a British king, particularly one so successful in battles against them!

However, when, around 1138, Geoffrey of Monmouth completes his Latin *History of the Kings of Britain*, the first text written in England to present a recognizable history of King Arthur, it is wildly successful. As Michael Faletra notes, "If the Middle Ages had a bestseller, surely Geoffrey of Monmouth's *History of the Kings of Britain* was it."[11] Survival of multiple copies is one of the ways in which we can gauge the relative popularity of a manuscript; given the labor of manuscript production, only those in demand would have been multiply produced. Many now-famous texts from the Middle Ages survive in only one or two copies. For example, only one single copy of *Beowulf* survives. But the *History of the Kings of Britain* survives in 215 manuscripts written between the mid-twelfth and sixteenth centuries.[12]

One way of accounting for the popularity of Geoffrey's *History* as well as the subsequent proliferation of Arthurian texts in this period is to recognize that the Anglo-Normans had a strong motive to take up the figure of King Arthur. By claiming identification with the heroic King Arthur, they legitimized Norman rule in England. They identified with a native figure, a hero actually from the island of Britain; at the same time, by identifying themselves through and with the figure of Arthur, they created an idea of Englishness which neatly co-opted the five hundred preceding years of Anglo-Saxon rule.

Geoffrey wrote in Latin, a language that continued to be used as the language of the Church, and also as the language of much historical, scholarly, and theological writing. Geoffrey wrote in prose, as had Bede in his *History* some 400 years earlier. But a number of other literary texts would take up the figure of Arthur and, later, all of the associated Arthuriana, in other genres, especially poetry.

THE IDEA OF THE AUTHOR

There is a considerable amount of poetry written in England during this period. In the early years, before the "re-emergence" of English, some of this poetry is written in French. Marie de France, writing in the late twelfth century, for example, produces a number of short poems called lais (also lays). Marie's exact identity is unknown, but

---

11   Geoffrey of Monmouth, *The History of the Kings of Britain*, ed. and trans. Michael Faletra (Peterborough, ON: Broadview P, 2008), 8.

12   Ibid.

while she may have written in Francien (a central French dialect), several manuscripts of her work show considerable Anglo-Norman influence.[13] She was likely French, but the Anglo-Norman manuscripts suggest that she was also likely to have been writing in England, perhaps around the court of Henry II. Marie identifies herself by that name in a preface to one of her poems titled "Guigemar":

Oez, seignurs, ke dit Marie
Ki en sun tens pas ne s'oblie...

Hear, my lords, the words of Marie,
who, when she has the opportunity,
does not neglect her obligations...[14]

The fact that Marie names herself, however vaguely, in this preface is significant, whether or not "Marie" was the actual name of the author. The bulk of literature from both the OE and ME periods is anonymous. We do not know who wrote *Beowulf* or *Sir Gawain and the Green Knight*. But the idea of the importance of identifiable authorship of a written text is developing during the ME period. The idea of identifying an author with the text that he or she puts down on the page marks a likely shift in attitude toward literature and toward the purpose and act of writing itself. While Marie still emphasizes hearing, rather than reading silently, and it was the case throughout the ME period that literature was still listened to for the most part, rather than read silently, by the end of the fourteenth century the idea of individual authorship of written literature is prevalent enough that Geoffrey Chaucer, in his *Canterbury Tales*, presents a character within his own work ironically discussing the merits of the poetic works of "Chaucer." Again, although throughout the ME period, the enjoyment of literature is largely a communal activity, the idea of the individual author as being in communication with an audience sows the seeds for the notion of a silent and more intimate relationship between the author and the individual reader. That relationship will become fully exploited in the EModE period, particularly in the marketing of the new technology of that period: the printed book.

END RHYME

Even without knowledge of French, it is easy to see that one way this poetry differs from poetry in OE is that it does not use alliteration extensively. Lines in the poem by Marie, cited above, are not linked by the repetition of initial sounds but rather they are linked by shared sounds at the end of the line. "Marie" and "oblie" share

---

13   William Kibler, *An Introduction to Old French* (New York: The Modern Language Association of America, 1984), 1.

14   Glyn S. Burgess and Keith Busby, *The Lais of Marie de France* (New York: Penguin, 1999), 9.

the same final sound. Poetry in French, like the lais of Marie de France, introduces the widespread use of **end rhyme** into the poetic traditions in England.

COURTLY LOVE

The fact that Marie is a woman is also significant. While certainly some women had been able to write in the OE period, no body of work clearly identifiable as written by a single woman author survives from that period. That a woman could name herself as the author of a series of poems reflects an increasing association of at least some kinds of literature with female patrons and audiences.

Women like Eleanor of Aquitaine, who married Henry II in 1152, brought with them both French literature and French literary tastes, and, as powerful noble patrons, disseminated that literature and those tastes in England. It is in this context that literature in French, like the lais of Marie de France would have been disseminated. While the actual transmission must have been more complex, Eleanor of Aquitaine herself is often credited with bringing to England the French literary discourse of **courtly love** which would become such a dominant set of literary ideas that it endures to the present day.[15]

In the literature of courtly love, a noble man binds himself to the service of a usually unavailable noble lady, often the wife of the noble man's superior, and accomplishes deeds of valor in order to prove his devotion, and to win the lady's love. In many ways, the ceremony of homage, by which a noble man pledged his service to his lord, is reflected in courtly love. In the courtly love triangle, the noble man often pledged his service to his lord's *wife*. An example of this kind of triangle easily accessible to present-day readers is clear in popular Arthuriana: Lancelot, pledging his service to Guenevere, his lord's wife, is a courtly lover.

Courtly love becomes so pervasive in literature of the period that it also extends to explicitly religious literature. Mary is represented in the later ME lyrics, for example, as a courtly lady, and Jesus as a courtly lover approaching that lady. Consider for example the following lyric, from the early fifteenth century.

I sing of a maiden	I sing of a maiden
That is makelees:	That is matchless
King of alle kings	King of all kings
To her sone she chees.	For her son she chose.
He cam also stille	He came as still
Ther his moder was	To where his mother was

---

15   Roberta L. Krueger, "Marie de France," in *The Cambridge Companion to Medieval Women's Writing*, ed. Carolyn Dinshaw and David Wallace (Cambridge: Cambridge UP, 2003), 173.

As dewe in Aprille	As dew in April
That falleth on the gras.	That falls on the grass.
He cam also stille	He came as still
To his modres bowr	To his mother's bower
As dewe in Aprille	As dew in April
That falleth on the flowr.	That falls on the flower.
He cam also stille	He came as still
Ther his moder lay	To where his mother lay
As dewe in Aprille	As dew in April
That falleth on the spray.	That falls on the branch.
Moder and maiden	Mother and maiden
Was nevere noon but she:	Was never any but she:
Wel may swich a lady	Well may such a lady
Godes moder be.	God's mother be.[16]

In this deceptively simply lyric, Mary is represented as a peerless and powerful maiden who chooses who her son will be. The approach of Jesus to his mother is depicted in terms that evoke the approach of a lover to the maiden's bower.

NEW GENRES

In addition to the discourse of courtly love, new genres enter into the literatures of England from French, among them the romance and the fabliau. Romance as a genre was different from what it has become in the present day. Romance was associated with literature in European vernaculars like French, rather than Latin, with elaborate plots involving noble men having adventures usually in faraway places. Many, many romances take up Arthurian themes and characters, but there are also romances that focus on the figure of Alexander, and on other exotic and heroic themes.

Fabliau is a comic genre, usually with bourgeois or peasant characters, a fair amount of violence and scatological humor. Most fabliaux include a succinct, often bawdy, moral to tie together the tale. While romance and fabliau are not native English genres, examples survive from the later ME period.[17]

---

16 "I Sing of a Maiden," MS Sloane 2593, c. 1430, http://www.luminarium.org, accessed 18 August 2016.

17 C.M. Millward, *A Biography of the English Language* (Forth Worth, TX: Harcourt, 1996), 219.

ENGLISH LITERATURE IN TRANSITION

Relatively speaking, there is very little literature in English that survives from the first century after the Conquest. One notable exception is the poem "The Owl and the Nightingale," from the late twelfth/early thirteenth century. The poem is an extended and often comic dialogue between an owl and a nightingale and as such has connections to texts like the beast fables written by Marie de France as well as other debate poems. The Nightingale first addresses the Owl in the following passage:

þe Niȝtingale hi iseȝ,	The Nightingale caught sight of her
& hi behold & ouerseȝ;	looked at her, and sneered.
& þuȝte wel vul of þare Hule,	To her the Owl seemed really repulsive,
For me hi hald lodlich & fule.	For she's regarded by people as hateful and filthy
"Vnwiȝt!" ho sede, "awei þu flo!	"You mutant!" she cried, "Why don't you fly away?
Me is þe wurs þat ich þe so!	Just looking at you is bad for me.
Iwis, for þine vule lete	In fact I'm frequently put off my singing
Wel oft ich mine song forlete.	because of your ugly countenance.
Min horte atfliþ & falt mi tonge,	Whenever you're shoved into my presence,
Wonne þu art to me iþrung.	my heart deserts me and my tongue falters.
Me luste bet speten þane singe	Because of your awful howling
Of þine fule ȝoȝelinge."	I'd rather spit than sing!"[18]

This passage provides many examples of English as a language in transition between OE and ME as it "re-emerges" in the later period. The vocabulary includes very few borrowings. The pronoun *she* does not appear in this text. Rather the form is *ho*. The thorn occurs throughout and has clearly not yet been replaced by the digraph <th>. The digraph <ch> for [tʃ] replaces <c> in the first-person singular pronoun *Ich*, but the final sound of that pronoun persists: it is still pronounced as the OE *Ic* was, and not, as it would become in most dialects by the end of ME, as [i]. Similarly, the passage shows a transition between Old English poetics and ME poetics. Already in this early Middle English poem, as in the poetry in French, end rhyme links two-line couplets (*Hule/fule, flo/so*, etc.). But the poem also retains a fair amount of the alliteration that characterized Old English verse. *Atfliþ* alliterates with *falt*, for example, and *speten* alliterates with *singe*.

As we have discussed, end rhyme becomes one of the most recognizable poetic devices of the ME period. Evidence of the dominance of end rhyme is clear, ironically, in the revival of the native tradition of alliteration. In the late fourteenth century, a number of poets eschewed rhyme in favor of a return to native poetic tradition in which lines of poetry were linked by alliteration. This movement is now called

---

18   Neil M. Cartlidge, ed. and trans., *The Owl and the Nightingale* (Exeter: U of Exeter P, 2001), 29–40.

the Alliterative Revival. Perhaps the most famous poem of the Alliterative Revival today is *Sir Gawain and the Green Knight*, an Arthurian romance. While *Sir Gawain* exploits end rhyme in its short rhymed stanzas (often referred to as the "bob and wheel"), much of the poem consists of long, alliterating lines, like those that had characterized English verse before the Norman Conquest. The following are the opening lines of the poem. We have underlined the alliterative sounds in the first few lines, as well as the end-rhymes of the final lines of the passage. After the passage we include the modern translation by Marie Boroff.

SIÞEN þe <u>s</u>ege and þe assaut watz <u>s</u>esed at Troye,
Þe <u>b</u>orȝ <u>b</u>rittened and <u>b</u>rent to <u>b</u>rondeȝ and askez,
Þe <u>t</u>ulk þat þe <u>t</u>rammes of <u>t</u>resoun þer wroȝt
Watz <u>t</u>ried for his <u>t</u>richerie, þe <u>t</u>rewest on erthe:
Hit watz Ennias þe athel, and his highe kynde,
Þat siþen depreced prouinces, and patrounes bicome
Welneȝe of al þe wele in þe west iles.
Fro riche Romulus to Rome ricchis hym swyþe,
With gret bobbaunce þat burȝe he biges vpon fyrst,
And neuenes hit his aune nome, as hit now hat;
Tirius to Tuskan and teldes bigynnes,
Langaberde in Lumbardie lyftes vp homes,
And fer ouer þe French flod Felix Brutus
On mony bonkkes ful brode Bretayn he settez
wyth <u>wynne</u>,
Where werre and wrake and <u>wonder</u>
Bi syþez hatz wont <u>þerinne</u>,
And oft boþe blysse and <u>blunder</u>
Ful skete hatz skyfted <u>synne</u>.[19]

Since the siege and the assault was ceased at Troy,
The walls breached and burnt down to brands and ashes,
The knight that had knotted the nets of deceit
Was impeached for his perfidy, proven most true,
It was high-born Aeneas and his haughty race
That since prevailed over provinces, and proudly reigned
Over well-nigh all the wealth of the West Isles.
Great Romulus to Rome repairs in haste;
With boast and with bravery builds he that city
And names it with his own name, that it now bears.

---

19 *Sir Gawain and the Green Knight* (Oxford: Clarendon P, 1967), lines 1–19.

Ticius to Tuscany, and towers raises
Langobard in Lombary lays out homes,
And far over the French Sea, Felix Brutus
On many broad hills and high Britain he sets,
Most fair,
Where war and wrack and wonder
By shifts have sojourned there,
And bliss by turns with blunder
In that land's lot had share.[20]

PDE readers of *Sir Gawain and the Green Knight* are often startled by how difficult the language appears, even if they are familiar with Chaucer's ME. In part that difficulty is only apparent: it is a matter of different editorial conventions and the retention of certain letterforms in modern edited texts of *Sir Gawain*. But many of the differences from Chaucer's English are significantly less superficial: they reflect differences in the dialects of ME in which the texts were written.

"RE-EMERGENCE" OF LITERATURE IN ENGLISH

The renewed interest in native poetic traditions parallels the re-emergence of English as a literary language. All kinds of literary production in English increase significantly during the fourteenth century. Today, while the anonymous *Sir Gawain and the Green Knight*, and perhaps other texts from the ME period, like the lyric "Loud sing cuckoo," may be familiar, almost all college students will have encountered at least part of Chaucer's *Canterbury Tales*. It is fair to say that today the single most famous English author from the Middle Ages is Geoffrey Chaucer, who lived between about 1340 and 1400. And although he wrote many other texts in English, Chaucer's most well-known work today is the collection of texts known as *The Canterbury Tales*. One of the reasons why *The Canterbury Tales* is so frequently taught in college and even high school courses has to do with the fact that it contains texts in almost all of the genres that are represented in literature from the ME period. Just reading *The Canterbury Tales* alone will expose students to both poetry and prose, and to the romance, the fabliau, the discourse of courtly love, the saint's life, the tragedy, the beast fable, the dream vision, and even a handbook on penance.

Furthermore, genres that Chaucer does not himself use within *The Canterbury Tales* are mentioned within the tales. The Miller's Tale, for example, shows clear elements of the fabliau, with its non-aristocratic characters, scatological humor and violence. But it also mentions dramatic performances as well as lyrics in a number of places. For example, the squeamish lover Absolon *pleyeth Herodes upon a scaffold hye* (3384) (plays the part of Herod on a high stage) to try to impress the married woman Alisoun.

---

20 Marie Boroff, trans., *Sir Gawain and the Green Knight*, ed. Marie Boroff and Laura L. Howes (New York: Norton, 2010).

Although manuscripts of medieval plays tend to appear later, from the fifteenth to the sixteenth century, dramatic performances are mentioned both in literature and in town records. These performances, as in the allusion from the Miller's Tale, were associated with Biblical narratives, the Flood, the Nativity, and the Crucifixion, but were not always Church productions. Often they involved trade guilds and other secular organizations in their performance. Drama will develop further during the EModE period, but it is clearly part of earlier traditions as well.

The same squeamish lover in the Miller's Tale not only acts the part of Herod to try to impress his would-be lover; he also sings to her and accompanies himself on a musical instrument: *He syngeth in his voys gentil and small,/"Now, deere lady, if thy wille be,/I praye yow that ye wole rewe on me"* (He sings in his gentle and small voice, "Now dear lady, if it be your will, I pray that you will have pity on me" (lines 3360–62). A large number of lyrics, short poems often with a personal focus and sometimes set to music, survive. Figure 8.5 is a page from British Library MS Harley 978, and shows the lyric "Sumer is icumen in" set to music. The topics of these lyrics range

FIGURE 8.5   British Library, Harley MS 978 f. 11v.

from mnemonics like "Thirty days hath November,/April June, and September," to meditations on the Annunciation, the Fall, or the Crucifixion, to bawdy drinking songs, to sometimes pointed social critiques.

While the literature written in England during the OE and ME periods was rich and varied on any number of levels—it was written in multiple languages, in many genres, in many forms—one unifying factor was the technology of its transmission: literature in the OE and ME periods was not printed but written by hand on vellum or parchment. Towards the end of the ME period, however, around 1476, William Caxton introduced the moveable type printing press into England. With the introduction of this technology, we will mark the end of the ME period.

CHAPTER NINE

Early Modern English

THE EARLY MODERN PERIOD AND THE AGE OF PRINT

During the Early Modern period (c. 1500–1800), the idea of Englishness changes dramatically. This change can be seen very clearly in the ways in which the positioning of England on maps of the world changes.

Figure 9.1 is a *mappamundi*, a medieval map of the world. In *mappaemundi* of this sort, the world is divided into three sections. The top half of the world is Asia. There, towards the top, is Eden. The center of the world is Jerusalem. The bottom right half is Africa. The bottom left is Europe. England is at the very edges of the bottom of the map, on the left, very far away from the center of the world. Of course, the *mappamundi* is not designed for actually guiding a traveler on a physical journey. One could never make one's way from England to Jerusalem, for example, by following a path on a map of this sort. The *mappamundi* is a different kind of map: it charts location with respect to Christian history, and it is explicitly ideological. As such, it provides a very clear sense of how the English positioned themselves ideologically. England in this typical medieval representation is far away from the center of the world; in fact, England is at the margins of this world, the edges of the world also inhabited by the "monstrous" figures illustrated in the band of images on the upper right.

In dramatic contrast, the nineteenth-century map shown in Figure 9.2 places England at the center of its representation of the world. In part, the map illustrates the greater geographical knowledge of the world that was the result of European exploration and colonization during the Early Modern English (EModE) period. But note that this map is in many ways no less ideological than the *mappamundi* reproduced in Figure 9.1. This map places England in the center of the world as the center of an Empire that stretches west across the Atlantic and east as far as Australia. The figures depicted on the periphery of this map represent the people the English have colonized. Looking at the thirteenth-century *mappamundi* and the nineteenth-century Imperial Federation map side by side enables us to see representations of

FIGURE 9.1   Psalter World Map, c. 1265.

England shifting from positioning England at the margins of the world to placing England at the center of the world. Obviously, this shift is important in the study of the history of the English language because it is also tied to shifting attitudes to English as a language.[1]

---

1   K. Aaron Smith and Susan M. Kim, "Colonialism: Linguistic Accommodation and English Language Change," in *Teaching the History of the English Language*, edited by Colette Craig and Chris Palmer (New York: MLA, forthcoming).

FIGURE 9.2   Imperial Federation Map of the World, Walter Crane, 1886.

We might choose a number of different external events to mark the end of the Middle English (ME) period and the beginning of the EModE period: the establishment of a new dynasty, the Tudors, on the throne of England; the break with the Church of Rome, and the establishment of the Church of England; or, exploration and colonization in the Caribbean, India, and the New World. While we will certainly take these events into consideration, we will mark the start of the EModE period not with a political event but with a technological innovation: William Caxton's introduction of the moveable type printing press into England in 1476.

As we discussed in Chapters 7 and 8, books during the Old English (OE) and ME periods were manuscripts. They were written by hand on prepared animal skin, called vellum or parchment. During the ME period a number of innovations increased the speed at which manuscripts could be produced. The use of cursive hands, for example, made copying much faster. Paper was available as early as the eleventh century in Spain, although it was not widely used in Europe until much later. Professional copying workshops made some texts more available; for example, they made it possible for readers like the students in the new medieval universities to purchase copies of manuscripts in pieces rather than as whole collections. But until the introduction of the moveable type printing press, it was impossible to produce and distribute written texts on a large scale.

Some kinds of printing predate the introduction of the moveable type press. These early technologies involved carving text into a plate that would then be used to print multiple copies of that text. The problem with these technologies was that they were cumbersome and expensive. Each plate could only be used for one purpose: each page of a book, for example, required a new plate. The innovation of the moveable type printing press was that it employed sets of letters that could be manipulated to produce any number of different texts. Once a printer had the sets of letters, he could print whatever he chose. Johannes Gutenberg is usually credited with the development of the moveable type printing press around the 1440s. **William Caxton** brought the moveable type press to England. In 1476 he set up a press in Westminster. By the end of his life (c. 1491), he had seen about 100 titles into production. Within a hundred and fifty years of the introduction of the press as many as 20,000 titles, with copies in the millions, had been printed and distributed.[2]

Because we live in an age of print—perhaps even an age beyond the age of print—we may not be conscious of how dramatically the introduction of the press changed not only the book, but attitudes towards language. Consider the following:

- No two manuscripts are the same. Because manuscripts were produced by hand, even copies of the same original would not be identical.
- Manuscripts reflect the identities of the scribes who copy them. Copyists introduced errors, or corrected errors, or wrote in asides, or edited out passages. They also reproduced their own dialects, or the dialects of their writing communities.
- Because manuscripts were so labor-intensive, even inexpensive productions remained prohibitively expensive. There was no such thing as a pamphlet or newspaper. Even "best-sellers" of the Middle Ages had very small distributions.
- Although literacy rates increased during the ME period, in the absence of widely accessible books, literacy rates remained quite low by modern standards.

However, after the introduction of the press:

- Hundreds, and eventually thousands, of identical copies of a single text could be produced in a single print run.
- Written texts became much more widely available. While early books remained costly, within a few generations, printing made written texts more available than had ever been possible before.

---

2   David Crystal, *The Cambridge Encyclopedia of the English Language* (Cambridge: Cambridge UP, 1996), 56.

- With increased access to written texts, more people became literate, and more people were able to write, and to publish their work.
- In addition, while book production for most of the Middle Ages occurred within the context of the Church, Caxton's press was secular, and it was a business.

It is not surprising that the period after the introduction of the press was marked by an increasing interest in the standardization of English. On one hand, the technology of the press itself contributed to the standardization of some aspects of written English. When thousands of readers encountered identical texts, features of the language of those texts were also disseminated. Readers who spoke one dialect of English sometimes encountered, and even eventually came to expect, quite another dialect of English in a printed text. On the other hand, the fact of the widespread dissemination of the printed text also provided the occasion for very self-conscious consideration of language choices. Caxton wanted to sell as many books as he could. To do so, he had to choose not only what kinds of books to print, but also in what language he would print them. On one level, these choices involved actual languages—French, Latin, or English, for example. Caxton himself translated as many as a quarter of the titles he published into English.[3] But on another level, they involved choices among dialects and registers. Very famously, Caxton narrated the following episode in a preface:

And that comyn englysshe that is spoken in one shyre varyeth from a nother. In so moche that in my dayes happened that certayn marchaũtes were in a ship in tamyse for to haue sayled ouer the see into zelande / and for lacke of wynde thei taryed atte forlond. and wente to lande for to refreshe them And one of theym named sheffelde a mercer cam in to an hows and axed for mete. and specyally he axyd after eggys And the goode wyf answerde. that she coude speke no frenshe. And the marchaũt was angry. for he also coude speke no frenshe. but wolde haue hadde egges / and she vnderstode hym not / And thenne at laste a nother sayd that he wolde haue eyren / then the good wyf sayd that she vnderstod hym wel / Loo what sholde a man in thyse dayes now wryte. egges or eyren / certaynly it is harde to playse euery man / bycause of dyuersite & chaũge of langage. For in these dayes euery man that is in ony reputacyon in his coũtre. wyll vtter his cõmynycacyon and maters in suche maners & termes / that fewe men shall vnderstonde theym / And som honest and grete clerkes haue ben wyth me and desired me to wryte the moste curyous termes that I coude fynde / And thus bytwene playn rude / & curyous I stande abasshed. but in my Iudgemente / the comyn termes that be dayli vsed ben lyghter to be vnderstonde than the olde

3 Elizabeth Evenden, "The Impact of Print: The Perceived Worth of the Printed Book in England, 1476–1575," in *The Oxford Handbook of Medieval Literature in English*, ed. Elaine Treharne, Greg Walker, and William Green (Oxford: Oxford UP, 2010), 97.

and aũcyent englysshe / And for as moche as this present booke is not for a rude vplondyssh man to laboure therin / ne rede it / but onely for a clerke & a noble gentylman that feleth and vnderstondeth in faytes of armes in loue & in noble chyualrye / Therfor in a meane bytwene bothe I haue reduced & translated this sayd booke in to our englysshe not ouer rude ne curyous but in suche termes as shall be vnderstanden by goddys grace accordynge to my copye. And yf ony man wyll enter mete in redyng of hit and fyndeth suche termes that he can not vnder-stande late hym goo rede and lerne vyrgyll / or the pystles of ouyde / and ther he shall see and vnderstonde lyghtly all / Yf he haue a good redar & enformer / For this booke is not for euery rude and vnconnynge man to see / but to clerkys and very gentylmen that vnderstande gentylnes and science.[4]

In this passage, Caxton claimed that regional differences in English were such that in some regions a man could ask for eggs and, because the local word for eggs was so different (i.e., *eyren*), be thought to be speaking French. While the events depicted are at least exaggerated, the point here is that as Caxton directed the lan-guage of the book he was printing to the unprecedentedly large audience it would reach, he was also making conscious choices about the forms he would use. As he made those choices, he shaped at once the written language and the reading audience that would receive it. As he wrote, "And for as moche as this present booke is not for a rude vplondyssh man to laboure therin / ne rede it / but onely for a clerke & a noble gentylman that feleth and vnderstondeth in faytes of armes in loue & in noble chyualrye," Caxton identified his audience as not "rude" (uneducated) or "uplandish" (northern) but rather educated and "gentle." He presented—and created—his target audience as speakers of a particular dialect (London) and of a particular class (the rising middle and "gentle" classes). And he explained that he had chosen language that was "a meane," a midway point, so as to increase its accessibility to the appro-priate audiences. Furthermore, he emphasized that in doing so he was making a foreign text accessible in "our English" ("our englysshe") but with his self-conscious manipulation, "by goddys grace accordynge to my copye."

OUR ENGLYSSHE, INKHORN TERMS, AND THE EXPANDING LEXICON

As we have noted, Caxton himself translated a number of the texts he published. The *Eneydos*, the preface of which we quote above, in fact has as its extended title, *Eneydos: Here fynyssheth the boke yf Eneydos, compyled by Vyrgyle, which hathe be translated oute of latyne in to frenshe, and oute of frenshe reduced in to Englysshe by me wyll[ia]m Caxton, the xxij. daye of Iuyn. the yere of our lorde. M.iiij.Clxxxx. The*

---

4   William Caxton, Preface to *Eneydos*, ed. Jack Lynch (http://andromeda.rutgers.edu/~jlynch/Texts/eneydos.html, accessed 14 September 2017).

fythe yere of the regne of kynge Henry the seuenth. Caxton's translation is a translation into English from French. The French was a translation from Latin. The movement here reflects the increasing sense that English was a language of sufficient prestige to merit such translation. Texts were translated not simply as an expedient, and in order to help students to learn enough that they could then go back and read the Latin, but rather with the aim of producing the text in English as an end in itself. As English accrued prestige as a literary language at the end of the ME period and into the EModE period, however, it also became the subject of scrutiny *as* a literary language. That is, languages like Latin and Greek for centuries had been the subject of academic study as well as the languages in which academic study was conducted. English, however, was new as a language both into which serious literature could be translated and in which academic study could be conducted. We will return in later sections of this chapter to the rather anxious attempts to bring English into line with the traditional understanding of grammar that came from the study of Latin and Greek. Here we consider first one consequence of the simultaneous increasing prestige of English as a literary language and the sense of its newness as a language for serious academic study.

During the EModE period, as scholars grappled with questions of how to use English in contexts that had been dominated by Latin and, to a lesser extent, Greek, they addressed what was perceived as a lack in the lexicon of English by borrowing from Latin and Greek, and sometimes by creating new words in English by combining elements from borrowings with English derivational affixes. These self-conscious scholarly introductions are often called **inkhorn terms**. The term refers to the act of writing itself, which is precisely the context in which a more "sophisticated" lexicon was considered desirable. During earlier periods, a number of scholarly borrowings had been introduced. During the Benedictine Reform in the tenth century, for example, a large number of words associated with scholarship in the Church were borrowed from Latin. Many of these words, however, have been lost: they were used in very specialized contexts and did not circulate widely. In contrast, however, many of the self-conscious scholarly borrowings of the EModE period remain. Although they too began in more specialized contexts, these EModE borrowings circulated much more widely because they were now disseminated in print. During the EModE period the lexicon of English quadruples, in no small part as a result of these self-conscious borrowings.

We have noted that we can still see the traces of the sociolinguistic distribution of French and English in the different meanings of closely related words, like *cow* (from English) and *beef* (borrowed from French) or *eat* (from English) and *dine* (borrowed from French). A similar tracing is possible with inkhorn terms. We have the native word *chew* but also the inkhorn term *masticate*, or the native word *youth* but also the borrowing *immaturity*. In fact we can see these traces across the history of English we have studied so far in a number of sets of synonyms like *ask*, *question*, and *interrogate*, in which *ask* is the native word, *question* the French borrowing from the ME period, and *interrogate* the borrowing from the EModE period. Such sets add considerably to the lexical complexity of English.[5]

There are several inkhorn terms that were used in the EModE period but that did not survive into later English. <u>*Perficate*</u> (to rub all over) and *pactation* (bargaining) appearing in Robert Cawdry's 1604 *A Table Alphabeticall*—a kind of early dictionary (see below)—are obsolete in ModE. It is not clear why certain inkhorn terms survived, and even become common, while others did not. Both *eradicate* and *derunciate* mean "to tear up from the roots," but while *eradicate* is commonly used, *derunciate* is not.

PHONOLOGY

MEDIAL AND FINAL [ç] AND [x]

During the EModE period, medial and final [ç] and [x], which continued on in many dialects throughout the Modern English (ME) period, were lost in nearly all dialects of English. For example, in ME *night* would have been pronounced [niçt]. During the EModE period, the sound [ç] in this context was lost.

In some words, however, the final velar fricative did not delete, but instead became an [f], as in *tough*, *laugh*, and *cough*.

LOSS OF POSTVOCALIC /r/

In many varieties of English in the EModE period (and continuing even today) there is the loss of /r/. At first the loss occurred before [s], as in *horse*, and then after back vowels, as in *quarter* and *March*. Eventually /r/ was lost before a consonant or at the end of any word, as in *car, river, clover*. This deletion is perceived by many as a significant marker of American (US and Canadian) and non-American Englishes (British, Australian, South African), although the actual distribution is more complex. We will return to the distribution of postvocalic /r/ in the next chapter.

PALATAL ASSIMILATION

Before the EModE period the combinations [sj], [zj], [tj], and [dj] would have been pronounced as two sounds in words like *tissue, fission, creature*, and *soldier*, and the unassimilated pronunciation is not unknown in some present-day dialects of English. However, in the EModE period, the two sounds coalesced into a single alveopalatal sound, i.e., [ʃ], [ʒ], [tʃ], [dʒ]. As was discussed in Chapter 7, the change is assimilatory in that the alveolar sounds in such pairs comes to sound more like the following sound, which in this case is a palatal glide.

---

5   Otto Jespersen, *Growth and Structure of the English Language* (Chicago: U of Chicago P, 1982), 124 ff.

EXERCISE

9.1 How would the italicized parts of the following words have been pronounced before and after palatal assimilation?

	Before	After
pre*ssu*re		
ti*ssu*e		
sei*zu*re		
crea*tu*re		
for*tu*ne		
sol*di*er		
gra*du*al		

THE GREAT VOWEL SHIFT

The **Great Vowel Shift** (GVS) started in ME and affected different dialects of English at different rates until about the end of the eighteenth century. The GVS is a drastic but (more or less) systematic reordering of long vowels. The fact that the GVS affected only long vowels is a central point in understanding how the change happened and for appreciating its effects on ModE, particularly on ModE spelling. The exact causes of the GVS are unknown.

Learning about the GVS in a class about the history of English is one of those moments when apparent chaos begins to make sense. After all, any English speaker who has studied another European language written in the Roman alphabet knows that there is something "odd" about the spelling of vowels in English. In Spanish, German, Latin, Italian, etc. the five vowels <a, e, i, o, and u>, are sounded very much like the phonetic value of those same vowels in IPA, most of the time, although with some very predictable variations: [ɑ], [e], [i], [o], and [u]. But in English, even our names for the vowels are very different from the names for the vowels in these other European languages. In English the names for the vowels are phonetically [ei, i, ɑi, ou, ju]. Clearly something has happened in English and that something has caused (or more accurately retained) a use of the vowel graphemes in English orthography quite different from their use in other languages.

Part of the mystery of vowels begins to unravel when we consider that each of the vowel graphemes in English represents at least two sounds:

Grapheme		Sound	Example
\<a>	→	[e]:	rate, make, bale
	→	[æ]:	path, fat, ram
\<e>	→	[i]:	beet, mete
	→	[ɛ]:	red, Beth, chef
\<i>	→	[ɑi]:	might, kite, bind
	→	[I]:	kit, miss, pig
\<o>	→	[o]:	bone, rote, spoke
	→	[ɑ]:	frock, lock
\<u>	→	[u]:	dune, dude, spruce
	→	[ʌ]:	buck, mud

Many will have learned that the difference between the first vowel and the second vowel in each set is that the first is "long" and the second is "short," as in the image in Figure 9.3, from a set of phonics cards for children reproduced below. However, because of the GVS, while there is a difference in length between these vowels, that difference is less important than other differences between the two sets of phonetic values for each vowel grapheme.

FIGURE 9.3   Phonics cards.

If we were to write the words from these cards phonetically, they would be [bɪb] and [kɑit].

In other words, one vowel is the diphthong [ɑi] and the other the monophthong [ɪ]. They are not merely long and short variants of the same vowel, as the terms "short" and "long" imply; they are different vowels.

In ME the difference between the vowels in *bib* and *kite* may certainly have involved quality, but the greater distinction was quantity. Phonemically we could write them as /bib/ and /kiːte/. Remember that the colon indicates a long vowel in phonetics and that the final /e/, our so-called silent <e>, was pronounced early on but was eventually lost. In ME, that is, one of these vowels was short and one was long. In Present-Day English (PDE), after the Great Vowel Shift, what had been mostly a matter of a difference in quantity became a difference in vowel sounds.

The GVS can be summarized as follows: *In the transition from ME to Early Modern English, long vowels moved to higher positions in the vowel space and the long, already-high vowels, /iː/ and /uː/ became the diphthongs [ɑiː] and [auː].*

For some changes, there were intermediate stages, which we will see below. The GVS can be visualized in the following chart:

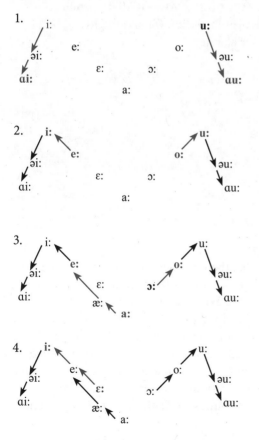

FIGURE 9.4   The Great Vowel Shift.

The GVS can also be visualized in the following table:

ME		ModE
i:	>	ɑi (there was an intermediate stage of [əi])
e:	>	i
ɛ:	>	e (sometimes a word would feed into the change above and go all the way to [i])
ɑ:	>	e (words showing this change went through [æ] and [ɛ])
u:	>	ɑu (there was an intermediate stage of [əu])
o:	>	u
ɔ:	>	o

EXERCISE

9.2   Consider the following words. What is the ME and ModE pronunciation? We have supplied the ME pronunciation when it might not be as easily reconstructed from earlier chapters.

	ME	ModE
name	_____	_____
moon	_____	_____
loud	_____	_____
feet	_____	_____
make	_____	_____
time	_____	_____
sea	sɛː	_____
bone	bɔːn	_____

It should be remembered, however, that there are a few out-of-pattern instances. Sometimes ME [ɛː], frequently spelled <ea>, remains [ɛ], as in *threat, head, death*. But others became [eː], which might be the expected outcome: *break, steak, great*. In many cases, [ɛː] goes all the way to [iː] (kind of takes two steps): *cheat, leaf*. In at least one word in PDE, both pronunciations can be heard, *deaf*: [dɛf] and [dif].

In some varieties of English, most notably Scottish English, and from there possibly Canadian English, the GVS seems not to have operated across the board. Thus the second vowel in Scottish *about* will in certain varieties sound like [u]. And in Canadian the second vowel in *about* often sounds like [əu], which may represent an intermediate step between [u] and [ɑu].

OTHER SPELLING AND SOUND CHANGES

As you know, one of the remarkable differences between ME and EModE is that the printed word became more available and over the EModE period more and more people became literate. We will note two corollary effects of this increased literacy as they affected spelling and sometimes pronunciation: **etymological spellings** and **spelling pronunciation**.

Not only does spelling become more regularized, but there is also a tendency to "reinstate" letters that were present in a given word only historically (and often from another language) even though the sound was not pronounced, and perhaps had never been pronounced with that sound. These reinstatements are called etymological spellings. Thus:

Middle English	Early Modern English	
dette	debt	(from Latin *debitum*)
doute	doubt	(from Latin *dubitum*)
ilond	island	(incorrectly thought to be from French *isle*. It came from OE *iegland*.)

A similar phenomenon to etymological spellings, and one that is sometimes to be observed in conjunction with it, is spelling pronunciation. Spelling pronunciation can be defined as the changing of pronunciation based on the spelling. So for instance, in ME the word *fault* was spelled <faute> and was pronounced [fɑut]. However, as with the <b> in *debt* discussed above, an <l> was "reinstated" into the word and later people began to pronounce the <l> even though it hadn't been pronounced before, e.g., [fɔlt].

The issue of spelling pronunciation continues even today. In recent years, *often*, which had been pronounced [ɔfɛn] is increasingly pronounced [ɔftɛn], and people will argue the point endlessly. Do you pronounce the <l> in *psalms*? Many young people will claim that they do, or should. Historically, however, the <l> was silent and in fact the Oxford English Dictionary gives the British pronunciation as [sɑːm] and the American pronunciation as [sɑː(l)m]; the <l> in parentheses recognizes that some speakers have reinstated the <l>.

MORPHOLOGY AND SYNTAX

CLITICIZATION

English is a **stress-timed** language. In stress-timed languages, timing is established between major stressed syllables. In contrast, in **syllable-timed** languages each syllable takes about the same amount of time to pronounce. So in English, in the sentence

The dógs rún (stress marks indicate major word stress), timing would be reckoned across the points of stress, from the beginning of the sentence to the stress on *dogs* to the stress on *run*. If we were to add function words (i.e., grammatical words like auxiliary verbs, prepositions, conjunctions, etc.) into this basic sentence structure, the timing between the stress points would stay about the same:

> *The dógs will rún.*
> *The dógs can rún.*
> *The dógs rún and the cáts júmp* (with an added set of stress points in the conjoined sentence—but note the phonetic reduction of *and*, the conjunction, and other words of a grammatical nature).

Notice that the function or grammatical words are quite reduced (in *The dogs will run*, say *will* in recitation style; then say it again in normal speaking rhythm). On the one hand the reduction affects the number of segments; often consonants will fuse (e.g., *gonna*) or they will elide (*will* → *'ll*). Also, such words may lose their independent status and become dependent on surrounding words, in which case they are called **clitics**. Specifically, they are called **enclitics** when they attach to the end of a word and **proclitics** when they attach to the beginning of the word. A feature of clitics is that such forms do not attach to a single word class but attach to whatever word happens to occur next to them; the word to which a clitic attaches is called a **host**:

> *He'll be here at noon.* (The host is a pronoun.)
> *The boy'll win the prize.* (The host is a noun.)
> *Crying'll get you nowhere.* (The host is a gerund.)

Clitics can even attach to phrases and clauses.

> *The player with the most points'll win the prize.* (The host is a prepositional phrase; this construction occurs in speech but is not generally accepted for writing.)
> *The player who gets the most points'll win the prize* (The host is the whole relative clause; this construction occurs in speech but is not generally accepted for writing.)

Cliticization was hardly a new phenomenon in EModE. English had a number of clitic formations before this period, e.g., ME *ich am* > *cham*, OE *ne wæs* > *næs* (both proclitics). The difference in EModE is that because of the perceived need to regularize spelling in a print culture, cliticization was recognized as a phenomenon that should be dealt with in some regular way. Thus clitics came to be spelled with the apostrophe in order to indicate the omission of letters: proclitics *'tis*, *'twas*, and enclitics *he'll*, *don't*, etc.

The apostrophe was also commonly used for "missing" letters in other parts of words too, not just those that resulted from cliticization. For example, the <e> in the regular past tense, which had been pronounced in earlier stages of English, was sometimes written with an apostrophe in EMODE, e.g., *talk'd*, *approv'd*, etc.

The use of the apostrophe to indicate deleted letters may also explain the use of the apostrophe for the possessive -*s*.

THE HIS-GENITIVE

One of the few noun inflections that remained in ME from OE was the genitive marker -*s*. However, because the marker continued to sound like [ez], [ɛz], or [ɪz], especially on words that ended already in a sibilant [s, z, tʃ, ʒ, dʒ, ʃ], e.g., Thomas's [tɑməsɪz], one account proposes that EModE speakers and writers thought that the syllable in such instances was an enclitic and that its full form was the possessive determiner *his*. In fact in EModE you can even see many instances in which *his* is written. Perhaps the most often-cited example of the *his*-genitive is "Mars his heart," from Shakespeare's *Twelfth Night*. But other examples from the period abound. John Donne, for example, titles a piece "Ignatius his Conclave," published 1611, in which he states that "every day affoords new Advocates to *Boniface* his side," that "Boniface his part is much releeved by that Order" and that "Boniface his successors... have ever beene fruitfull in bringing forth new sinnes, and new pardons, and idolatries, and King-killings." The *his*-genitive occurs in the King James Bible. Examples are common enough that by 1715, an early scholar of OE, Elizabeth Elstob, argues (as we do!) that the -*s* on words like *God's* and *man's* come from OE suffixes, and adds, "Some will say, that were better supplied by *his*, or *hers*, as Man *his* Thought, or the Smith *his* Forge; but this Mistake is justly exploded."[6]

Given the belief that the <'s> was clitic, based on its phonological and probably syntactic behavior (see below), the possessive, like other enclitics, began to be written with an apostrophe, so that we end up with our present day <'s/s'>, e.g., *dog's*, the *Flanders'*, etc. Even though the representation of the possessive with the apostrophe was based on partially false premises, it has continued to be used and it is certainly helpful in distinguishing the plural -*s* from the possessive -*s* in writing. However, because English speakers process language primarily through sound and only afterward consider its graphic representation, it is not uncommon to find errors in writing such as *The dog's like to run in the park*. The plural and possessive, although both realized with /s/, do not cause confusion in the spoken language: the confusion has to do with graphic representation, not the underlying grammar.

---

6   Elizabeth Elstob, *The Rudiments of Grammar for the English-Saxon Tongue, First Given in English: With an Apology for the Study of Northern Antiquities* (London: W. Bowyer, 1715), vi.

One additional fact about the *his*-genitive is that because people thought that constructions like *Mars his heart* were correct, they also extended it to other possessive determiners, like the plural and the feminine.

> *Wallings & Abbott there up land* (there = their)
> *Ann Harris her lot*[7]

In ModE the possessive -*s* does act very much like an enclitic, insofar as it will attach not only to nouns, but also to other structures modifying the noun, as we saw above with *'ll*. This "floatable" feature of possessive <'s> was probably already possible in Early Modern English.

> *The student's book* (The host is a noun.)
> *The student from Elgin's book* (The host is a prepositional phrase; this construction occurs in speech but is not generally accepted for writing.)
> *The student who you just spoke to's book* (The host is a relative clause; this construction occurs in speech but is not generally accepted for writing.)

Modern Dutch uses a contracted possessive construction very similar to the EModE his-genitive, with a form of the possessive determiner placed between the possessor and the possessed noun.

> Peter z'n fiets   Peter his bike *or* Peter's bike
> Marja d'r boek   Marja her book *or* Marja's book

As we noted in Chapter 5, Dutch is closely related to English and the appearance of such a similar pattern for possessives presents one of those tantalizing philological moments in which we strongly suspect that the similarity could not have arisen by accident. If the Dutch and English forms are historically co-developed from some earlier shared form, then an alternate explanation of the *his*-genitive might not be that it was merely a missegmentation in English.

PRONOUNS

While it may be said that nouns had essentially formed their present-day system in the ME period, pronouns overall have shown fewer changes, maintaining for example the older system of case. However, a few of the changes involving pronouns in the ME period were hardly superficial, for example the introduction of the *th*- forms of the third-person plural pronouns from Norse.

---

7   C.M. Millward, *A Biography of the English Language* (Fort Worth, TX: Harcourt Brace, 1996), 267.

In EModE, there also are a few noteworthy changes in the pronominal system: the new genitive form *its*; the loss of the singular/plural distinction in the second-person pronouns; and the development of the *wh-* forms of the relative pronoun.

THE NEW GENITIVE FORM, ITS

As we had left it in the ME period, the genitive form of *it* was *his*. Examples of neuter *his* persist in EModE:

How far that little candle throws his beams.[8]

However, in EModE the form *its* develops, perhaps because *his* seemed too animate, given that it was also the genitive form of *he*. Recall here that in ME the animate/inanimate distinction had gained in grammatical importance, as indicated by the loss of grammatical gender in favor of a gender system only relevant for higher animate nouns (people, domesticated animals). Hence, in ModE,

The table comes ready for assembly. Its hardware can be found in the box.

The composition of the *its* form with the regular genitive *-s* continues the long-term analogical spread of *-s* to signal possession, a process we saw affecting noun classes throughout the ME period.

THOU, THEE, YE, YOU

Students of any number of present-day European languages, including French, Spanish, German, Russian, etc., will know that using those languages involves a choice between different forms for second-person address, depending on the relationship of the speaker to his or her interlocutors. In its most general characterization, the choice is between formal (or polite) and informal discourse, although the decision about which pronoun form to use is considerably more complex. The following are forms for formal and informal second person singular address in a sampling of present-day European languages.

	formal	informal
Spanish	usted	tú
French	vous	tu
German	Sie	du
Italian	Lei	tu
Dutch	u	jij/je

---

8   Albert C. Baugh and Thomas Cable, *A History of the English Language* (5th edition) (Upper Saddle River, NJ: Prentice Hall, 2002), 243.

This formal/informal distinction is often referred to as the T–V distinction (T = *tu* and V = *vous*, as in French). While many languages naturally have varying forms of address based on social relations that are not copied from the European system (for example Japanese, Korean), European languages tend to have very similar systems that may well be imitative of one another to some extent, most likely influenced by French. In EModE a pattern of formal/informal distinctions analogous to those in other European languages was used, a pattern that emerged in ME. This emergent pronoun usage was in fact identical to the French custom. Thus:

French second-person pronouns

Singular	Plural and formal
tu	vous

EModE second-person pronouns

Singular	Plural and formal
thou	ye

In French the form *vous* is both the plural and the formal form. Early Modern English used *thou* and *ye* in this same pattern.

	Singular	Plural and formal
Subject	thou	ye
Object	thee	you

In informal or familiar address to one person:

I love <u>thee</u>.
<u>Thou</u> lovest me.

In plural address (talking to two or more people, regardless of social rank):

<u>Ye</u> love me.
I love <u>you</u>.

In formal address to one person:

<u>Ye</u> love me.
I love <u>you</u>.

The use of *ye/you* or *thou/thee* in EModE allowed speakers and writers to express subtle social and interpersonal connections, including changes in those relationships. This latter point stands out strongly in certain literary passages, as in those from

Shakespeare's *Romeo and Juliet* cited below. In the first passage, Romeo's and Juliet's first meeting, Juliet uses the polite and socially distancing *ye/you* forms, a discourse strategy appropriate for a young lady speaking to a young gentleman:[9]

> Good Pilgrime, you do wrong your hand too much,
> Which mannerly deuotion shewes in this,
> For Saints haue hands, that Pilgrimes hands do tuch,
> And palme to palme, is holy Palmers kisse.[10]

Romeo, however, in attempting to woo Juliet, uses the familiar pronoun in his playful speech to Juliet:

> O then deare Saint, let lips do what hands do,
> They pray (grant thou) lest faith turne to dispaire.[11]

At their second meeting, Juliet has clearly accepted the social contract of intimates and thus switches to familiar pronoun usage, as in this most famous line from the play:

> O Romeo, Romeo, wherefore art thou Romeo?[12]

Similarly, in Sir Thomas Malory's *Morte Darthur*, King Arthur and the Lady of the Lake speak with courtesy about the sword Excalibur, and in doing so they address each other with the *ye/you* forms:

> "Sir Arthur," said the damosel, "that sword is mine. And if ye will give me a gift when I ask it you, ye shall have it."
> "By my faith," said Arthur, "I will give you what gift that ye will ask."[13]

But just a few pages later, when King Roince demands that Arthur cut off his beard, Arthur haughtily addresses Roince's messenger with the *thou* forms:

> "Well," said Arthur, "thou hast said thy message, the which is the most orgulous and lewdest message that ever man had sent unto a king. Also, thou mayest see my beard is full young yet to make of a purfile. But tell thou thy king thus, that I owe him no homage, nor none of my elders...."[14]

---

9 Based on Baugh and Cable, *A History of the English Language*, 111. The edition of *Romeo and Juliet* cited here is René Weis, ed., *Romeo and Juliet (The Arden Shakespeare)* (New York and London: Bloomsbury, 2012).

10 Ibid., 1.5.96–99.

11 Ibid., 1.5.102–03.

12 Ibid., 2.2.33.

13 Thomas Malory, *Le Morte Darthur*, edited by Helen Cooper (Oxford: Oxford UP, 1998), I. 29.

14 Ibid., I.30.

Obviously at some point, likely by the eighteenth century, the pronouns *thou* and *thee* become obsolete. Interestingly enough, grammar books of the eighteenth century (and later!) continued to list the forms along with the *-st* and *-eth* verb inflections: *thou lovest, he loveth*, probably because they made English look structurally more like Latin or other European languages with fuller verbal inflectional systems, a clear case of inflection envy.

It is not terribly surprising that a form of the formal, rather than the informal pronoun survives. Obviously there was some confusion of the system and in such instances, it was better to err on the side of formality. Interestingly, a similar development has occurred in Brazilian Portuguese.

However, it is not the subject pronoun *ye* but the object form *you* that comes to take over all of the functions of the second person, both singular and plural. The form *ye* also becomes obsolete. Today *ye* survives in songs and literary texts, e.g., *God rest ye merry gentlemen*, but probably also as a fossilized form in the expression *lookee* (look ye), as in *lookee here*.

RELATIVE PRONOUNS

While we have not yet discussed relative pronouns at length in their historical development, in Chapter 7 we made the point that the clause structure of OE was largely paratactic (see pp. 149–50). Over the history of English, particularly as it came to be exercised more in literate domains, a number of hypotactic and subordinate structures were developed. The following is a review of important terms and concepts that we will need in order to talk about the development of clause-combining strategies in English. These terms and concepts are also discussed in Chapter 2:

Simple sentence: *I love you.* (A single independent clause.)

Compound sentence: *I love you and you love me.* (Two or more independent clauses joined by a coordinate conjunction: *and, but, or.*)

Complex sentence: *I love you because you are special.* (Independent clause + adverb clause.)

Complex sentence: *I love macaroni and cheese, which used to cost 19 cents a box.* (Independent clause + relative clause.)

Complex sentence: *I love that new house that they built on Hudson Street.* (Independent clause + relative clause.)

Complex sentence: *I love that they still make macaroni and cheese in a box.* (Independent clause + noun clause; in fact we say the noun clause is "embedded" in the main clause.)

Sometimes the various types of clauses involved in the complex sentences above are grouped together and called *subordinate clauses*, as they were in Chapter 2 of this book.

In this section we will focus on the development of relative clauses. As noted above, relative clauses are essentially adjective clauses because they modify or give more information about a noun. Relative clauses are introduced by a relative pronoun. The following sentences represent the kinds of relative pronouns used to introduce relative clauses. (Chapter 2 provides additional explanation of relative clauses.)

1. *I bought the computer that was on sale for $1000.*
2. *I saw the woman who gave the lecture last night.*
3. *The Sears Tower, which was built in 1973, was renamed the Willis Tower in 2009.*
4. *I found the book ø you left in class.* (The ø means there is no relative expressed.)
5. *He's the man ø will help you anytime.* (In some dialects.)

The relative pronouns *that, who, which* and ø are possible strategies in ModE. In OE, the main strategies involved the use of the invariable *þe* or *þe* with a pronoun:

Oð ðone dæg þe hi hine forbærnað
until the day that they him burn
until the day that they burn him

Þa com he on morgenne to þam tungeferan, se þe his ealdorman wæs
then came he in morning to the steward, who his superior was
then in the morning he came to the steward, who was his superior

In ME, *that* and ø became frequent. Both *that* and ø have their origins in OE, and are native to the language.

King Pluto ... and King Juno ... that sumtime were as godes yhold.
King Pluto and King Juno that were sometimes beheld as gods.

For hym ø thee boght.
For him who redeemed you.

However, in ME the *wh-* forms began to appear as relatives probably influenced by French/Latin models. *Which* is first attested as a relative pronoun from 1175, according to the Oxford English Dictionary, and *who/whom* from 1297.

> *sche which keepþ þe blinde whel*
> she who keeps the blind well

The development of relative pronouns is very interesting because it presents us with an area of language in which certain changes are clearly more intentional than others. In fact in historical language study we make a distinction between change from below and change from above. Changes from below are changes that have their source in casual, vernacular speech, while changes from above are prescriptive in nature, often the result of an ideology of correctness or sophistication. While certain of the relative strategies that we find in EModE were from below, i.e., *that* and ø, the *wh-* forms *which* and *who/whom* are more likely the result of changes from above, that is, introduced first in the ME period from the French model and propagated as a correct strategy for writing. If we compare *that* to *which* we find that the use of *which* increases drastically over the course of ME to EModE:

	1250-1350	1350-1420	1420-1500	1500-1570	1570-1640	1640-1710
that	130	45	26	16	14	15
which-constructions	31	22	63	40	47	50

(Chart from Smith 2011)

FIGURE 9.5   **That and Which Constructions.**

The EModE period, and especially the eighteenth century, has been much discussed as the age of correctness, a time when philosophers and grammarians sought to make sense of language. And in the EModE period, as the general concern of "correct" language arises, relative pronouns get caught up in the discussion. The following passage is from 1711 in a popular magazine called the *Spectator*. In this article the personified relative pronoun *which* complains about the relative pronoun *that*, claiming that it is "low."

We are descended of ancient Families, and kept up our Dignity and Honour many years, till the Jack-sprat THAT supplanted us. How often have we found ourselves slighted by the Clergy in the Pulpits, and the Lawyers at the Bar. Nay, how often have we heard in one of the most polite and august Assemblies in the Universe, to our great Mortification, these Words, That That that noble

Lord urged; which if one of us had had Justice done, would have sounded nobler thus, That which that noble Lord urged.[15]

Even in ModE, the rules for relative pronouns remain complex and they tend to be expressed as matters of style. The *Chicago Manual of Style*, for example, provides the following explanation of the "correct" uses for *that* and *which* in PDE:

> In polished American prose, *that* is used restrictively to narrow a category or identity a particular item being talked about {any building that is taller must be outside the state}; *which* is used nonrestrictively—not to narrow a class or identify a particular item but to add something about an item already identified {alongside the officer trotted a toy poodle, which is hardly a typical police dog}. *Which* should be used restrictively only when it is preceded by a preposition {the situation in which we find ourselves}. Otherwise, it is almost always preceded by a comma, a parenthesis, or a dash. In British English, writers and editors seldom observe the distinction between the two words.[16]

This recent manual of style acknowledges the fact that in British English, the words *that* and *which* often may be interchangeable. But it also emphasizes that the rather complex rules for choosing between *that* and *which* in PDE are a matter less of grammaticality than of writing in a "polished" style of American English.

It appears then that for present-day writers, *which* just becomes "fancier" and thus tends to appear more frequently in writing when writers want to sound authoritative. Consider, for example, the following excerpt:

> Slashdot reviews cover a wide range of topics and genres. Please use Slashdot's search engine to see whether the book you'd like to review has already been covered. Unless you have a special reason for doing so, don't choose a book which has already been reviewed on Slashdot. (Searching for the "Booktitle + Slashdot" on Google is your best bet). If multiple reviewers submit reviews of the same book, we may run more than one, or excerpt from several to present elements of both.[17]

In this instance, the writer, if he or she had followed the rules we have just observed in the *Chicago Manual of Style* passage, should have chosen *that* instead of *which*, because the relative clause describes a book that is new to the discourse (i.e., it's a

---

15 *Spectator* 78, 1711, cited in Aaron K. Smith, "Standardization after 1600 and Its Effects on Two Domains of English Structure," *Studies in Medieval and Renaissance Teaching* 18:1 (2011): 52.

16 *Chicago Manual of Style* (16th edition) (Chicago: U of Chicago P, 2010), 298.

17 http://slashdot.org/book.review.guidelines.shtml, cited in Smith, "Standardization after 1600," 53.

restrictive relative). The writer chose *which* most likely because it makes him or her sound more writerly. That notion of *which* as the fancier of the two relative strategies reflects those patterns of change from below and change from above that started in the ME period and were reinforced in the EModE concern for correctness.

EXERCISE

9.3   **For each of the passages below, identify what is unique to or new in EModE about the underlined forms.**[18]

  a. From a letter from Queen Elizabeth to James VI of Scotland (1587): "... for whan <u>you</u> make vewe of my long danger indured thes fowre— wel ny fiue—moneths time..." (for when you view my long danger endured these four, well near five months time)

  b. From the diary of Henry Machyn (1530–63): "... a prest of the ab[bay] dyd helpe hym that was the menyster [to] the pepull <u>who</u> wher reseyvyng of the blessyd sacrament..." (a priest of the abbey helped him who was the minister to the people who were receiving the blessed sacrament)

  c. From the diary of Henry Machyn: "The xxv day of Marche, the <u>wyche</u> was owre lade [day]" (The 25th day of March, which was our lady's day)

  d. From the diary of Henry Machyn: "my lord Russell <u>ys</u> sune" (my lord Russell's son)

VERBS

In ME strong verbs tended to become weak verbs by the process known as analogy. During the EModE period, the tendency for strong verbs to lose their ablaut past-forming strategies and replace them with a dental suffix continued. *Dread* and *wade* are two examples of verbs that became weak in the EModE period (formerly *drat* and *wod*), and other verbs such as *melt* appear to have resolved a long history in which strong and weak forms of the verb coexisted in favor of weak past tense morphology. In a few situations both a strong and a weak form of the verb coexist but with differentiated meanings, for example *melted* and *molten*.

---

18 All passages are taken from David Burnley, *The History of the English Language: A Source Book* (2nd edition) (Harrow, England: Pearson, 2000).

HYBRID VERBS

Up until EModE, the main division of verbs was into the categories strong and weak. However, in EModE a number of verbs developed in ways that made them somewhat "hybrid" between weak and strong types because they have a dental suffix but they also show a vowel change in the past tense. That vowel change, however, is not due to the original system of ablaut but arises because of the GVS. (So in that sense these verbs are not hybrid between strong and weak, but really a new kind of verb.)

During ME vowels became short in syllables closed by two consonants. This resulted in a number of verbs with a long vowel in the infinitive and in the present but a short vowel in the past when the dental suffix created a closed syllable, that is, a syllable ending in a consonant.

Present	Past
hi-de [iː]	hid-de [i]
ke-pe [eː]	kep-te [e]
sle-pe [eː]	slep-te [e]
he-re [eː]	her-de [e]

Since the GVS only affected long vowels, the vowels in the infinitive and present shifted, resulting in vowels of a different quality for the present and the past.

Present	Past
hide [ɑi]	hid [ɪ]
keep [iː]	kept [ɛ]
sleep [iː]	slept [ɛ]

Because of such verbs, among others, it is no longer customary to classify verbs as strong and weak for ModE, but instead verbs are generally regarded as regular or irregular verbs (although some grammar books do refer to verbs like *keep–kept* specifically as hybrids). Thus regular verbs are those that have an *-ed* to mark the past while keeping the same vowel. Irregular verbs include the hybrid verbs but also verbs that make their past tense through an older ablaut pattern (*speak–spoke*), no change (*hit–hit*), or other changes involving older processes (*bring–brought*).

INFLECTION

At the end of the ME period, we saw that the verb retained many of its inflections. However, as we move into the EModE period, many of the sound changes that had played some role in the loss of nominal inflection appear to have affected verbs as well. The loss of word-final [-n] and the loss of the vowels in the final syllable of verbs leveled distinctive inflections for the first person and any of the remaining forms with vowel + [-n].

Two other important changes involving verbs took place in the EModE period as well. First, the southern English -*th* inflection for the third-person singular is replaced by the northern –*s*:

3rd-person singular: *loveth* > *loves*

And eventually the -*st* inflection of the second-person singular is lost:

2nd-person singular: *lovest* > *love*

The loss of the inflection -*st* is an especially interesting problem in the history of English because the sounds that make up that inflection were not vulnerable to loss, e.g., the adjectival superlative inflection -*st* as in *fastest*, which was not lost. Also, the loss of verbal -*st* is accompanied by the loss of the pronoun *thou* at about this same time. While we generally think that the loss of the pronoun *thou* and the loss of the verbal inflection -*st* influenced each other, whether the pronoun or the verbal inflection was lost first is a bit of a chicken or egg question. The fact that -*th* was replaced and -*st* was lost at the same time suggests that changes in the verbal paradigm might have encouraged the loss of the distinct second-person singular pronoun. Other facts, however, suggest that the pronoun and the verb form were more independent of each other in their respective disappearance from the language, at least early on. Thus as we move into the EModE period, a typical paradigm for the past tense of the verb *be* was:

I was	we were
thou wast	ye were
he was	they were

But once *you* replaces *ye* and *thou*, we find the following:

I was	we were
you was	you were
he was	they were

So in EModE, at least with the past tense of the verb *be*, a distinction between singular and plural *you* was made through the form of the verb. In this case *was* signaled the singular, and *were* the plural. That is, *you was* probably developed through analogy, with the first- and third-person form *was* replacing *wast*, rather than through a simple loss of inflection. *You was* continued as acceptable, even preferable, English well into the eighteenth century. Later, of course, *were* became the preferred form for all combinations with *you*, although *you was* continues in many dialects, for example, *You was always too busy pullin' little girls' pigtails.*[19]

THE PROGRESSIVE

The origins and development of the progressive in English is a hotly contested issue. While there are some who posit a direct development of the English progressive from a similar OE construction, most scholars recognize that there must have been at least some input from the ME construction shown here:

and hii funde þane king; þar he was an hontyng.
and they found the king where he was (on) hunting (*Layamon*)

Over time, the *on* reduced and became an unstressed schwa, a form that we can still hear in some dialect varieties in PDE, e.g., *a-workin'*. (This unstressed schwa is also the source for the first syllable in words like *atop, asleep, ashore*). In EModE, instances of the progressive with the *a*-prefixed participle show up with some frequency, as in the example below:

Falstoffe: ... But are you sure of your husband now?
Mrs. Ford: Hee's a birding.[20]

The *a*-prefix on participles caused considerable anxiety among Early Modern grammarians and as we will see later in this chapter, those grammarians spilled some ink in their condemnation of the form.

AUXILIARY DO

The use of *do* as an auxiliary verb may have its origins as early as the OE period, but by ME, the construction that becomes the present-day pattern emerges more clearly.

This Nicholas no lenger wolde tarie,
But dooth ful softe unto his chamber carie
Bothe mete and drynke...[21]

Whan Phebus doth his bryghte bemes sprede...[22]

---

19 John Steinbeck, *The Grapes of Wrath* (New York: Penguin, 1992), 26.
20 From Shakespeare's *The Merry Wives of Windsor*, cited in CEPLAY 2A, Helsinki Corpus, University of Helsinki, Department of English.
21 *Canterbury Tales*, I.3409–11.
22 *Troilus and Criseyde*, I.54.

But the periphrases with *do* expanded considerably during the EModE period.

Consider the following statement: *John likes flowers*. Note that the verb is in the simple present and it is synthetic. However, if we make this sentence into a negative, we use the auxiliary verb *do* and the verb phrase becomes periphrastic: *John does not like flowers*. If we were to make this a *yes/no* question, we would also employ auxiliary *do*. *Does John like flowers?* If we make it a *wh-* question, we also use *do*. *What does John like?*

These same patterns apply to the simple past.

> John saw the circus.
> John didn't see the circus.
> What did John see?
> Did John see the circus?

The rule in PDE is the following: In the simple present and the simple past auxiliary *do* is used in the negative, *yes/no* questions and *wh-* questions when the *wh-*word is not the subject.

While native speakers of English tend to take such syntactic behavior for granted, use of auxiliary *do* is actually rather odd, from an Indo-European or even broader typological point of view. In Spanish for example, affirmatives, negatives and questions all have synthetic forms.

> *Juan tiene hermanos.* (Juan has brothers.)
> *Juan no tiene hermanos.* (Juan no has brothers.)
> *¿Tiene Juan hermanos?* (Has Juan brothers?)
> *¿Qué tiene Juan?* (What has Juan?)

In other words, questions and negatives in Spanish do not require an extra auxiliary; nor do they in most languages. Note also that auxiliary *do* in ModE may also appear in affirmative declarative contexts, but in such cases it is usually understood to be emphatic. *I DO love you.*

In EModE, *do* began to be used in all of these contexts (including the affirmative) and it was not always emphatic. The following sentences exemplify the use of auxiliary *do* across these syntactic environments in EModE. All examples come from Matti Rissanen, "Syntax."[23]

> *Thou must take hede howe thy hennes, duckes, and geese do ley, and to gather vp theyr egges.* (affirmative, non-ephatic)
> *Why do you not read Wiat's Accusation to him?*
> *What doe you call him?*

---

23 Matti Rissanen, "Syntax," in *The Cambridge History of the English Language*, 1476–1776, ed. Roger Lass (Cambridge: Cambridge UP, 2000).

What might be the reason for the development of auxiliary *do* in these situations? Explanation on the matter is elusive. Some have posited that a partial explanation may be the influence of Celtic, in which a similar pattern exists.[24] Whatever the ultimate explanation might turn out to be, we have noted in earlier chapters that over the ME and EModE periods, the verb phrase showed steady expansion, as is evident in the following synopsis of the PDE verb, repeated here for convenience.

	Simple	Progressive	Perfect	Perfect-Progressive
Present	he takes	he is taking	he has taken	he has been taking
Past	he takes	he is taking	he has taken	he has been taking
Future	he will take	he will be taking	he will have taken	he will have been taking

FIGURE 9.6   Synopsis of the Present-Day English Verb.

In every verb form other than the simple present and the simple past, we have an auxiliary verb. Given this pattern it is likely that the rise of *do* as a "dummy" auxiliary is due, at least in part, to analogy. We have so far used analogy to describe the process of the spread of the -*s* plural to most nouns (OE plural *word* > ModE *words*) and the spread of the weak verb dental suffix -*ed* to former strong verbs (ME past tense *wod* > ModE *waded*). Analogy describes a process but it is not an explanation per se. The way that analogy works is that a dominant pattern (often dominant because it is a frequent pattern) is more firmly stored in the mind; therefore when speakers and writers use language, the dominant pattern will be recalled first and sometimes even replace weaker patterns in the grammar (weaker may be an effect of lesser frequency or profound irregularity). In the case of *do*, once the verb phrase expands in English, the presence of an auxiliary becomes the dominant pattern and then the simple present and the simple past follow suit, using an "empty" auxiliary for the function of operator.

Also note that the syntax of the other verb forms with auxiliaries is exactly like the pattern we just observed with *do*:

John has taken the bus.
John has not taken the bus.
Has John taken the bus?
What has John taken?

---

24 Markku Filppula, Juhani Klemola, and Heli Paulasto, *English and Celtic in Contact* (New York: Routledge, 2008).

The rule for making a negative sentence is: place *not* after the first auxiliary; if there is no auxiliary, supply *do*. The rule for a *yes/no* question is: invert the subject and the first auxiliary. If there is no auxiliary, supply *do*. The rule for making a *wh-* question is: start the sentence with a *wh-* word. If the *wh-* word is not the subject, invert the subject and the first auxiliary. If there is no auxiliary, supply *do*. Thus the use of *do* greatly regularizes the syntax of negatives and questions in English.

EXERCISE

9.4   **Identify what is unique, new, or increasingly developing in EModE in the underlined forms.**[25]

   a.   From the diary of Henry Machyn (1550–63): "hundreds <u>dyd see</u> her grace" ("hundreds saw her grace")

   b.   From *Euphues or The Anatomy of Wit*, John Lyly (?1554–1606): "*yet <u>doth it not eate</u> into the Emeraulde*" ("yet does it not eat into the Emerald")

   c.   From *The Guls Horne-Booke*, Thomas Dekker (1609): "to make other fooles fall <u>a laughing</u>" ("to make other fools fall a-laughing")

   d.   From *The Guls Horne-Booke*, Thomas Dekker (1609): "it <u>skils</u> not if the foure knaues ly on their backs" ("it matters not if the four knaves lie on their backs")

STANDARDIZATION AND PRESCRIPTION

THE KING JAMES BIBLE

During the EModE period, England became the center of a developing Empire that stretched across the Atlantic and east to India. England also broke with the Church of Rome and established a new church with the English king at its head. English as a language was increasingly recognized during this period as a language with author-

---

25   All passages are from Burnley, *The History of the English Language*.

ity, even an authority that could challenge the authority of Latin, the language of the Church of Rome. The publication in 1611 of the **King James Bible** powerfully demonstrates this shift in attitudes towards English.

Throughout the ME period, the version of the Bible used in Church services was the Vulgate, Jerome's fourth-century Latin translation from Greek, Hebrew, and Aramaic. Scripture was encountered in Latin, and through the mediation of the Church: there was no private and secular Bible-reading. In fact, reading the Bible was explicitly against the law for individuals outside the Church. In the late fourteenth century, however, a powerful movement developed under the leadership of an Oxford don, John Wyclif (1330–84). Wyclif and his followers argued, among other things, for a radical predestination, for an idea of the church as the community of true believers rather than an institution, and for individual reading of Scripture. Individual reading of Scripture, in the ME period, required translation of the Latin Vulgate into English. It is because of the efforts of Wyclif and others associated with him that versions of the Bible were translated into ME.

The Wycliffite translations were considered extremely threatening both to the Church of Rome and to the English state. In the early fifteenth century, in response to the spread of Wycliffite teachings, reading or even owning a Bible in English could be punishable by death.

But the introduction of the press would make it increasingly difficult to control the dissemination of texts, among them new translations of Scripture and the books and pamphlets that supported the reforms that would become Protestant movements. When Henry VIII (ruled 1509–57) broke with the Church of Rome between 1529 and 1536, he initiated a period of unprecedented openness to the reforms that were gaining power in Germany under the leadership of Martin Luther. It is during the rule of Henry VIII in fact that the first complete Bible in English, the Coverdale Bible, is published in 1535. Although there would be intervals of Catholic rule and anti-Protestantism, the long rule of Elizabeth I (1558–1603) established Protestantism in England. One of the first initiatives by Elizabeth's successor, James I (ruled 1603–25) was to call for a conference at Hampton Court Palace, the royal residence at the time, to respond to a petition for reform. And a significant outcome of that conference was the plan for the King James Bible.

One observer at the conference recorded that:

> his Highness wished, that some especiall pains should be taken in that behalf for one vniforme translation (professing that he could neuer, yet, see a Bible well translated in English; but the worst of all, his Maiestie thought the Geneua to be) and this to be done by the best learned in both the Vniversities, after them to be reviewed by the Bishops, and the chiefe learned of the Church;

from them to be presented to the Priuy Councell; and lastly to bee ratified by
his Royall authority....[26]

The plan for the King James Bible thus reflected a number of the concerns with
language and the reification of language that occurred after the introduction of the
press. James commissioned "one vniforme translation," that is, a translation that
reflected the new concern with standardization of language. His plan involved the
consultation of experts "in both the Vniversities, after them to be reviewed by the
Bishops, and the chiefe learned of the Church." The translation experts would come
from the Church, but also in the new and increasingly secular universities. The plan
thus reflects the authority of a new kind of scholar: not only the theologian but also
the grammarian. Finally, the translation was "to bee ratified by his Royall authority."
That is, rather than threatening the authority of the state, this translation of the Bible
into English was seen as an extension of the power of the state, one that was ratified
by its authority, but also worked conversely to authorize that same state.

For the translators of the King James Bible:

- English is understood to be a language that has the power to convey Scriptural
  meaning;
- translation into English is not a threat to the Church of England but a means
  of securing its power;
- the translation into English is now a project of the state, not a potential threat
  to it; it is authorized by the King and supports his authority.

The King James Bible has been called "the most important book in the English
language"[27] in part because of its centrality to Christian cultures in English for the
last four hundred years. It is also a highly significant text because of its extremely
wide international circulation. Phrases from the King James Bible, like "the salt of the
earth," the "apple of his eye" and "sour grapes" have become idiomatic in English.[28]
Even when it is not used as a text to be actually read, we can see its pervasive cultural
significance as an artifact. In the United States, for example, many presidents ranging from George Washington to Barack Obama have chosen to lay their hands on a
copy of the King James Bible during the inauguration ceremony.

---

26   William Barlow, "The Summe and Substance of the Conference, which, it pleased his Excellent
     Maiestie to haue with the Lords, Bishops, and othe of his Clergie... at Hampton Court. Ianuary 14,
     1603," cited in *Translating the King James Bible*, ed. Ward Allen (Nashville: Vanderbilt UP, 1969), 4.
27   Gordon Campbell, *Bible: The Story of the King James Version 1611–2011* (Oxford: Oxford UP, 2010), 2.
28   Crystal, *The Cambridge Encyclopedia of the English Language*, 64.

LANGUAGE ACADEMIES

During the EModE period, many European countries formed language academies that were associated with the national government and charged with constructing a standardized grammar as well as an official dictionary for the language. In Italy, the Accademia della Crusca was founded in 1583, in France, the Académie Française (1635), and in Spain, the Academia Real Española (1713). In England, however, while a number of scholars argued for the founding of a similar academy, ultimately the project of constructing authoritative dictionaries and grammars fell not to a government-sponsored academy but to a class of grammarians, and eventually, in the case of the dictionary, to a university press in collaboration with a committee of scholars and a wide circle of amateur philologists.

Jonathan Swift, now perhaps more widely known as the author of *Gulliver's Travels*, was one of the most vocal supporters of the idea of an English language academy. In his 1712 tract, "A Proposal for Correcting, Improving and Ascertaining the English Tongue," Swift argued that the language of the King James Bible had provided a model for "ascertaining" or stabilizing language and that a standard might be established more broadly through an academy. He claimed,

> If it were not for the Bible and Common Prayer Book in the vulgar Tongue, we should hardly be able to understand any Thing that was written among us a hundred Years ago: Which is certainly true: For those Books being perpetually read in Churches, have provided a kind of Standard for Language, especially to the common People....[29]

Despite the interest by Swift and other scholars, the proposal for a language academy in England did not result in a project supported by the government. While the Accademia della Crusca was able to produce its official dictionary in 1612, and the Académie Française was able to produce its official dictionary in 1694, it was not until the mid eighteenth century that a dictionary attempting to list and define all of the words in English was published. And that dictionary was the work not of a government-sponsored academy, but of a single scholar and his assistants, with a private patron.

DICTIONARIES

Dictionaries have their roots in the tradition of glossing we discussed in Chapter 7. Texts in Latin, for example, were glossed in OE, sometimes with alphabetical word lists in both languages. Closer to the modern idea of the dictionary, however, were the dictionaries of hard words published in the EModE period. Especially given

---

29   Cited in Campbell, *Bible*, 144.

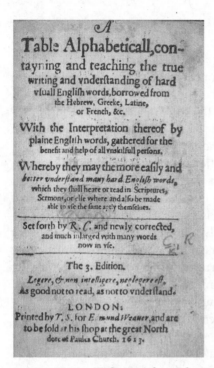

FIGURE 9.7   Title page from the 3rd edition of Cawdry's *Table*. Note that the address has changed from "for the benefit and help of Ladies, gentlewomen or any other vnskilfull persons" to "for the benefit and help of all vnskilfull persons."

the number of inkhorn terms and other borrowings that entered the lexicon in the EModE period, it is not surprising that scholars found the need to list and define these new and often fairly obscure words. Robert Cawdry's *A Table Alphabeticall*, first published in 1604, for example, is one of the first of these lists of hard words. Its full title explains that it is *A Table Alphabeticall, containing and teaching the true writing and vnderstanding of hard vsuall English words, borrowed from the Hebrew, Greeke, Latine, or French, &c, With the Interpretation thereof by plaine English words, gathered for the benefit and help of Ladies, gentlewomen or any other vnskilfull persons, Whereby they may the more easily and better understand many hard English words, which they shall heare or read in Scriptures, Sermons, or elsewhere and also be made able to vse the same aptly themselues.*[30] That is, it is explicitly a list of new borrowed words explained by "plain English words," and designed to help "ladies" or "other unskilfull persons" to read and use these words. As such, Cawdry's *Table* also provides much insight into the attitudes towards language that prompted its development. On one hand, English is understood to be increasingly complex, and

---

30 Text available through the University of Toronto Library at http://www.library.utoronto.ca/utel/ret/cawdrey/cawdrey0.html.

requiring the explanation and interpretation provided by the list. But on the other, by providing this explanation and interpretation, the list of hard words enables its readers to enter into new realms of discourse, not only to understand but also to "vse the same aptly themselues": English, "correct" English, is also represented as something to which readers *can* have access through these new resources.

Cawdry's *Table* was not an insubstantial text. It contained about 2,500 entries. It was not, however, a dictionary in the modern sense. Cawdry's aim was to explain hard words, not to define *all* the words of the language. Nathaniel Bailey's *An Universal Etymological English Dictionary* (1721) and later the *Dictionarium Britannicum* (1730), with about 48,000 entries, would come much closer to listing and defining the words of the language.[31]

When **Samuel Johnson** articulated his *Plan of a Dictionary of the English Language*, he described his project as the means "by which the pronunciation of our language may be fixed, and its attainment facilitated; by which its purity may be preserved, its use ascertained, and its duration lengthened."[32] Johnson appealed to exactly the concerns of those scholars like Swift who had argued for the establishment of a language academy: a concern with "fixing" and "ascertaining" or stabilizing the language, and thus preserving it from decay. Johnson proposed to approach the construction of his dictionary by first reading comprehensively, then, with his assistants, listing words, defining them, and illustrating them with quotations from his reading.

The first edition of his dictionary, published in 1755, contained around 40,000 entries illustrated by about 114,000 illustrative quotations. A typical entry, for the word *eternal*, follows.

Ete'rnal adj. [aeternus, Latin]
1. Without beginning or end
   The eternal God is thy refuge. Deut. xxxiii.27
2. Without beginning
   It is a question quite different from our having an idea of eternity, to know whether there were any real being, whose duration has been eternal. Locke.
3. Without end; endless, immortal.
   thou know'st that Banquo and his Fleance lives
   But in them nature's copy's not eternal. Shakes. Macbeth
4. Perpetual; constant; unintermitting.
   Burnt off'rings morn and ev'ning shall be thine,
   And fires eternal in thy temple shine. Dryd. Knight's Tale
5. Unchangeable.
   Hobbes believed the eternal truths which he opposed. Dryd.[33]

---

31 Millward, *Biography*, 240.
32 Baugh and Cable, *A History of the English Language*, 273.
33 Cited in Crystal, *The Cambridge Encyclopedia of the English Language*, 75.

The entry also provides some indication of the pronunciation of the word, with the stress marked in the second syllable, as well as information concerning its part of speech and etymology. It then details five possible meanings with illustrative quotations. Even examination of this one entry alone, however, suggests one weakness in this dictionary: more than half of the illustrative quotations come from just a handful of sources—Shakespeare, Dryden, and the King James Bible among them.[34] Other entries, such as the entry for *etch*, also reflect the fact that Johnson was working on his own, and he sometimes expressed his own opinions or simply identified his own lack of knowledge.

> Etch n.s. A country word, of which I know not the meaning.
> *Where you find dunging of land makes it rank, lay dung upon the etch, and*
> *sow it with barley.* Mortimer's Husbandry.[35]

Its idiosyncrasies aside, Johnson's dictionary quickly became *the* authoritative dictionary of English, and it remained so until well into the nineteenth century. One result of the authoritative reception of Johnson's dictionary was that it served as a model for correct spelling and consequently spelling in English even today continues to follow Johnson's plan. Even the makers of perhaps the greatest dictionary of English, the **Oxford English Dictionary**, conceived of their own project as a revision of Johnson's dictionary.

The *Oxford English Dictionary* (OED) began as *The New English Dictionary on Historical Principles*. The goal of this dictionary was to revise and expand Johnson's dictionary so that it included every word in English, with every meaning that word had ever had since its first appearance in written records. The scope of the project was staggering. Work began on the dictionary in 1858; however, the last volume of the first edition would not be published until 1928. The first edition of the OED was 15,487 pages long, and contained 414,825 words (240,165 main words).[36] The most recent edition includes close to 600,000 words with as many as 3,000,000 illustrative quotations.[37]

One of the innovations of the dictionary project was to employ amateur scholars. These amateur readers—schoolteachers, reading groups, armchair philologists, inmates—would write to the dictionary project and send in slips of paper for words to be defined, accompanied by an illustrative quotation with the citation, including the date, for the citation. Simon Winchester's *The Professor and the Madman* recounts the story of one particularly prolific contributor to the OED, an inmate at a facility for the criminally insane who submitted, in the end, close to 10,000 items to the project.

---

34 Crystal, *The Cambridge Encyclopedia of the English Language*, 75.
35 Ibid.
36 Ibid., 443.
37 http://public.oed.com/about.

The success of the OED is testimony to, among many other things, the tenacity of the attitudes towards language that develop in the EModE period: language is perceived as something to be collected and organized, not unlike the way physical artifacts might be collected and organized in a museum; this perception is the result of a growing sense that language is an object to be regulated by social institutions. But the OED makes clear that the institution of the English language is not something that only the elite can discover, but rather is a collection that all educated people can participate in amassing. In fact, the OED continues to accept contributions from amateur readers. It is still possible for you to contribute to this project. The OED homepage provides directions for readers who wish to contribute to the latest version of the dictionary.

Finally, readers of this book will appreciate too that the plan for the OED has always had the history of the word as an important part of its understanding. That is, a word, and indeed language more broadly, is a living entity shaped by its past. To know a language and to know it well is to know something of that history.

GRAMMARS AND GRAMMARIANS

In addition to the dictionaries produced by Johnson and others, the EModE period, and the eighteenth century in particular, also witnesses an explosion of grammars of English. In the first half of the eighteenth century 50 grammars were produced. However, in the second half of the century more than 200 grammars were published.[38] One explanation for the explosion of grammars has to do with changing social conditions, among the most important of which were the economic shift from land-based wealth to monetary wealth, and the concomitant effects of greater geographical and social mobility. Francis Austen provides a close study of the language of William Clift, who in 1792 left his birthplace of Cornwall and went to work for a wealthy London physician as his secretary.[39] In Clift's letters, Austin tracks shifts in language toward more prestigious and "correct" forms as Clift attempts to move in socially more prestigious circles. These shifts in language clearly reflect the association between certain correct forms and social class. In fact, many of the grammars of the eighteenth century were advertised as necessary for a person's social ascendency, a major marketing point of grammars and grammar teaching even today.

From the eighteenth century, two of the most famous grammarians to emerge, as judged by the number of editions and sales of their works, were **Robert Lowth** and **Joseph Priestly**. Lowth's 1762 *A Short Grammar of English* and Priestly's 1761 *The Rudiments of English Grammar* have long been set up in opposition to each other; Lowth has been constructed as the paragon of prescriptivism and Priestly as the

---

38 Joan C. Beal, *English in Modern Times* (London: Arnold, 2004), 90.

39 Frances Austin, "The Effect of Exposure to Standard English: The Language of William Clift," in *Towards a Standard English 1600–1800*, ed. Dieter Stein and Ingrid Tieken-Boon van Ostade (Berlin and New York: Mouton de Gruyter, 1994).

example of an early descriptivist.[40] The distinction is certainly not as stark as many would have it and was likely constructed by scholars in the early part of the twentieth century in order to build rhetorical space for what they saw as the superior approach of linguistic description; the idea was that there had been a glimmer of hope for more descriptive approaches in the EModE period, but that Lowth and his kind derailed scientific study of language for a long time and caused the split between linguistics and school grammarians, i.e., between prescription and description.[41]

Whatever the ideological differences between Lowth and Priestly may have been, the most popular English grammar in schools from the end of the eighteenth to the middle of the nineteenth century was Lindley Murray's 1795 *Grammar of English*. Murray's *Grammar* was decidedly prescriptive and served as a dominant model for grammars that came after it. It was especially popular in the US. Murray himself was an American, but fled to England during the Revolutionary War because of his loyalist position. Murray's grammar was based heavily on Lowth's, another matter that might have led to the twentieth-century over-evaluation of the prescriptive elements in Lowth's grammar.

EModE grammarians employed three chief means of justifying their grammatical positions. The first was an appeal to Latin. Up until the EModE period, the term "grammar" was essentially synonymous with "Latin grammar," and as thinkers turned their attention to making grammars for English (or discovering grammar in English, as they often saw it) they saw English through a Latin grammatical lens. For instance, the fact that the word *preposition* literally means "placed before," from the Latin grammatical term *praepositio*, led to the belief that it was ungrammatical to have a preposition that was not placed before a noun. Of course in a language like Latin, prepositions do not occur away from the nouns they govern (just as they do not in the modern Romance languages). But in a Germanic language, prepositions, and preposition-like words have a more varied set of uses like that in the sentence, *He gave up.* Note that in this instance *up* is part of a phrasal verb; there isn't a noun for it to govern. In other cases, prepositions may be stranded away from the noun (or more accurately the relative pronoun) that they govern, as in *I have read the book that the play was based on.* However, in written English, particularly conservative styles, the preposition should be before the word it governs and consequently preference has been to keep the preposition with the relative: *I have read the book on which the play was based.*

Early grammarians, like Lowth, recognized the variation and made their recommendations accordingly, decidedly on the side of pre-posing:

40 Ingrid Tieken-Boon van Ostade, "Lowth as an Icon of Prescriptivism," in *Eighteenth-Century English: Ideology and Change*, ed. Raymond Hickey (Cambridge: Cambridge UP, 2010).

41 Sterling Andrus Leonard, *The Doctrine of Correctness in English Usage 1700–1800* (New York: Russell and Russell, 1962).

The Preposition is often separated from the Relative which it governs, and joined to the Verb at the end of the Sentence, or of some member of it: as, "Horace is an author, *whom* I am much delighted *with*."... This is an Idiom which our language is much inclined to;[42] it prevails in common conversation, and suits very well with the familiar style in writing; but the placing of the Preposition before the Relative is more graceful, as well as more perspicuous; and it agrees much better with the solemn and elevated style.[43]

Another way that grammarians justified their strictures was through an appeal to logic, which they often called "analogy." Thus on the matter of double negatives, Lowth tells us, "Two negatives, in English, destroy one another, or are equivalent to an affirmative; as '*Nor* did they *not* perceive the evil plight in which they were.'"

One still finds such explanations among grammarians and teachers, and the persistence of these explanations highlights one of the most interesting and confounding aspects of language prescription: the notion that grammar exists independently of people's use of it. Indeed when a person exclaims, "I've never been nowhere!" he or she doesn't mean "I've been somewhere." This is not to say that double negation is not a rule of prescriptive grammar, but that prescriptive rule is an ideological convention, not a necessary rule or one based on observation of actual language use. Language prescription is socially meaningful but linguistically arbitrary.

Finally, some grammar rules in grammar books are simply **ipse dixit statements**. An ipse dixit statement is essentially "because I say so." For example, Lowth in his 1762 grammar remarks on the use of the simple past for the past participle, e.g., *I have saw*, calling such usage "barbarous" and "inexcusable."[44] But from the argument he makes, it is clear that his appeal is to his own sense of expertise in the language.

We saw above that Johnson's dictionary illustrated its definitions by quotes, most often from famous authors, including the King James Bible. This method of illustration was also a frequent method of the grammarians, as in the following example from James White's *The English Verb*, 1761.

As in the First Person singular, so in the First Person plural, shall and will are differently applied. Thus shall foretells what must happen; and may do so this sometimes ironically.
   "*We shall lose our time,*
   And all be turn'd to barnacles and apes." (*Shakespeare*)
   "*Shall, ignominious, we with shame retire?*" (*Pope*)

---

42 Much has been said about Lowth's use of a preposition at the end of his sentence in the grammar. Some conclude that the use is intentional and jocular, see Tieken-Boon van Ostade, "Lowth as an Icon of Prescriptivism."

43 Robert Lowth, *A Short Introduction to English Grammar* (London: R. Dodsley, 1762), 139.

44 Ibid., 89.

One might note that using literary authors to "prove" the grammar is based on a false notion that authors adhere to the standard; they don't. In fact, creative writers frequently break the rules; we even term this allowance for departure from language norms "poetic license."

Standard languages most often stem from the ideology of national singularity and thus they are very often shaped by the official language practices of government, an important historical element in the development of Standard English as well.[45]

CAN THE STANDARD AFFECT LANGUAGE USE?

Knowledge of the history of standardization in English should lead us to ask whether the standard can affect the way that people use language. After all, despite centuries-long attempts to eradicate *ain't* or multiple negation, such prescriptive infelicities still occur. Part of the answer to that question is obvious; of course it affects the way people write since most rules of standardization, at least in origin, have to do with the rules of good writing. However, for some matters of English use, the ideologies of proper usage may have spilled over into language behavior more generally, including the way people speak English, so that it is commonplace to talk about "speaking correctly."

Along those lines, consider the following sentences from *The Grapes of Wrath*, by John Steinbeck.

> *I ain't a-goin'. My pa come here fifty years ago. An' I ain't a-goin'.* (p. 64, spoken by a South Midland American English speaker)
> *They're a-workin' away at our spirits.*[46]

Forms such as *a-goin'* and *a-workin'*, known as **a-prefixed participles**, can still be heard today in quite a few dialects. Because dialects serve to cohere a group of people geographically or socially and because those groups often wish to maintain that identity against socially prescribed norms, dialects don't develop in line with the standard. In fact in some dialect groups, speaking too "standardly" may result in rejection from the group.

Verb forms such as *ain't* + *a-goin'* or *are* + *a-working* express progressive meaning, i.e., an event that is ongoing at a specific reference point. So if one says, "They're a-workin'," the action of the verb is occurring at the specific reference point of the present time, often the specific moment of speech. In Standard English the progressive appears with the "bare" present participle:

I'm not going.
They are working.

---

45 John Fisher, *The Emergence of Standard English* (Lexington: U of Kentucky P, 1996).
46 John Steinbeck, *The Grapes of Wrath* (New York: Penguin, 1992), 381.

The source of the *a*- prefix was discussed in the last section (p. 241); it developed out of the full preposition *on*. In the nineteenth century, grammarians were unequivocal in their proscription of the prefix for the present participle:

> *a* is used, but inelegantly, for *on* or *in*;... A is often redundant or superfluous at the Beginning of Words....

> In familiar conversation the Particle *a* is sometimes used before these Verbs; as, *the house is a building. The church is a repairing. The lottery is a drawing.* This particle is supposed to be a contraction of the Preposition on. It ought to be omitted.[47]

Given that the use of the auxiliary *be* + *on* > *a'* + *-ing* form is likely the source of our standard progressive (or some part of it), we note that the intervention of grammarians in ridding the construction of the *a*- prefix was successful. It makes us wonder too whether more speakers would use the *a*- prefix if not for the ideology of correctness among the early modern grammarians in regards to the progressive.

EXERCISE

9.5   How did grammarians justify the following rules?

a. The preposition should precede the noun or pronoun that is its object. Hence *He is a man whom I am fond of* should be *He is a man of whom I am fond.*

b. Two negatives equal a positive. Hence *I don't have nothing* should mean *I have something.*

c. The simple past should not be used for the past participle when an *-en* form exists. Hence *I have saw* is not correct.

---

47   James Buchanan, *The British Grammar* (Menston, UK: Scholar P, 1968) (first publication 1762), 148. George Neville Ussher, *The Elements of English Grammar* (Menston, UK: Scholar P, 1968) (first publication 1785), 60 (emphasis ours). Both cited in Aaron K. Smith, "The Development of the English Progressive," *Journal of Germanic Linguistics* 19:3 (2007): 205–41.

CHAPTER TEN

The Modern Period and Global Englishes

COLONIZATION

In this text we have studied the effects of a number of invasions, conquests, and waves of settlement in the history of English. We began with the conquest of Britannia by the Romans in 43 CE and moved through the large-scale settlement and political domination of the Anglo-Saxons after c. 450. We then considered the impact of the Scandinavian attacks, settlement, and rule of England, and the Norman Conquest in 1066. For much of the early history of English, that is, we have been concerned with what happens to English as a language when England as a country is invaded, settled, or colonized. But as we move to the Modern period, we must shift that focus. England is not successfully invaded again after 1066. And beginning in the Early Modern period, the English expand outwards: the English become the invaders, settlers, and colonizers of territories ranging from North America to the Caribbean to India, South Africa, Asia, and Australia.

The motivations for colonial expansion are complex and we will not be able to do justice to them here. But we can note that some of these motivations have already been presented in earlier discussions: the movement away from a system of landed wealth and what has been called feudalism to a market economy, with a new mercantile "gentry," an increasingly mobile middle class and an increasingly wage-driven working class. To this we can add the alliance between monarchical and mercantile interests, an alliance that resulted in the powerful royal monopolies granted most famously to the East India Company (1600) and the Massachusetts Bay Company (1629).

In the early part of the sixteenth century, it was the Spanish and Portuguese, not the English, who dominated European expansion. But after the English defeat of the Spanish Armada in 1588, the English established a number of settlements in the New World, South Asia, Australia, and Africa. In North America, the English established settlements in Jamestown (1607), Plymouth (1620), and Massachusetts Bay (1630). A sampling of subsequent conquests and settlements should provide an idea of the scope of the expansion of the British Empire during this period. In 1655, the English took control of Jamaica from the Spanish. In 1713, the British defeated the French in Atlantic Canada. Although the British, after the formation of the East India Company in 1600, already controlled much of India, in 1757 the British victory at Plassey ensured political dominance in South Asia for nearly a century.[1] Within 20 years of the British landing at Botany Bay in 1770, Australia became a British penal colony. In 1806, the British established political control in South Africa and in 1822 made English the official language of the country.[2]

Although above we have used, and we will continue to use, the comparatively neutral term "expansion" as we discuss the development of global Englishes, we emphasize that there was nothing neutral about these assertions of British political and economic power (or later assertions of power by the US). These colonies were not created in a vacuum: British settlement and British control of these territories around the globe occurred at the expense of the peoples who lived there, and without exception resulted in the exploitation, enslavement, or decimation of native populations.

WORLD ENGLISHES

Colonization is an obvious factor in the dramatic increase in the number of geographical varieties of English: English was used during the colonial period in territories around the globe. But we emphasize that as English comes into use around the globe, it also comes into contact with other languages in a wide variety of contexts: as the language of a colonial power, but also as a language of trade, as a lingua franca. With this in mind, although we will be considering the proliferation of Englishes during the Modern period, we must also remember that as the result of this language contact, changes occur in other world languages, and new languages called *creoles* develop (pp. 288–92).

The following chart, adapted from the *Cambridge Encyclopedia of the English Language*,[3] presents data from 1990 and tabulates populations of speakers of English as a first language in countries across the globe, with totals reaching 377,132,600 speakers. In the following chart, we have included only those countries listed with more than 115,000 speakers of English as a first language, and only those countries for which a count of speakers of English as a first language was available in 1990 (note that this excludes India, for example, with a total population of about 844,000,000).

---

1 Lynda Mugglestone, *The Oxford History of English* (Oxford: Oxford UP, 2006), 420.
2 David Crystal, *The Cambridge Encyclopedia of the English Language* (Cambridge: Cambridge UP, 1996), 100.
3 Crystal, *The Cambridge Encyclopedia of the English Language*, 108–09.

Even in such abbreviated form, however, the data should provide a clear sense of how enormously the number of varieties of English increased in the Early Modern and Modern periods as a direct or indirect consequence of colonial expansion.

Country	Number of speakers of English as a first language	% of estimated population
Australia	15,366,000	90
Bahamas	228,000	90
Barbados	257,000	100
Belize	123,000	65
Canada	15,972,000	60
Guyana	567,000	75
Hong Kong	117,000	2
Ireland	3,334,000	95
Jamaica	2,319,000	97
Liberia	2,491,000	96
Malaysia	358,000	2
Namibia	130,000	10
New Zealand	3,152,000	93
Nigeria	88,500,000	50
Papua New Guinea	2,423,000	66
Sierra Leone	3,943,000	95
South Africa	3,080,000	10
Trinidad & Tobago	616,500	50
United States	221,227,000	88

TABLE 10.1   Speakers of English in Selected Countries

The data from Table 10.1 is based on reports from 1990; the numbers will have shifted by now. However, updating the data from the table reveals complexity not only in the demographic distribution of speakers of English and other languages but also in the changing attitudes towards the use of English, particularly in relationship to other native and immigrant languages. Data for Australia, for example, shows that in 2012, with a total population of 22,683,600[4] and 16,500,000 speakers of English as a

4 Australian Bureau of Statistics, www.abs.gov.au, accessed 22 August 2016.

first language, the percentage of the population with English as a first language had dropped from 90 per cent to 73 per cent. Certainly patterns of immigration provide insight into that apparent drop in the percentage of speakers. But we should also consider the complexity of the linguistic make-up of the population in Australia. Ethnologue, an online catalogue of the world's languages, records 216 living native languages for Australia, as well as 44 immigrant languages. As attitudes towards the primacy of English shift, so too does assessment and reporting of competency in or preference for other languages within a country.

INNER, OUTER, AND EXPANDING CIRCLES

Kachru[5] developed the idea that world Englishes can be located within a set of concentric circles, comprised of the inner, outer and expanding circles. The **inner circle** is made up of those nations in which English is a native language for the majority of the population, such as the United States, Canada, the United Kingdom, Australia, and New Zealand. Obviously too, the standard Englishes of inner-circle countries, particularly the UK (and specifically England) and the US, have commonly been considered the basis for worldwide education in English as a second language as well, although there have been some significant shifts in attitudes toward the teaching of English as a foreign or second language and the ideology of language "ownership," a point we return to below.

Outer circle countries are comprised of those nations such as India, Singapore, and Ghana, in which English is not a native language, but is used extensively as a language of government, education, and business. And the **expanding circle** is composed of nations which have no great historical ties to English at the societal level but which increasingly use English, particularly in the international domains of commerce and science, e.g., Russia, Spain, Japan.

A remarkable fact about the linguistic structure of inner-circle varieties is that there is very little grammatical variation among them. Perhaps that is why when speakers of American English encounter differences in the language of UK English speakers, the changes often are not viewed as a hindrance to communication, but as quaint regionalisms. For example, speakers of American English, who say *in the hospital*, or *at the university*, are amused, and not confused, when hearing UK speakers say *in hospital* or *at university*. (But note that US speakers do say *at school*.)

Inner-circle varieties do show some degree of lexical variation. Of course we are familiar with geographically localized terminology from various parts of the world where English is spoken, giving rise to distinctive terms such as Australian English *boomerang* and *billabong*, or American English *skunk* and *mesa*, or South African English *lekker*, a word meaning *pleasant* or *nice*. In fact, each of these examples shows the influence of other languages coming into contact with English, whether they be

5 Braj Kachru, ed. *The Other Tongue* (Oxford: Pergamon, 1980).

aboriginal Australian or Native American languages, or other European colonial languages (*mesa* is from Spanish and *lekker* from Dutch, the other historical colonial power in South Africa). However, this type of geographical variation is superficial and creates no great impediment to communication among speakers of these various Englishes. Algeo distinguishes vocabulary common to all Englishes, items such as *computer, table, hair,* from vocabulary that is restricted to a given group of English speakers, such as the term *fit,* used by UK speakers to describe someone who is physically attractive.[6] Despite the far-flung geography of inner-circle Englishes, it is surprising in fact how little of the lexicon is actually distinctive to any one of them. Inner-circle world Englishes, in fact, share the great bulk of their core vocabulary.

If asked, many speakers would probably first point to differences in pronunciation as marking a given variety of inner-circle English as distinct from another variety. But these perceptions may be deceiving. Because we can communicate across Englishes, and do so fairly well, it is clear that while speakers of inner-circle Englishes are aware of phonological differences between and among global varieties of English, the similarities among these varieties obviously outweigh the differences.

Phonologically, Americans quickly point to "flapping" as distinguishing American and UK English. Flapping refers to the process by which a /t/ or /d/ located between two vowels is realized as a tap [ɾ] (see Chapter 4) when the stress precedes /t/ or /d/, e.g., US *better* [bɛɾəɹ], contra British [bɛtə].

Perhaps one of the most recognizable features that separate Canadian and US Standard English from the other Englishes of the world is the realization or deletion of postvocalic /r/. In Canadian and Standard US English, for example, the /r/ in *car* is pronounced, whereas that /r/ is absent in Standard UK, Australian, South African, and New Zealand English. We refer to the former as rhotic and the latter as non-rhotic varieties of English. The fact that Australian, South African, and New Zealand Englishes are, like Standard UK English, non-rhotic reflects their relatively later colonization. At the time America and Canada were made colonies of England, many speakers in England still pronounced the /r/ in words like *tar* or *cart*, although /r/-less pronunciations were spreading from the eighteenth century onward to a greater number of dialects and speakers. That pronunciation was retained in most dialects of American English. However, as we discuss later in this chapter, those regions of the US (e.g., New York, Boston, Charleston) that maintained ongoing contact with England tended to develop dialects that, like UK English, deleted postvocalic /r/.

Speakers may even be aware of slight differences in pronunciation and come to view these as markers of geography. For example, Americans are sensitive to the variations in diphthongs between American and Canadian English in a word like *about,* cf. American [əbaut] contra Canadian [əbəut], even to the point of stereotyping and exaggerating the difference.

---

6 John Algeo, "Vocabulary," in *The Cambridge History of the English Language,* Volume IV 1776–1997, ed. Suzanne Romaine (Cambridge: Cambridge UP, 1998).

The realities of shifting global politics have caused much re-evaluation of what constitutes the "English language." In the not-very-distant past, only inner-circle Englishes were considered legitimate Englishes. However, given that the majority of English speakers in the world today speak English as a second language, the centers of linguistic powers will inevitably shift. Some scholars have already begun to react to the changing realties of English and have argued for a definition of World English (English as an international language or English as a lingua franca) that includes input from outer and expanding circles.[7] However, such shifting demographics have not met with approbation from all. Prince Charles made headlines several times in the 1990s in his efforts to save what he considered to be the mother tongue. For example, in 1996, the *Guardian* quoted Prince Charles as he voiced his support for the British Council's plan to promote English. Charles argued specifically against American English as he declaimed, "We must act now to ensure that English—and that to my mind means English English—maintains its position as the world language."[8]

Outside of the inner circle, one finds greater variation among world Englishes in part due to more extensive language contact and in part due to speakers learning English as a second or additional first language. One example of such an English is Nigerian English, for which we offer a brief description.

NIGERIAN ENGLISH

One problem for describing an entity like **Nigerian English** is the difficulty in choosing which variety of the language to focus on. As discussed in the next section of this chapter, in many areas around the globe, English exists as "mixed" language, called a **pidgin** or a **creole**. A creole variety of English will show unique phonological, grammatical, and lexical characteristics, a fact that begs the question as to whether we ought to call it English or not. Nevertheless, in some areas, such as Nigeria, an English creole will exist alongside more standard varieties of English and so speakers will use a series of features or forms that range from fairly standard English to localized patois. The following description of Nigerian English leans toward the creolized variety and it is based on Faraclas (2004). The examples are generally from his description.

One feature of Nigerian English, at least in the variety we are describing here, is that it does not carry inflection for tense, aspect, mood or person, e.g., *mi sabi* (I know/knew), *yu sabi* (you know/knew), *im sabi* (he/she/it knows/knew), etc. In order to express time or mood, Nigerian English relies on auxiliary verbs, adverbs or context. This type of reduction of verb forms is regularly seen in global Englishes,

---

7   Jennifer Jenkins, *English as a Lingua Franca: Attitude and Identity* (Oxford: Oxford UP, 2007).
8   6 April 1996, quoted in Ans van Kemenade and Bettelou Los, *The Handbook of the History of English* (Oxford: Wiley-Blackwell, 2006), 596.

although again it is to be remembered that Nigerian English exists also in varieties in which verbs might inflect more like they do in Standard American or UK English. Some characteristics of the verb system in Nigerian English can be attributed to the indigenous languages spoken in the area. For example, free of any other context, a stative verb, that is one that denotes a state of being, will be understood to be present, e.g., *A sabi yu* (I know you.)[9] However, non-stative verbs, like those that show action, will be understood to be past, e.g., *A bay egusi fɔr markɛt* (I bought pumpkin at the market.)[10]

An important auxiliary verb in Nigerian English is *bin*, derived from English *been*. Nigerian auxiliary *bin* has the effect of shifting stative verbs into the past or non-stative verbs to the past before past.

> *A bin sabi yu*
> I been know you
> I knew you.

> *A bin go tawn*
> I been go town
> I had gone to town.

This use of *bin* is common in other varieties of global English as well.

Nigerian English shows another relatively common feature of global Englishes. In a copular sentence, e.g., one that uses *be* to link the subject to a noun, as in *I am a student*, or an adjective, as in *I am happy*, the verb is sometimes deleted, e.g., *A hapi* (I [am] happy). However Nigerian English also uses the copular verbs *de* and *bi*:

> *Uche bi ticha*
> Uche is teacher
> Uche is a teacher.

> *A de hapi*
> I am happy.

Nouns in Nigerian English, like those in many other varieties of global English, tend towards non-inflection for number or possession, and may or may not be

---

9 Nicholas Faraclas, "Nigerian Pidgin English: Morphology and Syntax," in *A Handbook of Varieties of English: Vol. 2, Morphology and Syntax*, edited by Bernd Kortmann, Kate Burridge, Rajend Mesthrie, Edgar W. Schneider, and Clive Upton (Berlin/New York: Mouton de Gruyter, 2004), 829.

10 Linguists working on lesser-known languages that do not have their own writing system use an adapted IPA-like alphabet for describing some of the letters. This is especially true of Africanists.

modified by the definite or indefinte article. Thus in Nigerian English the word *buk* may mean *a book, the book, books,* or *the books.* Articles do appear in Nigerian English as *di = the* and *wɔn = a/an. Wɔn* derives from English *one* and it is also common in many global varieties of English. (It will be recalled from Chapter 7 that Standard English *a/an* originally derived from the numeral *one* as well.)

Nouns may also be made plural by placing *dem* (<them) after the noun:

Di man dem de slip
The men are sleeping. (*dem* makes *man* plural and *de* means that the action is continuous.)

As mentioned above, nouns may also be uninflected for possession so that *di pikin plet* means "the child's plate." (*Pikin,* from the Portuguese word for "little," *pequinho,* is the word for *child,* and it is a very common word in global Englishes, attesting to the maritime flow and diffusion of English around the world.)

SINGAPORE ENGLISH[11]

Another example of an English in the outer circle is **Singapore English**. Singapore English shows some features in common with other global Englishes, including Nigerian English. For example, verbs tend to be uninflected for tense, aspect, mood, or person and instead time and temporal relationships are expressed by adverbials.

He eat here yesterday.
He not yet eat lunch.[12]

Perhaps related to the invariable form of verbs, tag questions of the sort *She is a doctor, isn't she?* also appear in the invariable form, *is it?*

He watching television, is it?
He is watching television, isn't he?

Invariable tags are known in other varieties of global English and even in some varieties of UK English where the invariable tag *innit?* has become increasingly used over the past several decades.[13]

---

11 Section based on Lionel Wee, "Singapore English: Morphology and Syntax," in *A Handbook of Varieties of English: Vol. 2, Morphology and Syntax,* edited by Bernd Kortmann, Kate Burridge, Rajend Mesthrie, Edgar W. Schneider, and Clive Upton (Berlin/New York: Mouton de Gruyter, 2004).

12 Wee, "Singapore English," 1059.

13 Jenny Cheshire, "Variation in the Use of Ain't in an Urban British Dialect," *Language in Society* 10:3 (1981).

In Singapore English, too, simple copular sentences may appear without the verb *be*, a feature we also saw in Nigerian English:

The house very nice.[14]

Be does not appear in progressive structures either:

The baby crying a lot.
The baby is crying a lot.

However, progressive aspect is still detectable in the *-ing* form of the verb.

Nouns, as in many other varieties of global English, like Nigerian English, often appear in an invariable form; that is, they are not inflected for number:

She queue up very long to buy ticket for us.
She lined up for a very long time in order to buy tickets for us.[15]

However, note that in *English in New Cultural Contexts*, Alsagoff and Ho suggest that *ticket* may not be merely an inflected noun but an example in which *ticket* has been reanalyzed as a non-count noun and thus unavailable for number distinction.[16] Also similar to nouns in Nigerian English, nouns in Singapore English tend to occur without an article.

In our short description of Nigerian English, we noted that certain unique features of that variety were due to influence from the indigenous languages spoken in the area. Singapore English too shows some features that appear to be influenced by grammatical processes in Chinese. For example, in Singapore English, speakers make use of the process of **reduplication**, that is the repetition of a word to derive a new meaning:

Where is your boy-boy?
Where is your boyfriend?

A similar process is also found in Chinese. Certain words may be reduplicated to derive a new word. For example, the verb *zǒu* means "walk," but reduplicated as *zǒu-zǒu*, it means *walk a little*.[17]

---

14 Wee, "Singapore English," 1060.
15 Wee, "Singapore English," 1061, from Lubna Alsagoff and Ho Chee Lick, "The Grammar of Singapore English," in *English in New Cultural Contexts: Reflections from Singapore*, edited by J.A. Foley, Thiru Kandiah, Bao Zhiming, A.F. Gupta, L. Alsagoff, Ho Chee Lick, Lionel Wee, I.S. Talib, and W. Bokhorst-Heng (Singapore: Singapore Institute of Management/Oxford UP, 1998), 144.
16 Alsagoff and Ho, 104.
17 Charles Li and Sandra Thompson, *Mandarin Chinese: A Functional Reference Grammar* (Berkeley and Los Angeles: U of California P, 1981), 29.

As noted earlier, the study of outer-circle varieties of English is more difficult in some respects than is the study of inner-circle varieties. In part, the difficulty has to do with availability of sources, and to this point we might note that Singapore English has a much "richer" set of descriptions in the literature than does Nigerian English, much of this literature having to do with the teaching of English. That fact is likely related to the emergence of Singapore as an economic center in Asia. However, both Nigerian and Singapore English are also difficult to study because it is not easy to talk about them in absolute terms. Speakers of those varieties shift their linguistic behavior between international and domestic varieties of English and local languages, like Igbo and Hausa (in Nigeria), and Chinese and Malay (in Singapore), creating a continuum of linguistic forms, a point we return to in the next section.

AMERICAN ENGLISH

The earliest settlement of English speakers in what would eventually become the United States was the colony founded in 1585 on the island of Roanoke, off the coast of what is now North Carolina. Although the Roanoke colony remains significant as the first settlement (and we will return to its significance to originary narratives for at least one variety of American English), that colony was completely abandoned within a few years of its establishment, leaving only traces of occupation on the island. The first permanent settlements of English speakers in North America were not until a generation later: the 1607 settlement at Jamestown, followed by the 1620 Pilgrim settlement in Plymouth and the 1630 settlement of Puritans in Massachusetts Bay. Although settlers arrived in relatively small numbers initially (the settlement at Jamestown began with only about 105 men and boys), and although, especially at Jamestown, violent conflicts with native populations continued, British settlement increased dramatically: by 1640 about 25,000 immigrants had settled near Plymouth.[18]

External factors that affect language change include geographic isolation and language contact, both clearly operative in the early colonies. The terms **founder's principle** and **colonial lag** are sometimes used to refer to the ways that transplanted languages are established and develop. The founder's principle refers to the fact that the features of a dialect of a certain area will be, at least in part, a reflex of the dialect(s) spoken by the population who initially settle in a new area. And this is certainly the case with certain of the features found in various American dialects. However, speakers from different dialect areas found themselves in situations in which accommodation of one another's language was necessary in the new American

---

18 Bruce Levine, Stephen Brier, David Brundage, Edward Countryman, Dorothy Fennell, and Marcus Redicker, *Who Built America? Working People and the Nation's Economy, Politics, Culture, and Society*, Volume 1 (New York: Pantheon, 1989), 41, and Crystal, *The Cambridge Encyclopedia of the English Language*, 92.

colonies, and under such forces some dialect features were lost. Colonial lag refers to the phenomenon that transplanted colonial languages will sometimes show apparent archaisms due to the fact that ongoing changes that affect the language in its original setting will not reach the colonial variety of the language until later, or even at all.

What is fair to say is that all languages change all the time, and while some things change, some stay the same. The original English dialects of the first settlers in England may have changed after settlement, but the new settlement varieties changed too in America, although perhaps in different ways. In some cases both the original and the American variety retained some shared features. Therefore we study dialects in terms of both **innovation** and **retention**.

Isolated from Britain by the expanse of the Atlantic, settlers sometimes retained features of English that characterized the English spoken in Britain at the time of their departure. As English in Britain changed, in some instances those changes were not carried to the colonies and incorporated into the English spoken in the colonies (for a discussion of rhotic/non-rhotic varieties of English, see pp. 276–77). Language contact also contributed to the development of American English, as English-speaking settlers interacted both with Native Americans and with French, Spanish, and Dutch settlers.

Part of the unique nature of American English is a result of its contact with Native American languages. During the period of early settlement, speakers of English borrowed a number of words from Native American languages, especially from the Algonquian languages, like Delaware. (Sometimes the words came into English from Spanish or French, which had in turn borrowed the word from a Native American language. The borrowed words that have survived in American English tend to be names for plants, animal species, and features of the landscape as well as some aspects of Native American life as the settlers experienced it. This pattern of borrowing we have already encountered in our discussion of borrowings into English from Celtic languages during the early Old English period. Borrowings from Native American languages into English from this period similarly reflect the nature of the contact, and include place names and words for native plant and animal species like *squash*, *moose*, *hickory*, and *pecan* as well as *canoe*, *wampum*, and *tomahawk*.[19]

A few of these borrowings take their current form in PDE as the result of a process called **folk etymology**. This process occurs across languages: it is not a phenomenon limited to borrowings during this period. In folk etymology, an unfamiliar-sounding word or phrase is changed so that it appears to make more sense within the lexicon of a language. In American English, the unfamiliar-sounding borrowed word *otchek* developed into *woodchuck*, by folk etymology. Similarly, *muskwessu* became *muskrat*, and *achitam* became *chipmunk*—all of which sound less foreign to English ears.

While one does have to conclude that the effect of Native American languages on English did not change the language to any great degree, and while one would be

---

19   Albert C. Baugh and Thomas Cable, *A History of the English Language* (5th edition) (Upper Saddle River, NJ: Prentice Hall, 2002), 362.

correct in understanding the tides of linguistic flow to be against Native American languages generally, including complete loss of many of those languages since the colonial period, a closer look at the linguistic situation in the early colonial period reveals instances in which the Native Americans held the upper hand in language negotiations. For example, some early settlers learned a simplified version of Delaware in order to be able to operate in their new environment. In 1643, Roger Williams published his book, *A Key into the Language of America, or an Help to the Language of the Natives in that part of America, called New England*. The appearance of such a book at that time suggests a desire to know the language of the Native Americans, knowledge recognized as necessary for successful settlement in the new land.[20]

The early period of colonial America spans from the early seventeenth century, when English-speaking settlers numbered in the hundreds, to the end of the eighteenth century, when European immigrants numbered as many as four million. Although it may certainly be argued that in the period from 1607 until the end of the eighteenth century a number of varieties of English developed which could be identified as American Englishes, as we have argued with respect to the development of English at other stages of its external history, the explicit association of a variety of English with a political identity underscores the distinctiveness of that variety of English. While a descriptive analysis of the varieties of English spoken in the North American colonies would certainly show differences from the varieties of English spoken in Britain, it is only during the Revolutionary period of the last quarter of the eighteenth century that American English began to be located rhetorically as positively identifying Americans, and as marking not just a linguistic, but also a political, and even a perceived moral distinction between Americans and the British.

The American lexicographer **Noah Webster** (1758–1843), for example, in his 1789 *Dissertations on the English Language*, wrote, "As an independent nation, our honor requires us to have a system of our own, in language as well as government. Great Britain, whose children we are, and whose language we speak, should no longer be our standard; for the taste of her writers is already corrupted, and her language on the decline."[21] In this passage, Webster acknowledges that Americans and the British speak the same language. But at the same time he argues that American *political* identity should correspond to a distinctive *linguistic* identity. As Webster argued for the importance of a distinctive American orthography, for example, he wrote, explicitly, that a "national language is a band of national union. Every engine should be employed to render the people of this country national; to call their attachments home to their own country, and to inspire them with the pride of national character."[22] Even spelling—or especially spelling—for Webster was political and inseparable from national identity.

---

20   K. Aaron Smith and Susan M. Kim, "Colonialism: Linguistic Accommodation and English Language Change," in *Teaching the History of the English Language*, edited by Colette Craig and Chris Palmer (New York: MLA, forthcoming).

21   Quoted in Baugh and Cable, *A History of the English Language*, 367.

22   Baugh and Cable, *A History of the English Language*, 368.

FIGURE 10.1   1829 edition of Webster's *The American Spelling Book*.

Webster would back up his argument with the creation of both a dictionary of American English, published in 1828, and a number of grammar texts that not simply recorded but also created and reinforced a number of distinctive American spellings. The preface to Webster's dictionary, not surprisingly, combined lexicography with explicit political content. He writes, "It is not only important, but, in a degree necessary, that the people of this country, should have an American Dictionary of the English Language; for, although the body of the language is the same as in England, and it is desirable to perpetuate that sameness, yet some differences must exist,"[23] and notes that words such as "senate," for example, must have different meanings in England than they do in America. Webster also published a revision of his *Dissertations on the English Language*, retitled *The American Spelling Book*. Similar to the dictionary in its explicit political association with American, rather than British identity, *The American Spelling Book* included an appendix featuring "a moral catechism" and "a federal catechism" with questions like "What are the faults of despotic

---

23   Noah Webster, *An American Dictionary of the English Language* (Online edition, accessed 26 May 2016).

governments?" and "What are the peculiar advantages of representative governments?" *The American Spelling Book*, used as a textbook throughout the States, sold as many as 80,000 copies in the century following its publication. Spellings Webster advocated and that continue in present-day American orthography include *-or* rather than *-our* in words like *color*, *-er*, rather than *-re*, in words like *center*, and the dropping of *-e* in words like *ax*. While small in number, Webster's unique American spellings made it possible for readers to know within a few words of any text whether the text was American or British, a rather effective way for a new country to assert itself. Canadian and Australian conventions tend to be a mix of American and British. Canadian orthography, for example, uses *-our* in words like *honour*, but spells *tire* as in the US, as opposed to the British *tyre*.

EXERCISE

10.1 **Based on the spellings in the following sentences, would you ascribe the sentence to an American author, a British author, or perhaps even an author writing in a different orthographic tradition? State explicitly why you make that assumption.**

a. You will find the most interesting museums located in the City Centre, near the National Opera House.
b. While the color scheme seemed shocking at first, Larry slowly began to appreciate the bold juxtaposition of the three primary colors in the landscape design.
c. Samuel and Franklin decided to go to the theater to see the revival performance of *Cat on a Hot Tin Roof*.
d. The general's honour has been fully restored with his exoneration for any wrongdoings in the battle.
e. Designed in 1924, the motorcar on display was rumoured to have been the first to utilize rubber tires.

IMMIGRATION IN THE NINETEENTH CENTURY

During the nineteenth century, a number of waves of immigration brought large numbers of settlers to the United States from countries other than England. For example, during and after the Great Potato Famine in Ireland in 1845–49 as many as one million people immigrated to the United States from Ireland. German settlers after the German revolutions of 1848 continued to immigrate to the United States, with total immigration in the millions before the end of the nineteenth century. Following the start of the Gold Rush, Chinese immigrants in the late nineteenth century arrived in increasingly large numbers, reaching the hundreds of thousands until the Chinese Exclusion Act of 1882. Scandinavians settled particularly in the Midwest, with 150,000 immigrants from Sweden alone arriving in the US between 1861 and 1881.[24] Patterns of settlement of these groups of non-English-speaking immigrants would contribute to the development of the regional dialects we will discuss below.

German immigrants in particular were a large and influential group in some parts of the colonies and in early America. Folk histories often maintain the myth that the new American republic nearly adopted German as its official language. The history of the German language (sometimes identified as Dutch, as in Pennsylvania Dutch) in America is certainly an interesting one, and its significance in certain areas should not be underestimated. The first Bible published in America in 1743 was in German (the first English Bible would not appear until 1782), and the signing of the Declaration of Independence was first reported in a German newspaper in Pennsylvania.[25] Still, the linguistic threat of German to the dominance of English is greatly exaggerated, and Bailey notes that the only well-known word borrowed into Colonial English from German was *sauerkraut*—hardly a very profound influence![26]

SLAVERY

Although immigration statistics include the coerced immigration of indentured servants from Europe, here we must pause to address the fact of slavery in pre-Civil War America, which involved the violent and forced "immigration" of millions of people from Africa and the Caribbean into the American colonies/United States. The effects of slavery are profound in terms of not only American identities but also American English.

European enslavement of Africans dates to the middle of the fifteenth century. During the three centuries of the racialized slavery that characterized the Early Modern and Modern periods, ten to twelve million Africans were enslaved and transported to the New World.[27] From a population of about 2,500 in 1700, the number of African slaves in the American colonies grew to 10,000 by 1800.[28] By the start of the Civil War in 1861, 4,000,000 enslaved African-Americans were living in the United States. The Civil War concluded in 1865, and the Thirteenth Amendment, ratified and adopted in 1865, abolished slavery as an institution in the United States. Many effects of centuries of racialized slavery remained, however, and persist to this day.

24   Library of Congress, "Scandinavian Immigration" (www.loc.gov, accessed 24 November 2012).
25   Richard W. Bailey, *Speaking American: A History of English in the United States* (Oxford: Oxford UP, 2012), 81.
26   Ibid., 84
27   Bruce Levine et al., *Who Built America*, 25.
28   Crystal, *The Cambridge Encyclopedia of the English Language*, 94.

The linguistic legacy of enslaved Africans and their descendants is a central topic in the history of English and we will return to it shortly.

GEOGRAPHIC VARIATION

In some ways, at least historically, the distribution of geographic dialects in the US reflects the variety of English that different settlers brought with them from England, or other English-speaking areas in the British Isles, Scotland, and Ireland, although such a scenario is not without controversies. While several scholars have put forward schemes in which the major dialect areas of the US even today are traceable to the dialects of the original settlers (Fischer[29] is an accessible and popular study along these lines, albeit one that has received considerable criticism), others have contended that the dialect distribution in the present-day US owes little to British antecedents.

Indeed, it is a very difficult task to link British dialect features to American dialect forms in any kind of very direct way and it is important to resist an oversimplified scenario of transplanted dialects. Immigration to and the settling of America has involved a series of protracted and heterogeneous processes, and the linguistic influences involved in those processes have depended on sociocultural ties of varying strengths with England (but of course with other nations too). Consequently any account of US dialects that attempts to locate its features in varieties of British English (or from influence from or contact with other languages) must be accompanied by immigration histories that would support specific diffusion scenarios. Too often it is the case that co-identity of a given form on both sides of the Atlantic has led to hasty transplant theories.[30] Here we present a broad view of those transplant theories that seem most likely while accepting the imperative that there is still much research to be done, much of it involving fairly straightforward description of US and British varieties of English.

When discussing dialects in the US, it is common to refer to dialect maps, like the one shown below. In that map we can see the four major dialect areas of US English: Northern, Midland, Southern and Western, with the Midland area broken into north and south regions. The map offers a broad view of US dialects; there are many subdivisions in each of the areas. For example, Pederson lists finer divisions within the Northern dialect region:[31] northeastern New England, southeastern New England, metropolitan New York City, southwestern New England, Hudson Valley, Inland North (western Vermont, Upstate New York, across the Great Lakes, and into Iowa, Minnesota, and the Dakotas). Similar divisions can be made for the other dialect areas too.

29   David Hackett Fischer, *Albion's Seed: Four British Folkways in America* (Oxford/New York: Oxford UP, 1989).

30   Michael Montgomery, "British and Irish Antecedents," in The Cambridge *History of the English Language, Volume VI: English in North America*, edited by John Algeo (Cambridge: Cambridge UP, 2001), 86–88.

31   Ibid., 289, and see Hans Kurath, *A Word Geography of the Eastern United States* (Ann Arbor, MI: U of Michigan P, 1949) for an earlier version of this general scheme.

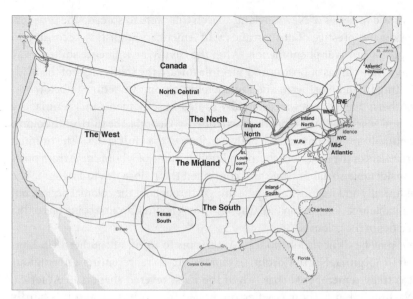

FIGURE 10.2   US dialect map. Labov, William, Sharon Ash, and Charles Boberg. Map 11.15, from *The Atlas of North American English*. Walter De Gruyter and Company, 2006. Reprinted with the permission of Walter De Gruyter and Company via Copyright Clearance Center, Inc.

The Northern dialect area was settled quite early and chiefly by Pilgrims and later Puritans. Puritan settlers tended to be upper or upper-middle class and in fact many of their leaders were Cambridge-educated.[32] The linguistic identity of the early settlers was considerably homogeneous since they tended to come from similar groups in England and were attracted to settlement towns for religious purposes; even those who might have come from different locations would have felt significant pressure to conform linguistically. Many areas of Coastal Northern, especially Boston and southward to New York City, are non-rhotic, while other Coastal Northern and virtually all Inland Northern varieties are rhotic. At the time when the Puritans settled New England, postvocalic /r/ would probably have been lost in a limited number of contexts, but the speech of the upper-class settlers would likely have favored some rhotic over non-rhotic forms. Postvocalic /r/ would remain over much of New England, but continued relationships with England, where the loss of postvocalic /r/ continued, influenced the non-rhoticity that we so strongly associate with places like Boston. At the time settlers moved westward into what would become the Midwest,

---

32 John Algeo, "External History," in *The Cambridge History of the English Language, Volume VI: English in North America*, edited by John Algeo (Cambridge: Cambridge UP, 2001), 8.

it was the rhotic varieties of New England speech that were to spread. The broader-scale adoption and prestige of postvocalic /r/ in American English is, according to Fisher,[33] a post–Civil War phenomenon. After the Civil War, influence shifted away from the non-rhotic areas of Boston and Virginia toward the rhotic areas of the Midwest (including Inland Northern) and Philadelphia, a point we return to below.

The Southern dialect area was originally rooted in settlements in Virginia, the Carolinas, and Maryland, and from there extended to Georgia, the thirteenth colony. It then eventually spread across most of the territory of the Gulf states. The original European settlers of the area were southern English, some of whom came from positions of considerable social prestige and continued their close ties to England. The area was ethnically and linguistically quite diverse throughout the colonial period, but it was a profitable area, Charleston (i.e., Charles Town), South Carolina being one of the wealthiest cities in the colonies.[34]

While it may be difficult for modern Americans to think of southern US English spoken in Virginia, North Carolina, Georgia, etc. as representing a prestigious dialect, it is to be remembered that two of the most revered shapers of America, George Washington and Thomas Jefferson, hailed from Virginia and it is hardly coincidental that the capital of the US came to be located in that general dialect area. However, the prestige of southeastern speech was always associated with the upper class and educated gentry, one that often enough owned plantations. While many of the original settlers would have been speakers of a rhotic variety of English, one consequence of the continued continental relationships was to follow fashionable trends in England, including speech. In fact, aristocratic families would often send their children to England to be educated, and that education would only inspire loss of postvocalic /r/. But loss of /r/ in certain southern varieties of English may well also be the influenced by the non-rhotic speech among the sizable slave population.[35]

The Midlands area is appropriately discussed in two stages of immigration, the first giving root to the northern Midland and the second to the southern Midland dialect. The Mid-Atlantic region was from the beginning settled by a more heterogeneous group than were the northern or southern dialect regions. Settled by Quakers and other groups from various parts of England and Germany seeking to escape religious persecution, speakers of that area likely found it necessary to accommodate one another's speech more than in other areas of the colonies. Although the English Quakers were predominantly from the north of England, linguistic accommodation of the sort described here had the effect of creating a variety of Colonial English different from northern or southern Colonial Englishes. The immigrants tended to be from the artisan classes whose skills in industries such as furniture making were highly valued in the early days of America. That early Quaker-settlement English, centered in Philadelphia (the City of Brotherly Love, founded by the Quaker leader

33   Algeo, "External History," 75–76.
34   Bailey, *Speaking American*, 48.
35   Algeo, "External History," 49.

William Penn) became the partial source of the northern Midland dialect, although there appear also southern English features.

A rather long wave of immigration, spanning the entire eighteenth century, brought a large number of immigrants from northern England, Scotland, and Northern Ireland, a group referred to collectively as the Scotch-Irish, sometimes called Ulster Scots. This wave of immigrants differed from the northern, southern, and Quaker settlers in that they did not seek refuge from religious or political persecution, but instead sought economic betterment in the so-called New World. Thus the Scotch-Irish immigrants tended not to be of the wealthy, educated, or artisan classes, but from those classes lower on the economic scale. However, if the Scotch-Irish hoped to escape prejudice and discrimination in the colonies and early American nation, their hopes were soon dashed. Upon arrival, they were encouraged to keep moving into the coastal hinterlands as the Quakers found them to be objectionable in dress, manners, and language.[36] The Scotch-Irish were thought to be bellicose and given to clan warfare.[37] As previously mentioned, some settled in the northern inland area of Massachusetts, but many more arrived in Philadelphia and from there moved to western Pennsylvania and the mountainous areas of Maryland and the Carolinas, and eventually settled the Appalachian region. Later speakers of that group moved into Arkansas, Missouri, and Texas. They are the source of the southern Midland dialect and also played a significant role in the development of the northern Midland dialect.

Even today there are a number of features that connect both the North and South Midland dialect areas to the source locations of the Scotch-Irish, as for example the use of the past participle after the verb *need*, as in *The car needs washed*. While the construction is current in Scotland and the north and south Midland regions, it is generally rejected by speakers of the Northern and New England dialect areas (even its acceptance in the south Midland area is not uniform).

Having just reviewed the geographically and linguistically diverse makeup of the colonial settlers, it may be somewhat surprising to learn that several British visitors and immigrants to the colonies remarked that Americans spoke in a remarkably uniform way. The Reverend Jonathan Boucher noted that "In North America, there prevails not only, I believe, the purest Pronunciation of the English Tongue that is anywhere to be met with, but a perfect uniformity."[38]

Some scholars have taken such accounts at face value, and used them to assert the theory that pervasive dialect mixing leveled variation in America.[39] By such theories, then, British antecedents would not be very relevant for the establishment of American dialectal patterns. Obviously American English did not exhibit "perfect uniformity," and indeed travelers to the colonies did from time to time comment on

36 Fischer, *Albion's Seed*, 605–06.
37 Fischer, *Albion's Seed*, 620ff.
38 Quoted in Daniel J. Boorstin, *The Americans: The Colonial Experience* (New York: Random House, 1964), 274.
39 J.L. Dillard, *Black English* (New York: Random House, 1972).

differences too. Furthermore, given that so many of the uniformity observations are accompanied by other statements of praise for the language in America, particularly in terms of correctness, we might assume that the reported uniformity may have been more apparent than actual, fueled by esteem for the democratic experiment of the new United States. Cooley[40] is probably correct in saying that variation was simply recognized by some and not by others.

A NOTE ON RHOTACISM

A phonetic feature that speakers of Englishes around the globe would be likely to list as a shibboleth of American and British English is the presence or absence of **postvocalic /r/**, introduced briefly in the first part of this chapter. The term "postvocalic" refers to the /r/ after a vowel. The impression that most Americans and British have is that postvocalic /r/ is pronounced in American but omitted in British English. That is, however, only partly the case. In reality, as we note above, some dialects in America and Britain pronounce postvocalic /r/ and some do not pronounce postvocalic /r/. As mentioned earlier, the founder's principle explains, at least in part, the American distribution.

In England, the southern varieties showed variable /r/-lessness already by the time of American settlement, although in a rather limited set of contexts. Northern England, although now showing increasing loss of postvocalic /r/, was presumably still mostly rhotic in the seventeenth and eighteenth centuries; that is, speakers articulated postvocalic /r/ at the time of the settlement of the colonies. Given that the Puritan settlers along coastal New England and the settlers of the southern colonies were often from the south of England, it is expected that the source speech for the coastal northern and southern dialect areas would have shown some variation in the pronunciation of postvocalic /r/ earlier on. However, the /r/-lessness of those dialect areas probably cannot be explained by that fact alone, and it is certain that sustained contact with southern England continued to influence the loss of /r/ (see above on southern Colonial English). The Midland US dialect region, however, remained rhotic in character.

The wider perception that US speakers have rhotic pronunciations of postvocalic /r/ while UK speakers have non-rhotic realizations of /r/ following a vowel stems from the fact that the standard varieties of American and British Englishes do follow such a rhotic/non-rhotic distinction. Again, there are some dialects in the UK that do remain rhotic in the north, and Irish and Scottish English are largely rhotic too. In America, non-rhotic varieties persist in many northern coastal and inland areas, e.g., Boston, and some parts of the southern dialect region are marked by non-rhoticism, although there is some evidence to suggest a wider-spread movement toward rhotic pronunciations in the south.

---

40   Marianne Cooley, "Emerging Standard and Subdialectal Variation in Early American English," *Diachronica* 9 (1992): 184.

In fact, non-rhotic varieties of American English maintained a certain amount of prestige until the middle of the twentieth century. However, after the Civil War cultural influence in the US shifted away from the non-rhotic areas of Boston and Virginia and towards the rhotic Midwest and Philadelphia thus establishing the pronunciation of postvocalic /r/ as the norm for American English.[41]

Study of the history of media in the US reveals an interesting competition regarding the prestige of postvocalic /r/. In the early part of the twentieth century the movie industry had settled on a mid-Atlantic pronunciation, so called because it wasn't really American and it wasn't really British, but rather was located somewhere in between. One feature of that mid-Atlantic English was the dropping of postvocalic /r/. One can listen to the /r/-less diction of actresses like Joan Crawford in 1930s and 1940s films. Joan Crawford was born and grew up in the American West (Texas, Oklahoma) and would not be expected to drop postvocalic /r/ as a natural feature of her dialect. However, while the movie industry promulgated /r/-lessness, the American standard had moved westward and would come to be based on an ill-defined "Midwestern" dialect, perhaps in part linked to the growing turn-of-the century prestige of Chicago as an American metropolis.[42] It would be that vague Midwestern that broadcasters would adopt as the standard for radio and television, thereby "making" American English rhotic.

MAPPING DIALECTS

A dialect map shows dialect boundaries (represented by the lines on the dialect map above), and a key concept in establishing dialect boundaries is the **isogloss**. An isogloss is the line of demarcation between two linguistic variants. For example, a linguist might collect data from speakers in the Midwest to discover the line that separates out the places where speakers use *paper bag* versus *paper sack*, as in the figure below.

Additional isogloss tests in the same area would reveal a number of variable features that would likely run roughly along the same general line as the *paper bag ~ paper sack* isogloss, e.g., the pronunciation of [ɔ] versus [ɑ] in *caught*, the use of *pail* versus *bucket*, etc.[43] When a number of such isoglosses occur together, then the geographic line etched out by so many changing features represents an actual dialect boundary. In this case, the **dialect boundary** established is that between the northern Midland and Northern dialect areas seen on the larger dialect map that appears at the beginning of this section.

One further interesting note is the fact that some dialect boundaries run along major US interstates, a fact that is not mere coincidence. Dialect boundaries frequently reflect older migration patterns and the interstate system was often built on

---

41 John Hurt Fisher, "British and American Continuity and Divergence," in *The Cambridge History of the English Language, Volume VI: English in North America*, edited by John Algeo (Cambridge: Cambridge UP, 2001), 59–85.

42 Bailey, *Speaking American*, Chap. 9.

43 George Yule, *The Study of Language* (4th edition) (Cambridge: Cambridge UP, 2010), 243.

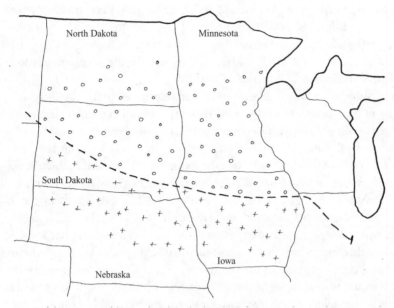

FIGURE 10.3 **Dialect map showing the distribution of "paper bag" and "paper sack" in the Midwest, from *The Study of Language*, 6th Edition, by George Yule. Cambridge University Press, 2017. Reprinted with the permission of Cambridge University Press.**

US highways, roads that had been earlier migration routes. Even today the relationship between dialect and the interstate system can be seen in so far as dialectologists will talk of the "Chicago–St. Louis corridor" an area in which certain dialect features are shared that are not found outside of that stretch of land. The corridor is the site of the former and famed Route 66 and is today Interstate 55 in Illinois.[44]

The map also shows that the western part of the US has fewer dialect areas than in the eastern part of the country. We can attribute this fact to two causes. First of all, settlers in the west came from many different locations in the east and Midwest, and therefore there was much dialect mixing. In conditions of dialect mixing, speakers tend to accommodate one another and dialect differences are reduced. Secondly, the west was settled much more recently and there has not been as much time for new dialect differences to become entrenched.

Impressionistically, most of us have noticed that geographical dialect variation appears to have reduced or leveled out, particularly among speakers of classes that

---

44 Lauren A. Friedman, "A Convergence of Dialects in the St. Louis Corridor," *University of Pennsylvania Working Papers in Linguistics* (*Selected Papers from New Ways of Analyzing Variation*), 21.2 (2015).

have access to certain kinds of education and mobility that puts them into contact with speakers from other geographical areas. In addition to exposure there is yet another reason for the apparent reduction in regional variation in modern American English: migration into cities. In 1910, only 28 per cent of Americans lived in cities, while that percentage grew to 80 per cent in 2000.[45] Obviously, in such a scenario there is considerable dialect mixing and in such cases there occurs leveling, that is, loss of distinctiveness of geographical dialect. This is not to say that geographical variation will be lost or is no longer of interest to a history of English, but it does impel us to look at other ways that language may vary among speakers as well.

One remarkable thing about the study of dialect forms is that they reoccur over many different dialects, and this fact may well contribute to the perception of American sameness discussed earlier. In other words, it is rarely the case that a given feature marks exclusively a single dialect. Take for example dialect features that mark the "Okie" dialect in John Steinbeck's *Grapes of Wrath*:[46]

"Pa," he said, "if <u>you was</u> to rush her one side an' me the other an' then the res' pile on...." (p. 232)

"I didn' even know it when I was <u>a-preachin'</u> aroun.... " (p. 233)

"If I <u>ain't</u> gonna preach <u>no</u> more, I gotta get married." (p. 233)

"if we'll bring <u>our'n</u> over and breed 'em...." (p. 38)

The features found in these passages include paradigm leveling (*you was*), *a*-prefixed present participle (*a-preachin'*), use of *ain't* and multiple negation (*ain't... no*), and possessive -*n* (*our'n*). The "Okie" dialect that Steinbeck represents would be from the south Midland dialect area.

Sarah Orne Jewett, in her novel *The Country of the Pointed Firs*, offers a representation of New England English:[47]

"When <u>we was</u> young together his mother didn't favor the match...." (p. 7)

"an' we get <u>a-talkin'</u> together an' have real pleasant times." (p. 51)

"I <u>ain't nothin'</u> like so handy with a conveyance as I be with a b'ot." (p. 85)

"I been lottin' all the way on a cup o' that best tea o' <u>yourn</u>." (p. 57)

---

45 United States Census Bureau. "Demographic Trends in the 20th Century." Census 2000 Special Reports. By Frank Hobbs and Nicole Stoops. November 2002, 33. https://www.census.gov/history/pdf/1970suburbs.pdf.

46 Originally published in 1939. Here we cite the 1992 edition by Penguin.

47 Originally published in 1896. Here we cite the 2000 Signet Classic edition by Penguin.

We find Jewett using the exact same dialect features to represent the speech of her characters speaking a dialect far-flung from the south Midland dialect area. Why then do we have the impression that these dialects are so different? One reason may be phonological; we tend to perceive differences in accent as being highly significant when determining language varieties and pay less attention to morphology and syntax, a point made earlier. We also tend to focus on differences in lexicon, and in fact there are real differences in vocabulary between dialects.

However, another reason that we may have the impression of so great a difference among dialects that otherwise may share a number of forms is that we do not only "hear" with our ears. We appear to carry with us an expectation of dialect difference and that expectation is closely tied to cultural stereotypes. An approach to dialect study known as perceptual dialectology is based in this notion of evaluative variation.[48]

It is for this reason that speakers can associate the same linguistic form, like *ain't*, with quaintness when encountered in one dialect, but with ignorance and even immorality when encountered in another. The problematic association between language prejudice and speaker identity becomes especially acute when we consider variation that occurs among speakers that correlates with social affiliations.

EXERCISES

10.2 The following are questions excerpted from the questionnaire administered by the researchers for the *Dictionary of American Regional English* between 1960 and 1975.[49] All of these questions came under the heading "food."

Work through the questions yourself. Are you aware of a difference between what you would say in response to the question, and what you would recognize as a term used in your household, or in your community as you were growing up?

  a. The meal that people eat around the middle of the day:
  b. The meal that people eat at the end of the day:
     (The same every day?)
  c. Are the names of meals the same on Sundays as on weekdays?
  d. If somebody never eats very much food, you say he's a _____.

---

48   Dennis Preston, *Perceptual Dialectology: Nonlinguists' Views of Areal Linguistics* (Berlin: de Gruyter, 1989).

49   DARE Surveys and Fieldwork, 1965–70 (http://dare.wisc.edu, accessed 14 September 2017).

e. If somebody eats rapidly and noisily, you say he _____.
f. Bread that's made with cornmeal: (Explain differences.)
g. What do you mean by a biscuit?
   How are they made?
h. Kinds of soup favored around here:
   —any specialties? (Open question)
i. Kinds of sausage that people around here especially favor:
j. Other kinds of roll or bun sandwiches favored around here—in a round bun or roll:
k. Dishes made with meat, fish, or poultry that everybody around here would know, but that people in other places might not:
l. Dishes made with beans, peas, or corn that everybody around here knows, but people in other places might not:
m. Names for different kinds of pickles favored around here:
n. Kinds of desserts especially favored by people around here:

Try asking family members these questions. Do they provide answers congruent with those you provided? Do you notice a difference in the pattern of answers that corresponds to generational differences among the respondents?

SOCIOLECTS

Despite a certain degree of geographical dialect leveling, it is apparently human nature to mark perceived differences among ourselves by language; in fact, expression of social identities, which may sometimes be due to geographic allegiance, may be an underrated function of language. In recent years especially, linguists have gained new perspectives on variation that is defined not only by geographic location but also by social identities, such as racial affiliation or socioeconomic class. Linguists refer to such varieties as **sociolects**, a blend of the words *social* and *dialect*, hence a sociolect is a social dialect.

Sociolectal variation may be studied along any number of lines involving social identities. Some of the most common varieties to have been studied are those defined by identities involving gender, age, socioeconomics, and ethnic affiliation. The term "defined" here is being used in a fairly technical way, referring to the fact that the boundaries of a given sociolect are established by isoglosses that can be established between speakers of differing social groups. As with geographic isoglosses, there is much overlap and continuity. An important caveat is to remember that social identities *are not essential*. In fact, social identities are arguably less important in terms of what is and more relevant as we consider what a person believes himself or herself to be. For example, a person may be extrinsically identified as male, but may identify as female. That person's speech then may show features of language more in line with typical female speech or speech typical of male-to-female-identifying individuals, a sociolect that may be similar to but not identical with female speech, i.e., may share overlapping isogloss boundaries.

GENDER AND LANGUAGE

Sociolinguists have spent much time studying the language of men and women in attempts to find differences in language form and usage. Some of the differences that have been suggested are that women use more descriptive and flattering language, e.g., adjectives like *fabulous, adorable, cute*, or that they employ more hedges such as, *you know, sort of*, and *kind of*.[50] Others have suggested those differences may be more perceptual than empirical.[51] Other studies have considered the question of male and female language in terms of discourse patterns or conversations. H. Leet-Pelligrini, for example, reported on observations of pairs of individuals in which one of the interlocutors was made "expert" on a given topic.[52] Males who had been made expert in such instances were interpreted as using the expert information as a source for dominance in conversation, whereas women were said to have taught the expert information to their conversation partner. It is important again to remember that what is at issue is not whether a person is a biological male or female; what gives rise to different patterns of speech associated with gender is about acculturation and (self) identification as a "man" or "woman."

Languages other than English sometimes show even greater differences between male- and female-identifying speakers; in some cases resulting in different grammatical forms. For example, in Japanese, there are different forms of the first-person pronoun. While all Japanese speakers can use the unmarked form *watashi* for *I*, other forms of the pronoun are only available to males or females. Thus, *boku* is another way of saying *I* in Japanese by males and *atashi* is used to say *I* by females. In Koasati, a Native American language spoken in Louisiana, words have different grammatical endings depending on whether the speaker is a male or a female

Another way in which gender and language have been studied is through analysis of discourse patterns used by individuals who identify as gay men, for instance. In such studies it has been suggested that interlocutors in gay male groups participate in **cooperative discourse**, that is using certain discourse strategies to build and continue discursive exchanges.[53] Those strategies include verbal sparring and allu-

50 Robin Lakoff, *Language and Women's Place* (New York: Harper and Row, 1975).

51 Suzanne Romaine, *Language in Society* (2nd edition) (Oxford: Oxford UP, 2000), Chapter 4.

52 H. Leet-Pelligrini, "Conversational Dominance as a Function of Gender and Expertise," in *Language: Social Psychological Perspectives*, ed. Howard Giles, W.P. Robinson, and Philip Smith (Oxford: Pergamon, 1980).

53 William L. Leap, *Word's Out: Gay Men's English* (Minneapolis: U of Minnesota P, 1996).

sion to popular figures in gay culture. The development and maintenance of such lects provide a site of co-identifying behaviors for individuals who view themselves as part of groups that at times feel set apart from mainstream society.

SOCIOLECT AND SOCIAL CLASS

A pioneering and widely cited example of sociolectal variation along socioeconomic lines is William Labov's study of speakers in New York City in the mid-1960s. Specifically, Labov was interested in the rates of variation of postvocalic /r/, a feature discussed earlier in this chapter in several places. Labov had noticed that /r/-less (non-rhotic) pronunciations in NYC were more likely among working-class individuals and /r/-ful (rhotic) realization of words among affluent classes. In order to test his hypotheses (which were more complex than mere socioeconomic identities, also involving the dimensions of gender and age), he visited various department stores in New York City and asked for the location of items that he knew to be on the fourth floor.

The phrase *fourth floor* contains two possible opportunities to observe the deletion of postvocalic /r/: the /r/ in *fourth* and the /r/ in *floor*. The three department stores that Labov chose were Saks, Macy's, and S. Klein, stores targeting the affluent, middle, and working classes, respectively. Not too surprisingly, Labov found that speakers in Saks rarely deleted postvocalic /r/ and that speakers in S. Klein did so most frequently. Labov's method also involved asking for a repetition, as if the person asking for the item hadn't understood the response. Speakers at Macy's were most likely to change their pronunciation toward the prestige form, that with postvocalic /r/, in the repeated utterance.

Thus Labov was able to confirm his hypothesis that the further one moved toward affluent class identity, the more likely one was to realize the /r/ in postvocalic position. However, Labov's study also shows us a couple of other interesting aspects of sociolectal variation. First we can note that it is the middle classes that show the most variation, a fact that has been replicated in many sociolinguistic studies since. Mostly the explanation for this phenomenon lies in the position of the middle classes between working-class identities and affluent-class aspirations. In ways very similar to the desire for cultural capital that drove the sales of the many, many grammar books produced just before and during the Industrial Revolution in America and Britain, middle-class speakers may regard, mostly subconsciously, more standard forms as prestigious, and thus attempt to use those forms as a way of asserting cultural capital in the form of perceived erudite language.

However, it is not at all uncommon for middle-class speakers especially to overshoot the mark of correctness, resulting in a phenomenon called **hypercorrection**. Hypercorrection is the "correcting" of a feature of language use that wasn't wrong in the first place. Many readers of this text are familiar with the hypercorrected prepositional phrase *for you and I* based on the mistaken belief that the correct form of the combined pronoun pair is always *you and I*. Of course in this case the pronouns *you* and *I* are objects of the preposition and in standard usage they should be in the objective forms *you* and *me*. In fact, if one takes *you* out of the phrase, the remaining pronoun would sound odd to speakers of English, *for I*.

Even New Yorkers who know that they have a tendency to delete the /r/ in words like *fourth* or *thirty* sometimes hypercorrect and insert the /r/ where it never was. Hearing the diphthong [oi] in [toidi] as the same as that in *toilet*, NYC English speakers will sometimes put in what they believe to be a missing /r/, yielding [tɛɹlɛt] for *toilet*.[54] In fact, the pronunciation of *idea* with an intrusive /r/, *idear*, has become a stereotype of certain varieties of New England English.

Another interesting aspect of Labov's study is that it shows the linguistically arbitrary nature of social correctness. While /r/-less pronunciations are deemed to be non-standard and socially stigmatized in NYC, /r/-lessness is not stigmatized in this way at all in British English; pronouncing the /r/ makes one look rustic and unsophisticated in London, but is the standard in US English. Even in the US, deleting the /r/ in Boston is associated with long-established, wealthy, and politically influential Irish Catholic families like the Kennedys. In Charleston, /r/-less pronunciation is considered genteel and classy. However, as these regional features continue to diminish in use, the social evaluations of /r/-less pronunciations are changing too.

EXERCISE

10.3 In this section, you read about William Labov's famous 1960s' New York City study regarding postvocalic /r/. Part of the elegance of his study was his creative way of collecting data from different sociolinguistic groups by targeting shopping locations frequented by customers from different economic groups. It is not so clear that Labov's assumptions about shopping and the clientele from different socioeconomic classes would work today. Nearly everyone, from time to time, visits large discount stores where one can buy items as varied as toothbrushes and heads of lettuce under the same roof, and high-end boutiques like Saks Fifth Avenue and Tiffany's are now chains with shops in upscale, yet accessible, sites in malls all through suburbia.

Describe a feature of language that you think varies by social class in your region. Identify locations around your town/city where you believe you could establish the socioeconomic distribution of the feature you described. Below is an example from the speech community in which one of the authors grew up.

---

54 Romaine, *Language in Society*, 77.

Speakers vary in how they express the third-person singular contraction of the present tense auxiliary do *so that some speakers say* he/she/it doesn't *and some say* he/she/it don't. *The difference appears to be stratified by socioeconomic class, with speakers from the working class using* he/she/it don't, *and speakers from the white-collar workforce using* he/she/it doesn't. *In order to test that distribution, one could observe the speech among clientele in different bars around town. It is hypothesized that patrons of certain bars near the town's manufacturing area would use* he/she/it don't *at a higher rate than would patrons of bars in the newly renovated downtown area, which has a number of upscale pubs and restaurants that cater to the growing sector of white-collar professionals in the town's burgeoning medical industry.*

AFRICAN-AMERICAN ENGLISH

Another parameter of sociolinguistic variation that has been widely studied is that of ethnic affiliation, and there is no sociolect associated with racial identity that has been more studied than the variety that has come to be known as **African-American English**. African-American English is comprised of a set of linguistic forms that have their roots in the English used by enslaved Africans in the US South during the eighteenth and nineteenth centuries. During the 1950s and 1960s, many African-American families and individuals migrated into large metropolitan areas out of the South, e.g., Chicago, New York City, Detroit, Philadelphia, Los Angeles, etc. Many of those émigrés continued to use African-American English, and today those varieties of English are probably more associated with general urban rather than rural Southern identities.

Again, it cannot be stressed enough that we are talking here about socially negotiable identities; not every African American speaks African-American English, nor are all African-American English speakers African American. The term *African American* as it applies to a variety of English is to be understood in terms of the historical origins of that variety, and not exclusively because of its association with a group of people. In fact, to focus solely on racial identity ignores the fact that there are growing numbers of non-African Americans who use forms that originate historically with Southern African Americans, including Caucasian Americans and Asian Americans. It may well be that in the next one hundred years or so, the variety of English we now call African-American English (or AAE) will become more a matter of urban versus suburban identity; even so, it is appropriate to continue to call it African American in order to identify and honor its roots in our larger cultural history.

There exists a large literature on the linguistics of AAE and since the 1960s, many book-length treatments have been produced,[55] and many features of AAE have been identified on several levels of linguistic description. One interesting feature of AAE is the broad use of *ain't* as an auxiliary verb. The origin of *ain't*, which we showed earlier to appear in many dialects of English, is a somewhat mysterious topic in the history of English. From what we can tell it would appear to have its source in two equally possible forms. On the one hand, it may have descended from the naturally contractive form of *am + not, amn't*. Note that the other forms of the verb *be* contract with the negative, *aren't/isn't*, and *amn't* would be expected. From there, the form may have undergone certain phonological changes in the vowel and consonant to yield *ain't*.

In another scenario, *ain't* develops from *have not* (or *has not*) with appropriate phonological changes. While there are reasons to support and reject both historical analyses,[56] the fact is that *ain't* does appear in many varieties of English just where *am not, have not* or *has not* would occur.

I am not angry. ~ I ain't angry.
We have not seen him in a while. ~ We ain't seen him in a while.
He has not left yet. ~ He ain't left yet.

Of course, the trouble with identifying the historical source has to do with the fact that whatever the origins of *ain't* might have been, it has spread such that it is used in all contexts of negative *be* in the present, both as an auxiliary verb, *He ain't tellin' you nothin'*, and as a copular verb, *She ain't here right now*. As we have seen above, it is also used for all auxiliary uses of *have/has + not*, but apparently not when *have* is the main verb, even in those varieties of English that allow for *have* contraction as in, *I haven't a penny*.

However, in AAE, *ain't* shows considerably wider distribution, occurring also in contexts where we might expect *doesn't/don't* and even *didn't*.[57] For example in the use of *ain't* in the sentence, *If they ain't have they ain't complain*,[58] the most likely paraphrase would be *If they don't have [anything], then they don't complain*.

---

55 Dillard 1972, Fasold 1972, Labov 1972, Rickford and Rickford 2000, Smitherman 1977, Green 2002, and many others.

56 Otto Jespersen, *A Modern English Grammar on Historical Principles, Part V* (Copenhagen: Ejnar Munksgaard, 1940); Cheshire, "Variation in the Use of Ain't in an Urban British Dialect"; K. Aaron Smith, "Historical Development and Aspectual Nuances of Ain't-Periphrases," in *Ain'thology: The History and Life of a Taboo Word*, ed. Patricia Donaher and Seth Katz (Newcastle upon Tyne: Cambridge Scholars Publishing, 2015).

57 K. Aaron Smith, "Historical Development and Aspectual Nuances of Ain't-Periphrases"; Walt Wolfram and Natalie Schilling-Estes, *American English: Dialects and Variation* (2nd edition) (Malden, MA: Blackwell, 2006).

58 From Colin Channer's novel, *Passing Through* (Penguin, 2004), 62.

Another feature of AAE is the future auxiliary *finna*. *Finna* has its roots in Southern US English where it is still frequently used by most speakers in its fuller form *fixin' to*, or any number of reduced variants, *fissa*, *fitna*, etc. The form *finna*, however, appears to be more specifically the form in AAE and as such can be heard in almost every variety of AAE throughout the US. The development of *finna* from *fixing to* is phonologically analogous to the development of *gonna* from *going to*.[59]

Fixing to originally meant arranging things in such a way to create an outcome, but as *fixing to* came to mark a future prediction, the two words fused. In many ways, *finna* has become more grammatical, and certainly more frequent than *fixin' to* and other reduced variants, suggesting that the system of future auxiliaries in AAE has become very complex, a system in which very subtle differences between *will*, *gonna* and *finna* can be expressed. Another even newer futurate auxiliary has emerged within the verb system of AAE, *tryna* (from *trying to*), that does not simply mean *attempt* and instead seems to signal yet another level of future prediction or intention.

Certain aspects of the linguistic structures we have been looking at so far show unique patterning in AAE, like the use of *ain't* as a present-tense auxiliary and the actual form *finna*. However, in another sense, the constructions that are involved in that patterning are certainly shared with other varieties of English. We have already discussed the broad usage of *ain't* in many Englishes and most non-AAE Southern US varieties use *fixing to*, or some reduced variant of it. While isogloss overlap is no more surprising in this instance than it is in any other instance of identity or geographical boundary, scholars have used facts like these to evaluate the origins of AAE.

While evidence of shared features between AAE and other varieties of English suggest a native English origin, other kinds of evidence point to other explanations for the development of AAE. For example, certain features of AAE attest to the African roots of its earliest speakers. Single words originally associated with AAE, like *okra* for example, are likely from West African languages, Igbo in the case of *okra*.[60] And certain songs and stories migrated with Africans into the Caribbean and American South, such as the much-studied Ananse stories, tales of a spider character believed to have originated in Ghana and later appearing as tales of "Aunt Nancy" (from *Ananse*, a case of folk etymology). However, in grammatical terms, the connections between AAE and African languages are relatively few. The strongest counter-argument to English origins for the grammatical structures found in AAE is the creolist position. However, to appreciate the arguments of dialectal origins, we first need to look again at a group of languages known in linguistics as pidgins and creole languages.

---

59   K. Aaron Smith, "The History of *be fixing to*: Grammaticization, Sociolinguistic Distribution and Emerging Literary Spaces," *English Today* 97, 25.1 (2009).

60   OED online.

PIDGINS AND CREOLES

The linguistic designation of pidgin is given to a class of contact languages that emerge among speakers of different languages. Every instance of language mixing of the type that gives rise to pidgin communication systems is unique and so there are essentially as many different types of pidgins as there are pidgins. The term pidgin is believed to be the Chinese Pidgin English pronunciation of the English word *business*.

When a pidgin becomes the native language of a group of speakers, it develops into a creole (see below). Since pidginization occurs in the context of language accommodation among speakers of different languages, the process is marked by linguistic simplification of the target language, that is, the language toward which non-native speakers move (also known as the **lexifier language**). That simplification occurs on all levels of linguistic structure: phonological, morphological, syntactic and semantic. Some examples of simplification on these various levels in pidgins/creoles follow.

Phonological

Consonant clusters tend to be simplified, and there may be mergers of sounds, particularly when the sounds are not present in the source language of the users of the pidgin. For example, in Tok Pisin, a language spoken in Papua New Guinea, *fruit* is often *prut* for a number of speakers since /f/ is absent or non-phonological in the native languages of some of its speakers.[61]

Morpho-Syntactic

The morphological distinction between singular and plural is often lost, *aal di animal* (all the animals).[62] In Jamaican (and some other creoles), *dem* (them) may be added as a new plural indicator, *di gyal dem* (the girls),[63] a feature also seen in the short description of Nigerian English in the first part of this chapter.

Semantic

Often in pidgins, fine distinctions among senses of different words are lost, and a single word may become generalized to include multiple senses. For example in Tok Pisin the word *gras* (< English *grass*) can be used to mean "hair, beard, moustache, eyebrow, bird's feather, dog's fur, and weed."[64]

Although it may be difficult for speakers of the lexifier language(s) to appreciate or recognize, the process of simplification in language contact situations is not evi-

---

61   Romaine, *Language in Society*, 185.
62   John Holm, *Pidgin and Creole Languages*, 2 vols. (Cambridge: Cambridge UP, 1989), 193.
63   Mark Sebba, *Contact Languages: Pidgins and Creoles* (London: Macmillan, 1997), 209.
64   Romaine, *Language in Society*, 189.

dence of cognitive or social degeneration and in fact reveals considerable complexity. For instance, in the expression *two dogs*, the numeral *two* expresses the plural and does so with great precision; the plural marking on *dogs* is, strictly speaking, redundant. Thus, morphological simplification often strips away superfluous grammatical adornment, streamlining, if you will, the linguistic signal. Outside of grammar, the example of semantic generalization in Tok Pisin shows not merely the loss of the lexical items *fur* and *feathers*, but a gain in the nuances of the word *gras*. Thus from a different perspective, semantic simplification in the overall lexicon may be balanced by semantic/pragmatic complexification.

There is also the question of who is responsible for the kinds of simplifications seen in pidginization. In the late nineteenth century, Hugo Schuchardt suggested that it was speakers of the lexifier languages who provided the simplified linguistic input to the pidgin, and there is doubtless some truth to this view, although imperfect learning of the lexifier language must also provide some of the negotiated structure of the pidgin.[65] One good piece of evidence that native speakers of the lexifier languages contribute to the simplification is the fact that they also speak the pidgin in interactions; that is, it is not as if native speakers use the lexifier language in its "full" form and only second language speakers use it in its "stripped down" version. In Delaware Pidgin for example, all nouns take the inanimate form (actual Delaware had two genders, inanimate and animate). As Ives Goddard points out, the non-native speakers of the pidgin would have heard a mix of animate and inanimate nouns so that for the pidgin to be so consistent it would have required control of the grammatical form, something that could only be exercised by speakers who knew the language.[66] Again it is important to remember that these are negotiated languages and that negotiation, at least in the linguistic realm, occurs on both sides.

While pidgins in their beginning stages are quite limited in terms of the social domains they are used in and often variable in terms of structure, some pidgins expand and come to be used in multiple domains. At that stage they often show a more fixed and describable grammatical structure as well. Given the linguistic, ethnic, and social context of the pidgin, some children are born into societies in which the only or most consistent linguistic input is the pidgin. In other words, these children acquire the pidgin as their first language. In such cases the pidgin is said to have become a creole language. Thus the definition of a creole is, most straightforwardly, a nativized pidgin.

---

65 Glen G. Gilbert, ed. and trans., *Pidgin and Creole Languages: Selected Essays by Hugo Schuchardt* (Cambridge: Cambridge UP, 1980), 65, 69.

66 Ives Goddard, "Pidgin Delaware," in *Contact Languages: A Wider Perspective*, ed. Sarah G. Thomason (Amsterdam: John Benjamins, 1997), 69.

A creole is a full language in the way that any other human language is a language. It is the native language of some population of speakers; it is used across a wide set of domains, the core of which is intimate for the speakers, e.g., home; and it contains complex structures on all levels of analysis. In analyzing creoles, however, it is very important to consider the structure of the creole objectively and not merely to compare it to the lexifier language. Each speaker of a creole has acquired that creole as his or her first language; creole speakers did not acquire the standard form of the lexifier language and then subsequently misuse it.

Since they were first identified as a class of languages, creoles have intrigued researchers because of the structural similarities that persist across creoles from completely different parts of the globe. One persistent explanation for those similarities has been the idea that under conditions of simplified input, like the structurally stripped-down pidgin, language learners are forced to rely on innate linguistic structuration principles in reconstructing a full language. This theory has been attractive to linguists, particularly those whose theories are built on the tenet that language is part of our genetic endowment as a species. Bickerton[67] renders one of the strongest biological claims linking universals and creole structure in the statement that certain structures are "rooted in specific neural properties of the brain" (his reference is to verbal constructions).

Suzanne Romaine presents the use of the verb *get* to mean *exists* in four creoles, three English-lexified and one Portuguese-lexified. The sentences below all mean "There is a woman and she has a daughter." Note that the verb *get* is used for both the existence (there is) and possession (has) portions of the sentences.

Guyanese Creole:	get wan uman we get gyal pikni
Hawai'i Creole English:	get wan wahine shi get wan data
Tok Pisin:	i gat wanpela meri i gat wanpela pikinini meri

In Malacca Creole Portuguese, similarly, the same verb *tem* (to have/possess) is used for both meanings. Thus in Malacca Creole Portuguese the sentence *irmang machu teng na rua* (literally "brother have in street") means "(my) brother is in the street," that is, *teng* (have/possess) is used here to mean *exists/is*.[68]

Since these creoles are spoken in different parts of the world, arose under different sociohistorical conditions and do not always share a common source or lexifier language, an appeal to some underlying universal language structure or structuration principles is seductive. But universal language structure is not the only explanation that linguists have put forward. Some pidgin and creole scholars

---

67   Derek Bickerton, *Roots of Language* (Ann Arbor, MI: Karoma, 1981), 12.
68   Romaine, *Language in Society*, 179.

have theorized that all modern European-based pidgins and creoles have a single source in a Portuguese creole spoken in West Africa, a remnant of the Medieval and Early Modern Mediterranean pidgin, Sabir.[69] This has come to be known as the **monogenesis theory**.

Monogenesis as an explanation for the widespread similarities among pidgins and creoles is, however, difficult to sustain. It is certainly the case that the multiple occurrences of certain lexical items are due to diffusion, and, at least in some cases, quite probably diffusion from that West African Portuguese creole. For example the word *pikinini* (or some variation of it), from Portugese *pequininho/a*, referring to a child or children, appears frequently in a number of European-based pidgins and creoles both in the Atlantic and the Pacific. We also saw it in the description of Nigerian English in the first part of this chapter. It is not at all likely that a word so similar in form and meaning would have sprung up by chance in multiple languages. And in fact, the far-flung orbit of sailors speaking pidgins and creoles is well documented. For example, in the 1820s groups of Hawaiian sailors were found in New England ports of call, and the use of the Hawaiian word *kanaka* (human being) in many pidgins and creoles around the Pacific also attests to the presence of Hawaiian sailors and the force of lexical diffusion among pidgins and creoles.[70]

A diffusion scenario seems less likely, however, in the example discussed above concerning the possessive verb *get*. While lexical items may be borrowed rapidly in contact situations, grammatical influence requires more sustained contact and some periods of considerable bilingualism. As another way of explaining the similarity in grammatical patterns that have arisen, probably independently in creoles of various origins, it is possible to invoke the notion of universals, but in a different sense from the theory discussed earlier which views cross-linguistic similarities as a product of the genetic blueprint for language in the human species. It may be possible instead to understand the structural similarities among creoles as arising from similarities in human cognition and communicative pressures common to all humans.

When viewed in terms of the latter functionalist principles, structuration of a creole may not be distinct from well-attested, cross-linguistic paths of change that occur in many languages—not merely creoles. For example, the same verb used for both possession and existence occurs in many non-creole languages as a result of the two meanings overlapping in their conceptual domains; after all, to possess something is to know that it exists. If the possession part of the meaning is suppressed or erodes, what is left is an existential construction. Zeitoun et al.[71] show such a

---

69 Holm, *Pidgin and Creole Languages*.

70 Romaine, *Language in Society*.

71 E. Zeitoun, L.M. Huang, M.M. Yeh, and A.H. Chang, "Existential, Possessive, and Locative Constructions in Formosan Languages," *Oceanic Linguistics* 38(1) (1999): 1–42.

pattern in the Formosan languages and Clark[72] identifies 27 of the 30 or so languages in her study in which existentials and possessives are expressed by the same verb. And although Clark's study is synchronic in nature, other studies have shown that existence meanings frequently grow out of possessive meanings.[73] Even in English, a similar semantic overlap is found in sentences like *You go up two blocks and there you got a big billboard. Turn left and....* The purpose of the verb *get* in the sentence is to indicate not possession, but the existence of the billboard.

The failure to acknowledge the similarities between what has been studied as normal language change and creole structuration has led to some criticism of pidgin and creole studies. One vein of this line of criticism has come to be known as **creole exceptionalism**.[74] Certainly the constraints of the genetic model/metaphor of language relatedness have encouraged the view that creoles are different from other languages, but sometimes that difference has been exaggerated, or at least not considered against the larger spectrum of language difference and similarity within typological studies. It is ultimately important to remember that the definition of a creole, or of any language, is partly linguistic, partly social, and partly historical.[75] Creoles do probably constitute a language type, but as with any type, closer study reveals much internal variation, empirically documented cross-type patterning, and thus challenges to facile universal assumptions.

CREOLE EXCEPTIONALISM

Creoles continue to occupy an uneasy position in linguistic politics. Around the world wherever creoles are used, they are almost invariably regarded as corrupted versions of their lexifiers. Consider for instance that creoles, despite their status as full languages, rarely figure on genealogical language trees, like that given for Indo-European in Chapter 3. One of the most politically successful creoles is Tok Pisin, which holds official status for the nation of Papua New Guinea. Papua New Guinea is an independent nation occupying the eastern half of the island of New Guinea and several surrounding islands in Melanesia. Papua New Guinea contains no fewer than 840 indigenous languages. Under such conditions recognition of the creole for official purposes has undoubtedly fostered the ability of the federal government to represent all peoples and groups of the nation by avoiding the appearance of privileging one group and one language.

Even when a creole assumes official status, however, the anxiety surrounding its legitimacy is still apparent. In Vanuatu, where the creole Bislama is the official

---

72 Eve Clark, "Locationals: Existential, Locative, and Possessive Constructions," in *Universals of Human Language, Volume 4: Syntax*, edited by Joseph Greenberg (Stanford, CA: Stanford UP, 1978), 85–126.

73 Bernd Heine and Tania Kuteva, *World Lexicon of Grammaticalization* (Cambridge: Cambridge UP, 2002), sc. "possess".

74 Michael DeGraff, "Against Creole Exceptionalism," *Language* 79.2 (2003): 391–410.

75 Romaine, *Language in Society*, 167.

language, that same official language has been forbidden in schools.[76] Even young Papua New Guineans with financial means to do so prefer to go to Australia for school and consider acquisition of that variety of English to be a marker of their high social status in Papua New Guinea.

Given the kinds of discrimination that speakers of a creole may experience, there often arises a set of variants within the creole with some forms closer to and some further away from the lexifier language. Such sociolinguistic patterning has come to be known as the **post-creole continuum**. The forms of creole in a post-creole context represent various lects referred to as basilectal, mesolectal, and acrolectal varieties. The **basilectal** variety is the one that is most like the pidgin source of the creole, or put another way, the one that is most different from the lexifier source, while the **acrolectal** variety approaches a structure more like the lexifier language. **Mesolectal** varieties fall between the two.

The term post-creole continuum is used to distinguish language situations in, say, Jamaica from those in societies like Haiti.[77] In the latter, speakers use Haitian Creole (also known as Kreyol), but a more standard French is also used in certain domains, those perceived as requiring more official or formal language. However, in Haiti the switch between Haitian Creole and French is presumably more abrupt than in a post-creole societal context; a person speaks either Kreyol or French and not something in between. This type of language situation is known as **diglossia**, which can be defined as the co-existence of two historically related varieties of a language, each variety being preferred in certain social domains. The varieties are sometimes referred to as H(igh) and L(ow), H forms being used in domains like government offices, higher education, etc., and L forms at home, among familiars, etc. Of course, no society maintains such a sharp distinction between language use and domains, and even in diglossic societies there is overlap in language use.

A post-creole continuum is one in which the space between the lexifier language and the historically related creole is not abrupt, but instead gradual as it is in the Jamaican context. David DeCamp illustrated the gradual nature of the post-creole continuum by looking at a set of six features that showed variation between Jamaican Creole and English.[78] Those features included Eng. *child* versus Jamaican Creole (JamC) *pikni*, Eng. *eat*: JamC *nyam*, Eng. [θ] and [ð] for <th>: JamC [t] and [d], Eng. *granny*: JamC *nana*, and Eng. *didn't*: JamC *no ben*. Speakers do not use all Jamaican Creole forms or all English forms, but instead mix them, with some speakers using more Creole features and other using more English features. Presumably, then, a speaker using more English features would be more intelligible to a Standard English speaker than

76 Romaine, *Language in Society*, 194.
77 David DeCamp, "Toward a Generative Analysis of a Post-Creole Speech Continuum," in *Pidginization and Creolization of Languages: Proceedings of a Conference Held at the University of the West Indies, Mona, Jamaica, April 1968*, ed. Dell Hymes (Cambridge: Cambridge UP, 1971), 351.
78 DeCamp, "Toward a Generative Analysis of a Post-Creole Speech Continuum," 355.

a speaker using a preponderance of creole features. From these features one could create a series of sentences ranging from basilectal to mesolectal to acrolectal form:

Basilectal: Mi nana no ben go de
Mesolectal: Mi granny didn't go de
Acrolectal: My granny didn't go there

However, it is not only societal attitudes towards creoles, and their speakers, that make them seem so exceptional. In linguistics too, creoles have been treated as if the processes that create them are unique and even primal, but in fact the same processes that have given rise to creoles are seen to operate in those languages not identified as creole, as we saw with the verb *get* earlier. For example, copula deletion, a feature discussed above in connection with AAE and creoles, is an extremely frequent feature of many languages, including Arabic, Russian, and Japanese.

In terms of the history of English, the reductive features seen to have operated in the morphology of the noun and verb systems between Old and Middle English have sometimes been attributed to contact situations with the Norse and possibly the Normans, and likened to the kinds of changes witnessed in pidginization and creolization processes.[79] While scholars like Thomason and Kaufman attempt more data-driven, empirical refutation of the creole status for English,[80] for others, the problem is more ideological.

Returning to the question of the origins of AAE in light of our discussion of pidgin and creole languages, we will note that AAE has some features in common with languages commonly identified as creoles, such as Gullah, spoken on the Sea Islands and southern east coast US.[81] However, there are many features of AAE that have their sources quite firmly in English, and no recourse to creolization is necessary. The two grammatical features of auxiliary *ain't* and future *finna* (from *fixing to*) are found in other varieties of English. *Ain't* is especially common in varieties of English all over the globe, showing its origin in insular English at the time of colonialization. Whether it is useful to apply creolistics to the study of AAE is something we cannot answer here. However, care should be taken so that we do not become blind to similarities among Englishes based, perhaps, on a perception of otherness that has no place in language study.

---

79 Charles James Bailey and K. Maroldt, "The French Lineage of English," in *Langues en contact: Pidgins, creoles = Languages in Contact*, ed. J.M. Meisel (Tübigen: TBL Verlag, G. Narr, 1977).

80 Sarah Thomason and Terence Kaufman, *Language Contact, Creolization and Genetic Linguistics* (Berkeley and Los Angeles, CA: U of California P, 1988).

81 Tracey L. Weldon, "Gullah Negation: A Variable Analysis," *American Speech* 82.4 (2007).

EXERCISE

10.4 In Nigerian English, different senses of a verb are expressed through the use of auxiliary verbs. Look at the following sentence patterns and try to fill in the missing sentences or translations based on the patterns you observe.

Present
A de haws.	I am home.
A layk nyam.	I like yams.
A feel kol.	I feel cold.
A luv ma fren.	I love my friend
A sabi di pikin.	I know the child.
A nid di moto.	I need the car.
A get di moni.	I have (got) the money.
A ste di tawn.	I stay in the town.

Past
A bin de haws.	I was home.
A bin layk nyam.	I liked yams.
A bin feel kol.	I felt cold.
A bin luv ma fren.	_____
A bin sabi di pikin.	_____
_____	I needed the car.
_____	I had (gotten) the money.
_____	I stayed in town.

Future
A go de haws.	I will be home.
A go layk nyam.	I will like yams.
A go feel kol.	_____
_____	I will love my friend.
A go sabi di pikin.	_____
A go nid di moto.	_____
_____	I will have the money.
I go ste di tawn.	_____

Perfect

A don de haws.	I have been home.
A done layk nyam.	I have liked yams.
A don feel kol.	I have felt cold.
_____	I have loved my friend
A don sabi di pikin.	_____
A don nid de moto.	_____
_____	I have had the money.
_____	I have stayed in the town.

Habitual

A de de haws.	I am always home.
A de layk nyam.	I always like yams.
A de feel kol.	_____
_____	I always love my friend.
_____	I always know the child.
A de nid di moto.	_____
_____	I always have the money.
A de ste di tawn.	_____

LUMBEE ENGLISH

Throughout this chapter, we have presented information on language change in America and we conclude by offering a brief discussion on a variety of American English that highlights some very interesting societal and linguistic intersections. While many discussions of dialect and sociolect in American English focus on a single variety in its contrast to the standard, varieties develop in complex contexts and from complex social and linguistic circumstances, often involving multiple varieties in contact with each other. One very clear example of multi-ethnic contact in the development of a variety of American English is **Lumbee English**.

The largest Native American group east of the Mississippi, the Lumbee were recognized, though "without entitlements," by a Congressional Act in 1956, "by reason of tribal legend, coupled with distinctive appearance and manner of speech."[82]

The center of the Lumbee population is in Robeson County, North Carolina, not far from the site of the earliest attempted settlement of English speakers in North America, the "lost" colony at Roanoke. Tribal legend includes narratives involv-

---

82 Wolfram and Schilling-Estes, *American English*, 208.

ing the incorporation of members of that lost colony, thus linking the Lumbee to the earliest English-speaking community in America. The Lumbee do not have a surviving ancestral language, and the loss of the ancestral language seems to have taken place as long as centuries ago. The "distinctive... manner of speech" cited in the Congressional Act is not a Native American language, in the sense that, for example, Cherokee is a Native American language, and wholly unrelated to European languages like English. The "manner of speech" associated with Lumbee identity is a variety of American English.

Robeson County is unique in the division of its population into affiliations with three major social and ethnic identifications and three corresponding varieties of English: in 1999, 40 per cent of its population identified as Native American, 35 per cent as European American, and 25 per cent as African American.[83] Varieties of English spoken in Robeson County have a number of overlapping features. The European American, African American, and Lumbee English spoken in Robeson County share the regularization *was/is* (*they was dancin' all night*), for example. Lumbee English also shares retentive features with other varieties of American English, like Appalachian English, such as *a*-prefixing (*my head was just a'boilin'*). Both BE-paradigm leveling and the *a*-prefix are evident in other varieties of English: the examples we cited were from the South Midland dialect and from New England English. But Lumbee English of course also has features that are not shared by the varieties it develops in proximity to, such as the regularization of negative *were* (*she weren't here*) and the perfective *be* (*I'm been there*). There are also lexical items unique to Lumbee English, like *ellick* (coffee with cream).[84]

While some features of Lumbee English as it is spoken by younger speakers seem to indicate increasing overlap with the variety of African-American English spoken in Robeson County, Lumbee English remains distinctive enough that a majority of local speakers were able to identify audio samples as Lumbee, African American, or European American English as often as 80 per cent of the time.[85]

There are many, many more varieties of American English we might survey here: more, in fact, than we could ever include in a history of English textbook. What these varieties share, however, is an evolving set of features, both retentive and innovative, that not only serve communicative desires but also represent geographic, cultural, or ethnic affiliation through the use of a specific combination of features, underscoring the axiom: all languages are changing, have changed and will continue to change.

83 Wolfram and Schilling-Estes, *American English*, 206.
84 Walt Wolfram and Clare Dannenberg, "Dialect Identity in a Tri-Ethnic Context: The Case of Lumbee American Indian English," *English World-Wide* 20.2 (1999): 208.
85 Walt Wolfram, Clare Dannenberg, Stanley Knick, and Linda Oxendine, quoted in Wolfram and Schilling-Estes, *American English*, 207.

Glossary

A-prefix: The a-prefixed participle is a form of the verb of the type *a-runnin'*, *a-clappin'*, *a-singin'*, etc.

Accusative: The case used chiefly to indicate that the noun phrase is the direct object, or the object of some prepositions.

Acrolectal: The acrolectal variety of a creole approaches a form more like that of the lexifier language.

Active voice: In a sentence in the active voice, typically the subject is the doer of an overt action upon some affected entity (*Dmitri kicked the ball*).

Adjective: Adjectives can be described semantically as qualitative words that describe or modify nouns. Adjectives can also be defined by their structural behavior: adjectives can enter into superlative and comparative morphosyntactic patterning (*more intelligent, smartest*) and they may occur in both attributive (*a smart dog*) and predicative (*the dog is smart*) positions.

Adverb: Adverbs have multiple functions: an adverb may modify a verb, an adjective, another adverb, or an entire clause.

Adverb clause: Adverb clauses are one kind of subordinate clause; adverb clauses modify some aspect of the predicate, usually the main verbal idea (*Mike left after the prizes had been distributed*).

Affricate: An affricate is a combination of a stop and a fricative. When making the sound [tʃ], as in *church*, for example, first the flow of air is stopped at the alveolar ridge, and then it is allowed to continue at the place of the palate.

African-American English: A set of varieties of American English with roots in the speech of enslaved Africans in the southern US in the eighteenth and nineteenth centuries.

Alfred the Great: Alfred ruled Wessex between 871 and 899. He defended Wessex against the Scandinavian attacks, eventually establishing the Danelaw. Alfred also proposed a plan for translation of texts from Latin into English and for education in English.

Alliteration: The repetition of initial word sounds. Alliteration characterizes Old English poetry.

Allophone: While the phoneme is an abstract mental category of a sound, in actual speech, that abstract mental category may manifest itself in different sounds. The various manifestations of a phoneme in speech are referred to as allophones of the phoneme.

Alveolar: Alveolar sounds have the alveolar ridge as their place of articulation. See p. 83 for an illustration of the vocal apparatus.

Analogy: The process whereby forms pattern alike based on internal linguistic pressures.

Anglo-Saxon Heptarchy: The seven major Anglo-Saxon kingdoms before the conflicts with the Scandinavians in the ninth century are called the Heptarchy (Wessex, Sussex, Essex, East Anglia, Mercia, Northumbria, Kent).

Aorist: A verb category that places a verb in the past without regard to its beginning, end, or other relations of temporal relevance.

Appositive: A noun phrase in any position can be expanded, defined or exemplified by a following noun phrase, *John, the butcher, lives in Oakland*. It is usually set apart by commas in writing and by a lowered and separate intonation contour in speech. Apposition is a characteristic of Old English literature, and can be extended to larger syntactic and even narrative units.

Approximant: An approximant sound is so called because in the production of these sounds, the articulators approach one another but with minimal constriction of air. These sounds can be contrasted with fricatives, in which the articulators approach one another so closely that an audible friction is made. With approximants, the airflow is much more open than with fricatives.

Arthur: King Arthur is a figure likely based on a British leader during the period of conflict between the Anglo-Saxon invaders of Britain and the native British Celts around 500 CE. King Arthur as a literary figure begins to appear in the literature of England only after the Norman Conquest.

Ash: In Old English, the letter ash, <æ>, represents the first sound in Present-Day English *at*. Ash is also a letter of the International Phonetic Alphabet, [æ], representing the first sound in Present-Day English *at*.

Aspect: Aspect refers to the finer distinctions concerning the temporal contours of a verb. Progressivity, for example, *He is running*, is an aspectual category that refers to actions that are ongoing at a time of reference.

Assimilation: Assimilation can be defined as two sounds becoming more alike, for example when the [t] of *at* becomes [tʃ] because of a neighboring [j] sound in *you*, e.g., *atchu*.

Attributive adjective: An attributive adjective occurs in the position in front of the noun it modifies (*Once in a blue moon*).

Auxiliary verb: Auxiliary verbs occur in combination with other verbs, as in *is playing* or *has been playing*. The four subclasses of auxiliary verbs in Present-Day English include HAVE-auxiliary, BE-auxiliary, DO-auxiliary, and modal auxiliaries.

Basilectal: The basilectal variety of a creole is most like the pidgin source of the creole or, put another way, the one that is most different from the lexifier source.

Battle of Hastings: The Norman defeat of the Anglo-Saxons in 1066 established William the Conqueror as the king of England.

Battle of Stamford Bridge: The Anglo-Saxon defeat of Harald Hardrada in 1066 is often used to mark the end of the Viking Age.

Bayeux Tapestry: Perhaps commissioned by Odo, Bishop of Bayeux, the Bayeux Tapestry is an embroidery narrating many of the events of the Norman Conquest.

BE-auxiliary: The auxiliary verb *be* is used in the progressive forms. The auxiliary verb *be* is also used in the passive.

Bede: The Venerable Bede, writing in the early eighth century, provides in his *History of the English Church and People* (731) one of the most important histories of the early Anglo-Saxon period.

Bilabial: Bilabial sounds have both the speaker's lips as their place of articulation. See p. 83 for an illustration of the vocal apparatus.

Black Plague: The Black Plague was a catastrophic epidemic that struck England and most of Europe in 1348. As much as a third of the population of England was killed in the first wave of the plague alone.

Bound morpheme: Morpheme that is attached to or bound with another morpheme, usually a free morpheme. Bound morphemes like *-s* must occur in combination with a free morpheme. Bound morphemes can be inflectional, like *-s*, or derivational, like the suffix *-ly*.

Britannia: The Roman name for the Roman territory (43–410) in what would eventually become England. *See also* Britons.

Britons: Celtic-speaking peoples for whom the Romans named the island Britannia. The Anglo-Saxons conquered the Britons in the mid-fifth century.

Caesura: An extra-metrical pause. In Old English poetry, the caesura occurs between half-lines.

Case: A system in which a noun or pronoun (and often the words that modify it, like adjectives or definite articles) changes form according to whether it is being used as the subject, direct object, indirect object, object of a preposition, etc.

Caxton, William: (c. 1422–c. 1491) In 1476, Caxton brought the moveable type printing press to England.

Clitic: A bound morpheme that attaches to hosts of different syntactic categories (a noun, a phrase, a verb), e.g., *'ll* (<will). Contrast: inflection, which always attaches to the same syntactic category, e.g., *-ed*, which always attaches to a verb.

Cnut: Cnut was the son of the Danish king Swein Forkbeard who ruled England as part of a Scandinavian empire between 1016 and 1035.

Colonial lag: The hypothesis that transplanted colonial languages will sometimes show apparent archaisms due to the fact that ongoing changes that affect the language in its original setting will not reach the colonial variety of the language.

Comparative: The comparative degree is used when comparing two nouns according to some quality (*the taller of two buildings, the more affordable of two cars*).

Complex sentence: A sentence in which at least one subordinate clause is contained within the main clause (*She became a veterinarian because she loved dogs*).

Compound sentence: In a compound sentence one or more simple sentences are joined with a coordinate conjunction (*and, or, nor, but, so,* and *yet*), e.g., *I tasted the dessert and it was delicious.*

Conditioned sound change: Changes that do not affect every single instance of a given sound, but only the sound as it occurs in certain phonetic (and sometimes morphological) environments.

Conjunction: Conjunctions are words used to join words, phrases, or clauses to other words, phrases, or clauses (*and, but*).

Consonants: Sounds that impede the flow of air from the lungs to some degree. They are usually contrasted with vowels.

Cooperative discourse: Using certain discourse strategies to build and continue discursive exchanges.

Copular verb: The copular verb (or copula) links the subject to some information in the predicate. These verbs are sometimes called linking verbs. Among the most common copular verbs are *to be, to become, to appear,* and *to seem.*

Courtly love: A literary discourse pervasive in the Middle English period. In courtly love, a male lover woos a usually unavailable lady, who spurs him to acts of valor.

Creole: A nativized pidgin, i.e., a pidgin that becomes the first language for a population of speakers. (Note that the line between pidgin and creole is less abrupt in many actual situations than this definition might suggest.)

Creole exceptionalism: The theoretical notion that creoles constitute a unique set of languages and that the forces that shape creoles are unique to that class of languages.

Danelaw: Established after the Treaty of Wedmore in 878, the Danelaw allowed for Scandinavian settlement within Anglo-Saxon territory.

Dative: The case that indicates that the noun phrase is the indirect object or the object of most prepositions.

Definite article: The form of the definite article in Present-Day English is the invariable form *the.*

Deletion: The loss of a sound or group of sounds.

Demonstrative: Demonstratives are deictic words (pointing words) that express relations of distance to the speaker/writer. In Present-Day English, demonstratives are either proximal (near) (*this*) or distal (away from) (*that*) and either singular or plural (*this/these, that/those*).

Derivational morpheme: Derivational morphemes can change the meaning of a word and thereby create a new word. They sometimes change the grammatical category to which a word belongs.

Diachronic: Diachronic approaches link synchronic descriptions or analyses in order to consider language changes across time.

Dialect boundary: When a number of isoglosses occur together, then the geographic line etched out by so many changing features represents an actual dialect boundary.

Diglossia: The co-existence of two historically related varieties of a language, each variety being preferred in certain social domains.

Digraph: A digraph is a combination of two letters used to represent a single sound. <ch> is a digraph in Present-Day English that represents the sound [tʃ].

Diphthong: A diphthong is the articulation of two vowel sounds in a single syllable.

Direct object: Semantically, the direct object is the noun that is affected by the verb. Syntactically, the direct object is the noun that will become the subject in a passive transformation; that is, the noun that will become the subject if we make the verb passive but maintain the general meaning of the sentence (*The girl threw the ball* → *The ball was thrown by the girl*).

Dual: Dual is a distinction of number, referring to two and only two of something.

Emma of Normandy: Emma was the sister of Richard, duke of Normandy, and the wife of both Æthelred and his successor Cnut. She was the mother of both Harthacnut and Edward the Confessor.

Enclitic: A clitic which attaches to the end of a word, phrase, or clause.

End rhyme: The repetition of final syllable sounds. End rhyme becomes a characteristic of verse in English during the ME period.

Eth: The letter now called eth represented two sounds in Old English, both of which are represented in present-day orthography with <th>. In IPA these two sounds are represented as [θ] and [ð]. The letter eth represents the same two sounds in Old English orthography as thorn.

Etymological spelling: The "reinstating" of letters that were present in a given word only historically (and often from another language) even though the sound was not pronounced and perhaps had never been, for example the inclusion of <b> in <debt>.

Expanding circle: Nations which have no great historical ties to English at the societal level but which increasingly use English, particularly in the international domains of commerce and science, e.g., Russia, Spain, Japan.

External motivations: Motivations for language change that have to do with the lives of their speakers and include pressures like the prestige of one dialect over another, or economic advantage/imposition, political domination, language contact, etc.

First Germanic Sound Shift: The sound changes described by Grimm's Law are also called the First Germanic Sound Shift.

First person: First-person pronouns refer to the speaker(s)/writer(s).

Folk etymology: In folk etymology, an unfamiliar-sounding word or phrase is changed so that it appears to make more sense within the lexicon of a language. In American English, the unfamiliar-sounding borrowed word *otchek* developed into *woodchuck* by folk etymology.

Founder's principle: The hypothesis that features of a dialect of a certain area will be, at least in part, a reflex of the dialect(s) spoken by the population who settled the area.

Free morpheme: Free morphemes can occur independently as a word. They can be lexical, like *cat*, or they can be grammatical, like *is* in *is writing*.

Fricative: Fricatives are consonants whose manner of articulation involves constricting the flow of air.

Genetic model: In genetic models, a language is said to descend from a parent language, and languages that descend from the same parent are said to be sister languages.

Genitive: The case used chiefly to indicate that the noun phrase is possessive.

Germanic: The reconstructed ancestor language for East, West, and North Germanic languages. Germanic languages share features such as a two-tense system, a system of strong and weak verbs, the dental preterit, a system of strong and weak adjectives, fixed root initial stress, and a consonant system which differs from that of other Indo-European languages as explained by Grimm's Law.

Gerund: A verb form that functions as a noun. *Taking*, in *Taking a walk is good for your heart*, is a gerund because it functions as the subject of the sentence and subject is a noun function.

Glossing: Glossing is the practice of annotating texts, most often by writing in the margins or between the lines of those texts.

Glottal: Glottal sounds have the glottis as their place of articulation. See p. 83 for an illustration of the vocal apparatus.

Grammatical gender: An arbitrary classification of nouns into masculine and feminine (and sometimes neuter) categories. That classification most often has nothing to do with a perception of femaleness or maleness for inanimate nouns.

Great Vowel Shift: A systematic reordering of long vowels. Likely begun in the fifteenth century, the Great Vowel Shift is a systematic reordering of long vowels upward in the oral space. The two high vowels [i] and [u] became [ɑi] and [ɑu] respectively in that shift.

Grimm's Law: Published by Jakob Grimm in the early nineteenth century, Grimm's Law describes a series of changes in the consonant system of Germanic which differentiated that system of those of other Indo-European languages.

Harold Godwinson: Son of the most powerful earl in England, Harold Godwinson was appointed king in 1066.

HAVE-auxiliary: The auxiliary verb *have* is used in the perfect forms.

High West Germanic: High Germanic languages are grouped together on the basis of similar changes in the sound system of the language; these languages tended to be spoken historically in the southern and mountainous areas of the Germanic-speaking area. It is the basis for Modern Standard German. Yiddish is also a High West Germanic language.

Host: The syntactic structure to which a clitic attaches.

Hundred Years' War: Waged between 1337 and 1453, the Hundred Years' War pitted England and France against each other as primary antagonists. By the end of the war, England lost all holdings in France except the port of Calais.

Hypercorrection: Hypercorrection is the "correcting" of a feature of language use that wasn't wrong in the first place, for example the "correcting" of *between you and me* to *between you and I*.

Hypotaxis: In hypotaxis, the placement of clauses is such that one is dependent on the other but still somewhat independent of it grammatically, i.e., not part of the independent clause grammar (contrast subordination).

I-mutation: The assimilation of a vowel to a high front vowel in the following syllable. Its effects on English are dated to the pre-Old English period.

Imperative: The imperative is a grammatical mood in which the speaker commands an outside agent, cf. a command (*Dmitri, throw the ball!*).

Indefinite article: The indefinite article in Present-Day English has two forms, *a* and *an*.

Indefinite pronoun: Indefinite pronouns refer to unspecified entities. Indefinite pronouns in Present-Day English include the following: *someone, somebody, anyone, anybody, something, anything, everyone, everybody*.

Indicative: The indicative is a grammatical mood that refers to situations that the speaker asserts as true in the real world.

Indirect object: An indirect object is the noun phrase for whom the direct object is intended (*The child gave the dog a bone*).

Inflectional morpheme: Inflectional morphemes carry grammatical meaning, like the past tense marker *-ed*.

Inkhorn terms: Learned borrowings usually from Latin and Greek introduced during the Early Modern period.

Inner circle: Those nations in which English is a native language for the majority of the population, such as the United States, Canada, the United Kingdom, Australia, and New Zealand.

Innovation: In dialectal terms, a form that springs up in a dialect for which the source is not directly found in the language variety of the original settlers.

Interdental: Interdental sounds have the tongue between the teeth as their place of articulation. See p. 83 for an illustration of the vocal apparatus.

Interjection: Interjections are emotive expressions that one utters in surprise, pain, glee, etc., and are syntactically independent from the rest of the utterance. For example, _Ouch! You are on my foot!_

Internal motivations: Motivations for language change that have to do with the ways that languages—all languages—work: they are not about the lives—social, cultural, political—of their speakers so much as about what all languages tend to do. Internal motivations for language change include grammaticalization, analogy, and assimilation.

Ipse dixit statements: Statements about grammar that do not provide argumentation other than the judgment, opinions, or preferences of the grammarian.

Isogloss: The line of demarcation between two linguistic variants.

John Lackland: John Lackland, ruled 1199–1216, famously lost control of Normandy to Philip, the king of France, in 1204, hence the sobriquet "lackland."

Johnson, Samuel: (1709–84) Samuel Johnson was a lexicographer. His dictionary, first published in 1755, is often cited as the first modern dictionary.

Jones, Sir William: (1746–94) Sir William Jones is often cited as the first scholar to observe that many of the older and contemporary languages of Europe and India were remarkably similar and to propose on the basis of such similarities that those languages are related to each other in that they share a common ancestor language.

King James Bible: English translation of the Bible published in 1611 and commissioned by James I.

Kurgan hypothesis: Marija Gimbutas linked the culture of the Indo-Europeans to the Kurgan culture of the Caucasus steppe, a culture reconstructed from archeological evidence in the 1970s.

Labial: Labial sounds have the lips as their place of articulation. See p. 83 for an illustration of the vocal apparatus.

Labiodental: Labiodental sounds have the lips and teeth as their place of articulation. See p. 83 for an illustration of the vocal apparatus.

Lexicon: The set of vocabulary items in a language.

Lexifier language: The language that provides the lexical base of a pidgin.

Lindisfarne Gospels: Latin Gospels produced in the late seventh/early eighth century with later Old English glossing.

Liquid: Liquids are a class of sounds that have historically been characterized as flowing out of the mouth, i.e., l-sounds and r-sounds.

Locative construction: The verb *be* + a preposition (usually *on*) + the gerund, one of the likely sources for the development of the progressive.

Low West Germanic: Low West Germanic languages did not undergo the set of changes in the sound system of the language that characterized High West Germanic languages. These Low West Germanic languages tended to be spoken in the lowlands and in the north of the Germanic-speaking areas. English, Frisian and Dutch are Low West Germanic languages. Sometimes a distinction is made between English and Frisian on the one hand and Dutch on the other. The group has also been referred to as Ingvaeonic in some historical work on the Germanic languages.

Lowth, Robert: (1710–87) Eighteenth-century grammarian often associated with the prescriptivist (and complaining) tradition in grammar (*A Short Grammar of English*, 1762).

Lumbee English: A variety of American English with its roots in European, African American, and Native American sources.

Manner of articulation: The way in which air is constricted as it leaves the lungs in speech. For example sounds may be stopped or forced to pass through the nose, etc.

Mesolectal: A variety of a creole that falls between the basilectal and acrolectal varieties in terms of its similarity to the lexifier source.

Middle voice: The middle voice conceptualizes the action as a process and makes the affected entity into the subject. Some consider sentences like *The window broke* to be a kind of middle voice construction in English.

Monogenesis theory: Theory that all modern European-based pidgins and creoles have a single source in a Portuguese creole spoken in West Africa, a remnant of the Medieval and Early Modern Mediterranean pidgin, Sabir.

Monophthong: A single vowel articulation in a syllable.

Morpheme: The smallest part of a word with meaning. The word *cat* consists of only one morpheme, *cat*. We cannot divide the word into any smaller units that have meaning.

Morphology: Morphology has to do with the composition of words and their meaningful parts.

Nasal: Nasal consonants are made by raising the velum such that the flow of air through the mouth is closed off, thus forcing air through the nasal cavity.

Natural gender: Gender based on the biological gender of the referent.

Nigerian English: The name used for the variety of English spoken in Nigeria. Nigerian English exists as a range of varieties, some closer to UK/US forms and others more like a pidgin/creole.

Nominative: The case used chiefly to indicate that the noun phrase is the subject or subject complement.

Norman Conquest: 1066 conquest of England by the Normans, who spoke a dialect of French.

Normandy: Normandy originated as a settlement of Scandinavians in French territory in 911, analogous to the Danelaw in England.

Noun: Semantically speaking, a word for a person, place, thing, or idea. Other ways of defining nouns include morphological and syntactic tests. For example, nouns can immediately follow the definite article (*The _____ ate my breakfast*) and most nouns can be made plural with the suffix <-s>/<-es>.

Noun clause: Noun clauses are subordinate clauses that function as nouns, i.e., as subjects, direct objects, etc. (*I noticed that Maria speaks French*.).

Noun phrase: A group of words functioning as a syntactic unit in which the headword is a noun, *the big house, a little mermaid, my funny Valentine*, etc.

Number: *See* singular; plural

Object complement: A noun or adjective occurring directly after the direct object (i.e., not after a preposition) and providing another quality or further reference for the direct object.

Object of a preposition: When a noun phrase follows a preposition and forms a constituent with that preposition, it is said to be its object (*on the table, with the coupon*).

Optative: The optative is a grammatical mood used to make a wish.

Orthography: Orthography refers to the system for representing a language in writing. We sometimes use the term "conventional spelling" for orthography.

Outer circle: Those nations such as India, Singapore, and Ghana, in which English is not often a native language, but is used extensively as a language of government, education, and business.

Oxford English Dictionary: Dictionary attempting to define and illustrate the meaning of every word in English. The final volume of the first edition was published in 1928. The dictionary also provides the etymology for most of the entries.

Palatal: Palatal sounds have the palate as their place of articulation. See p. 83 for an illustration of the vocal apparatus.

Parataxis: Parataxis involves the placement of clauses such that each has parallel independent status.

Parchment: Prepared animal skin used as the surface for writing in Medieval England.

Passive: *See* passive voice

Passive voice: In a sentence in the passive voice, the affected entity of an active sentence is transformed into the subject of the passive verb form. The doer of the action is optionally expressed in a by-phrase (*The ball was kicked by Dmitri*).

Peasants' Revolt: Revolt of peasants and artisans in England in 1381.

Perfect: Perfect forms tend to express completion of the verb (*Maria has/had seen him*).

Periphrastic: Periphrastic constructions signal meanings with multiple-word phrases. The progressive in Present-Day English, for example, is periphrastic: it is made up of *is* + present participle, as in *is walking*.

Person: *See* first person; second person; third person

Personal pronoun: Personal pronouns refer to a noun that has already been used in the sentence or is known from the immediate environment (*Jane started a new job last week and she loves it*). For a summary of the personal pronoun forms in Present-Day English, see Chapter 2.

Phoneme: The basic unit of phonology is the phoneme, an abstract mental category of a sound.

Phonology: The systematic patterning of sound units in a language.

Pidgin: A contact language that emerges among speakers of different languages, most often used in trade or under conditions of slavery and/or indentured servitude.

Place of articulation: The place in the vocal tract that is active in producing a speech sound, e.g., a sound like [m] is made at the lips (a labial sound), or [f] is made through contact of the lips and teeth (a labiodental sound).

Plural: Plural is a distinction of number, referring to more than one, as in *horses*.

Positive: The positive degree of an adjective is its use to describe a noun without comparison to any other noun (*the white cat*) in contrast to the comparative and superlative forms/uses.

Post-creole continuum: Set of variants within the creole with some forms closer to and some further away from the lexifier language.

Postposition: Postpositions are like prepositions in function, but they follow rather than precede their objects, similar to expressions like *thereby* or *herewith* in formal/archaic English.

Postvocalic /r/: The /r/ after a vowel. The presence or absence of postvocalic /r/ (rhotic/non-rhotic) is commonly noted as a marker of dialect difference.

Predicate adjective: A predicate adjective appears after a copular verb and states some quality about the noun that is functioning as the subject of the copular verb (*Kwame is successful*).

Preposition: A preposition is generally a small word that is used to establish a specific relationship of a noun to the rest of the clause in which it appears (*of, to, for*). Prepositions may also be compound, that is, composed of several words, e.g., *in spite of*.

Priestly, Joseph: (1733–1804) Eighteenth-century grammarian often associated with a more descriptive approach to grammar (*The Rudiments of English Grammar*, 1761).

Proclitic: A clitic which attaches to the beginning of a word.

Progressive: An aspectual category that refers to actions that are ongoing at the time of reference (*The plan is succeeding as we speak*).

Proto-Indo-European: The reconstructed ancestor language for Germanic, Celtic, Italic, Hellenic, Balto-Slavic, Indo-Iranian, Tocharian, Hittite, and Armenian.

Reduplication: The repetition of a word to create a new lexical item or build a different grammatical form. As a lexical example, *boy-boy*, in Singapore English, means *boyfriend*.

Relative clause: Relative clauses are one kind of subordinate clause; relative clauses are sometimes also called adjective clauses, and modify a noun (*The man who just spoke to us has returned to the stage*).

Relative pronoun: Relative pronouns are used to introduce relative or adjective clauses that function to describe a noun (*We elected the candidate who was more qualified*).

Retention: In dialectal terms, a form that has its source in the language of the original settlers.

Runes: Symbols in a Germanic alphabet. Runes could represent sounds or words. The symbol <þ> for example could represent the sounds [θ] and [ð] or the word meaning *thorn*.

Second person: Second-person forms refer to the person(s) being spoken or written to.

Simple sentence: A sentence in which there is a single subject and a single predicate (*The caterpillar became a butterfly.*).

Singapore English: A variety of English spoken on the island of Singapore, with some features common to world varieties of English and others influenced by other languages spoken in Singapore.

Singular: Singular is a distinction of number, referring to one entity, as in *horse*.

Sociolect: Variation that is defined not only by geographic location but also by social identities, such as racial affiliation or socioeconomic class.

Spelling pronunciation: Pronunciation based on spelling, for example *often*, which had long been pronounced [ɔfɛn] has increasingly been given the spelling pronunciation [ɔftɛn].

Stop: A consonant whose manner of articulation involves stopping the flow of air.

Stress-timed: In stress-timed languages, timing is established between major stressed syllables.

Strong adjective: Strong adjective forms occur without a determiner or after the indefinite article in Germanic languages. The distinction between strong and weak adjective forms is lost in some modern Germanic languages such as English.

Strong verb: Strong verbs express tense through ablaut, or vowel gradations, *sing–sang, write–wrote*.

Subject: The subject is often defined semantically as "what the sentence is about" or "the noun that is performing the action of the verb." Morphosyntactic descriptions for the subject include the following: the subject is the noun with which the verb agrees in number; and the subject is often the noun that appears immediately to the left of the verb (*The mouse squeaked*).

Subject complement: The subject complement is the noun or adjective following the copular verb; the subject complement restates something about the subject (*Raul is a good student*).

Subjunctive: The subjunctive is a grammatical mood that refers to situations that the speaker asserts as hypothetical, probable, or contingent.

Subordination: Subordination entails the placement of clauses such that one is subsumed within the grammar of the other (*see* Complex sentence).

Superlative: The superlative degree is used to compare more than two nouns (*the largest planet, the most successful species*).

Swift, Jonathan: (1667–1745) Eighteenth-century author and thinker responsible for a proposal for establishing a language academy in England.

Syllable-timed: In syllable-timed languages each syllable takes roughly the same amount of time to pronounce.

Synchronic: Synchronic approaches to a language involve description and analysis of the language at a single moment in time.

Syntax: The meaningful arrangement of words into phrases and clauses.

Synthetic: Grammatical relations that are expressed through word-forming processes are synthetic. For example, the comparative can be expressed synthetically with the suffix *-er*, as in *smarter* (contrast "periphrastic").

Tap: In this text, tap refers to the IPA symbol [ɾ], which represents a voiced alveolar tap articulation. A tap differs from other consonant articulations in that it involves very brief contact with the place of articulation.

Tense: Tense may be understood as the grammaticalization of location in time; tense is the linguistic means of placing utterances within a general time frame, present, past, etc.

Third person: Third-person forms refer to a person being spoken or written about.

Thorn: Thorn is a letter from the English runic alphabet. It represented two sounds, both of which are represented in present-day orthography with <th>. In IPA these two sounds are represented as [θ] and [ð]. The letter eth represents the same two sounds in Old English.

Unconditioned sound change: Changes that occur to a sound regardless of where the sounds happen to occur.

Velar: Velar sounds have the velum as their place of articulation. See p. 83 for an illustration of the vocal apparatus.

Vellum: Prepared animal skin used as the surface for writing in Medieval England.

Verb: Semantically, a word that describes an action, or expresses a state or event. Verbs are more effectively defined by their structural properties: a verb is a word that can be made past or present and can take an -*ing* inflection.

Verb phrase: A group of words functioning as a unit in which the headword is a lexical verb.

Verner, Karl: (1846–96) Linguist who demonstrated that Grimm's Law operated predictably when the stress in the word followed the sound in question, but it did not operate in the same way if stress preceded the sound in question.

Viking Age: The period during which Scandinavians explored, raided, and settled in territories ranging from Anglo-Saxon England to North America, dating between c. 793 and c. 1066.

Voicing: Voicing refers to the state of the vocal folds in the glottis. See p. 83 for an illustration of the vocal apparatus.

Vowel: A sound that involves minimal constriction of the flow of air from the lungs in speech. Vowel sounds can be described according to (1) tongue height along a vertical axis; (2) horizontal location in the front, central, or back regions of the vocal tract, and (3) sometimes a third or fourth descriptor such as lip rounding and/or tenseness versus laxness. Vowels are typically contrasted with consonants.

Weak adjective: Weak adjective forms occur following a determiner (other than the indefinite article) in Germanic languages. The distinction between strong and weak adjective forms is lost in some modern Germanic languages such as English.

Weak verb: Weak verbs form their past tense with the dental preterit, e.g., the -*ed* in Modern English, *loved*.

Webster, Noah: (1758–1853) American lexicographer whose dictionary and spelling book codified a number of distinctive American spellings.

Wessex: The only kingdom of the Heptarchy to withstand the Scandinavian attacks in the late ninth century. The kings of Wessex eventually reclaimed land from the Danelaw and ruled Anglo-Saxon England.

Wynn: A letter from the English runic alphabet. It represents the sound [w].

Symbols

~	Indicates that two forms vary with one another. The selection of one form or the other may have to do with linguistic/sociolinguistic patterning or speaker/writer choice.
*	Indicates that the form or sentence is not one that a speaker of writer of English would likely produce.
*	In historical linguistics, an asterisk before the form means that it is reconstructed.
ø	Indicates the absence of a form in morphology or syntax.
>	Refers to a historical change or development.
→	Refers to a synchronic process.
/ /	Indicates that a sound is phonemic, that is, a sound in the phonological system of the language.
< >	Indicates the orthographic representation of a sound or word.
[ ]	Indicates the phonetic realization of a sound in speech.

Abbreviations

AAE	African-American English
EModE	Early Modern English
GVS	Great Vowel Shift
IE	Indo-European
ME	Middle English
ModE	Modern English
NP	Noun phrase
OE	Old English
PDE	Present-Day English
PIE	Proto-Indo-European
VP	Verb Phrase

Answers to Exercises

1. Introduction

1.1

    a. Synchronic. The statement is concerned with language at one broad but particular point in time ("In OE…").

    b. Synchronic. The statement is more complicated than the statement in (a) but it is still concerned with language at one broad but particular point in time ("In OE…").

    c. Diachronic. The description links a synchronic statement about OE and early ME to one about EModE.

    d. Diachronic. The description links a synchronic statement about OE to one about PDE.

1.2

    a. Internal. This motivation for language change is not specific to a particular language, or related to the lives of its speakers. It is concerned with how language is organized and processed in the mind.

    b. External. This motivation for language change—settlement and language contact—is specific to the social and political lives of its speakers.

2. Grammar Fundamentals

2.1

that	determiner
large	adjective
man	noun
in	preposition

the   determiner
yellow   adjective
hat   noun
spoke   verb
loudly   adverb
about   preposition
monkeys   noun
and   conjunction
literature   noun

2.2

a. noun; noun
b. adjective; adjective; adjective
c. verb; verb; verb

2.3

a. she   3rd-person feminine singular
b. we   1st-person plural
c. they   3rd-person plural
d. I   1st-person singular
e. you   2nd-person singular and plural

2.4

a. a, a/an   indefinite article
b. his   possessive determiner
c. that/this   demonstrative determiner
d. our   possessive determiner
e. the   definite article

2.5

a. goes   present
b. walked   past
c. feel   present
d. is   present
e. has   present

2.6

a. is going   progressive
b. has gone   perfect
c. was talking   progressive

    d. has talked   <u>perfect</u>
    e. will be talking   <u>progressive</u>
    f. will have gone   <u>perfect</u>

2.7

    a. talking
    b. talked
    c. going
    d. gone

2.8

    a. *On, of,* and *at* are prepositions.
    b. *And, but,* and *or* are conjunctions.

2.9

    a. *The <u>biggest</u> dog goes to his <u>best</u> doghouse and sleeps soundly.*
    b. *The big <u>dogs</u> go to their good <u>doghouses</u> and sleep soundly.*

Note that to maintain agreement, when you change *dog* to *dogs*, you must also change the verb *goes* to *go*, the verb *sleeps* to *sleep*, and the possessive *his* to *their.*

    c. *The big dog <u>went</u> to his good doghouse and <u>slept</u> soundly.*

2.10

    a. possessive
    b. subjective
    c. objective

2.11

    a. subject
    b. object of the preposition
    c. indirect object; direct object

2.12

    a. Subject   <u>the captain</u>
    b. Direct object   <u>a toy</u>
    c. Indirect object   <u>the child</u>
    d. Object of the preposition   <u>the ship</u>

2.13

In sentence a., *The woman is a doctor*, the verb is the linking verb *is*. The noun phrase following that verb is the *subject complement*.

In sentence b., *The woman sees a doctor*, the noun phrase following the verb *sees* is the *direct object*.

2.14

In sentence a., *The pro gave the golfer a good tip*, the noun phrase *the golfer* is the *indirect object*.

In sentence b., *The pro gave a good tip to the golfer*, the noun phrase *the golfer* is the *object of the preposition*.

2.15

a. Main clause = *she loaned it to Marguerite*
b. Main clause = *The parrot and the budgie ate the birdseed*
c. Main clause = *Machiko was able to catch him easily*
d. Main clause = *the whole mantle shook*

2.16

a. Relative clause = *that we saw last week*
b. Relative clause = *which provides an emergency exit*
c. Relative clause = *who really knows his antiques*
d. Relative clause = *I love*

2.17

a. That the cat was sleeping pleased the mouse.
b. That the fish could sing surprised many people.
c. Carla is always asking if the parrot can speak Italian/Carla is always asking whether or not the parrot can speak Italian.
d. I need to know where the remote is.

3. Before English

3.1

a. Finnish
b. Turkish
c. Basque

3.2

    c. Finnish, spoken in present day Finland

3.3

    a. False
    b. False
    c. True
    d. False

3.4

    a. False
    b. False
    c. False
    d. False

English *shares* an ancestor language with Latin, Greek, and Sanskrit: Proto-Indo-European. Hebrew is not an Indo-European language.

3.5

Case is the concept that explains why the noun takes these different forms in these sentences.

    Discipulus amat canem.
    The student loves the dog.

    Canis amat discipulum.
    The dog loves the student.

Note that in the first sentence, the form of the Latin word meaning *student* is *discipulus*. In this sentence, *discipulus* is the subject of the sentence. In the second sentence, the form of the word is *discipulum*: in the second sentence *discipulum* is the direct object.

3.6

    b. is walking
    c. have walked
    d. will be walking

4. Introduction to Phonetics and the International Phonetic Alphabet

4.1

Conventional Spelling	IPA
1. <maze>	*[mez] or [meiz]
2. <mouse>	[mɑus]
3. <mice>	[mɑis]
4. <thigh>	[θɑi]
5. <sign>	[sɑin]
6. <quick>	[kwɪk]
7. <shake>	[ʃek] or [ʃeik]
8. <churches>	['tʃɹ̩tʃɪz]
9. <move>	[muv]
10. <yeast>	[jist]
11. <ought>	[ɔt]
12. <look>	[lʊk]
13. <feet>	[fit]
14. <note>	[not] or [nout]
15. <racket>	['ɹækɪt]
16. <rocket>	['ɹɑkɪt]
17. <gateway>	['getwe] or ['geitwei]
18. <poster>	['postɹ̩] or ['poustɹ̩]
19. <backache>	['bækek] or ['bækeik]
20. <pizza>	['pitsə]
21. <oblige>	[ə'blɑidʒ]
22. <candle>	['kændl̩]
23. <recipes>	['ɹɛsɪpiz]
24. <certain>	['sɹ̩tən]
25. <peanuts>	['pinəts]

*Remember that for most English speakers, monophthongal [e] and [o] do not occur and instead occur as the diphthongs [ei] and [ou]. The [e] and [o] alone will suffice for very broad transcriptions.

5. Germanic

5.1

The Indo-Europeans likely inhabited a common homeland between the 5th and 4th millennia and 2,500 BCE.

5.2

Germanic develops between 2,500 BCE and 100 BCE.

5.3

a. West Germanic language

5.4

c. Present-Day Dutch: both are Low West Germanic languages.

5.5

Germanic languages have a two-tense system. Note that while Latin (like, for example, Italian, French, or Spanish) uses a suffix to mark the future, English, as a Germanic language, uses a suffix only in the present and past. To form the future, English uses an auxiliary verb.

Germanic languages have a system of strong and weak adjectives. Weak adjective forms occur after a determiner other than the indefinite article. Strong adjective forms occur with the indefinite article or without a determiner.

Germanic languages have both strong and weak verbs. Strong verbs indicate tense through ablaut, changes in the vowel of the stem. Weak verbs indicate tense with the dental suffix.

Germanic languages have fixed root initial stress. Note how the stress in the Latin forms falls on the first syllable of *laudō*, but the second of *laudāre*. In Germanic languages, stress tends to fall on the first syllable of the root.

5.6

A voiceless alveolar stop in IE became a voiceless interdental fricative in Germanic.
A voiceless velar stop in IE became a voiceless velar fricative in Germanic

5.7

PIE	Germanic
*pisk-	f
*trei-	θ
*dent-	t
*gen-	k
*kerd-	h

5.8

   a. Retention: IE had a system of case which included different inflections to mark the subject, the object, and the possessive.

   b. Innovation: a two-tense system exists in Germanic but not in IE.

   c. Retention: IE had a system of grammatical (not natural) gender.

   d. Innovation: both strong and weak verbs, i.e., both the dental preterite and ablaut, exist in Germanic but not in IE.

   e. Innovation: a system of strong and weak adjectives exists in Germanic but not IE.

7. Old English

7.1

	OE	PDE
1.	ðis	this
2.	æt	at
3.	þæt	that
4.	pæð	path

7.2

	OE	PDE
1.	scield	shield
2.	fisc	fish
3.	wecg	wedge
4.	micg	midge

7.3

	OE	PDE
1.	god	god
2.	græs	grass
3.	græġ	gray
4.	ġear	year
5.	ċild	child
6.	ċin	chin
7.	ċicen	chicken
8.	clæġ	clay

7.4

OE	PDE
1. bōc	book
2. cōc	cook
3. cwēn	queen
4. fēt	feet

7.5

eald	[æɑld]
ċild	[tʃild]
scīnan	[ʃiːnɑn]
wecg	[wedʒ]
cwēn	[kweːn]

7.6

scūfan	[ʃuːvɑn]
wīse	[wiːze]
forþ	[forθ]
assa	[ɑssɑ]
eft	[eft]

7.7

a. Þæt wīf   lufode þone hund.
   The woman loved the dog.

b. Sē hunta bindeð/bint þone hund to morgenne.
   The hunter (will) bind   the dog   tomorrow.

c. "Iċ   lufi(ġ)e þone hund," cwæð þæt wīf.
   "I   love   that dog," said   the woman.

d. "Þū   lufast hund?" ascode sē hunta.
   "You love   (a) dog?" asked   the hunter.

e. Þæt wīf   band þone huntan.
   The woman bound the   hunter.

7.8

a. Those words were enormous.
   þā word

b. The student lifted the book from the stone.
                                  þām stāne

c. That teaching was profound.
   Sēo lār

d. The woman knew <u>the stones'</u> properties.
   　　　　þara stāna

7.9

Sē   <u>gōda</u> leorningcniht (m. sg. nom.) hæfde   bōc.
The good student   had   (a) book.

<u>Gōde</u> bēċ (f. pl. nom.)   sindon for eallum.
Good books   are   for all.

Hēo ġeaf þæm <u>gōdan</u> hunde (m. sg. dat.) bān.
She gave the   good   dog   (a) bone.

Ðæs <u>gōdan</u> wīfes (n. sg. gen.) hund wæs hungriġ.
The good   woman's   dog   was hungry.

7.10

a. Sē gōda mann lufode þā bōc.
b. þā gōdan menn bundon þā bōc.
c. Lufa þæs mannes word!
d. þā menn lufiað þā lāra.
e. Wit lufiað inc.
f. Hīe bindað menn tō þæm stānum.
g. Hēo lufað word.
h. þū lufast gōd word.
i. Ġē lufodon gōdne nāman.
j. þæt gōde wīf lufode þæs mannes ēagan.

8. Middle English

8.1

OE	<u>ðis</u>	ME	<u>this</u>
OE	<u>scip</u>	ME	<u>ship</u>
OE	<u>ecg</u>	ME	<u>edge</u>
OE	<u>mūþ</u>	ME	<u>mouth</u>
OE	<u>nū</u>	ME	<u>now</u>
OE	<u>ċild</u>	ME	<u>child</u>
OE	<u>miht</u>	ME	<u>might</u>

8.2

OE	ðē	ME	thee
OE	gōd	ME	good
OE	fēt	ME	feet
OE	cwēn	ME	queen
OE	cniht	ME	knight
OE	gilt	ME	guilt

8.3

grief	[gɹif]	to grieve	[gɹiv]
breath	[bɹɛθ]	to breathe	[bɹið]
belief	[bəlif]	to believe	[bəliv]

8.4

OE spelling	OE pronunciation	ME spelling	ME pronunciation
wæs	[wæs]	was	[wɑz]
is	[is]	is	[iz]
ðis	[θis]	this	[ðis]
ðæt	[θæt]	that	[ðat]
of	[of]	of	[ov]

8.5

ME form	IPA
I	[i]
Me	[me]
Min	[min]
Thou	[ðu]
Thee	[ðe]
Thin	[ðin]
He	[he]
Hit	[hit, hɪt]
She	[ʃe]
We	[we]
Us	[us]
Ye	[je]

8.6

The following perfect periphrases with *have* occur:

| Whan that Aprille with his shoures soote | When April with his showers sweet |
| The droghte of March <u>hath perced</u> to the roote, | The drought of March has pierced to the root, |

...

Whan Zephirus eek with his sweete breeth	When Zephirus (the west wind) also with his sweet breath
<u>Inspired hath</u> in every holt and heath	Breathed has into every grove and field
The tender croppes, and the yonge sonne	The tender crops, and the young sun
<u>Hath</u> in the Ram his half cours <u>yronne</u>,	Has in the Ram (Aries) his half course run,

...

That hem <u>hath holpen</u> whan that they were seeke.	That them has helped when they were sick

8.7

Examples of the periphrastic infinitive:

Thanne longen folk <u>to goon</u> on pilgrimages,	Then long people to go on pilgrimages
And palmeres for <u>to seken</u> strounge strondes,	And pilgrims to seek faraway shores

...

The hooly blissful martir for <u>to seke</u>,	The holy blissful martyr to seek

Note that the *-n* suffix is not lost all at once. Note that both the form *to seken* and the form *to seke* occur in this passage!

8.8

The third-person plural present suffix is *-n* here.

And smale foweles <u>maken</u> melodye,	And small birds make melody,
That <u>slepen</u> al the nyght with open ye	That sleep all the night with open eyes

Final *-n* in the third-person plural present forms is lost during the ME and EModE periods.

8.9

The third-person singular present suffix in this passage is *-th*, as in *The droghte of March <u>hath</u> perced* and *So <u>Priketh</u> hem Nature*. That suffix will be replaced by *-s*.

8.10

In this representation of the speech of the north, the third-person singular present suffix is -s: nede _has_ na peer, and the corn _gas_ in.

9. Early Modern English

9.1

	Before	After
pre<u>ssu</u>re	[sj]	[ʃ]
ti<u>ssu</u>e	[sj]	[ʃ]
sei<u>zu</u>re	[zj]	[ʒ]
crea<u>tu</u>re	[tj]	[tʃ]
for<u>tu</u>ne	[tj]	[tʃ]
sol<u>di</u>er	[dj]	[dʒ]
gra<u>du</u>al	[dj]	[dʒ]

9.2

	ME	ModE
nam(e)	nɑːmə	nem
moon	moːn	mun
loud	luːd	lɑud
feet	feːt	fit
make	mɑːkə	mek
time	tiːmə	tɑim
sea	sɛː	si
bon(e)	bɔːn	bon

9.3

a. While the choice of the _ye/you_ forms may indicate formality, the form _you_ was the object form for most of the EModE period. The subject form was _ye_. But during the later part of the period, the form _you_ replaces _ye_ in most contexts.

b. The _wh-_ forms of the relative pronoun develop in the EModE period.

c. The _wh-_ forms of the relative pronoun develop in the EModE period.

d. The _his_-genitive develops during the EModE period as the genitive inflection comes to be interpreted as a clitic.

9.4

    a. During the EModE period the *do*-periphrasis develops and occurs *both* emphatically and non-emphatically.

    b. During the EModE period the *do*-periphrasis develops and occurs with negation.

    c. During the EModE the *a*-prefixed participle develops out of the older preposition *on* + gerund construction.

    d. During the EModE period the -*s* suffix eventually replaces the -*th* suffix in the third-person present indicative.

9.5

    a. The rule is justified through an appeal to Latin.

    b. The rule is justified through an appeal to logic.

    c. This is an ipse dixit prescription.

10. The Modern Period and Global Englishes

10.1

    a. British because of the spelling "centre."

    b. American because of the spelling "color."

    c. American because of the spelling "theater."

    d. British because of the spelling "honour."

    e. Canadian because of the spelling "rumoured" as in British English, but "tires" as in American English.

10.4

Past

A bin de haws.	I was home.
A bin layk nyam.	I liked yams.
A bin feel kol.	I felt cold.
A bin luv ma fren.	I loved my friend.
A bin sabi di pikin.	I knew the child.
A bin nid di moto.	I needed the car.
A bin get di moni.	I had (gotten) the money.
A bin ste di tawn.	I stayed in the town.

Future

A go de haws.	I will be home.
A go layk nyam.	I will like yams.

A go feel kol.	I will feel cold.
A go luv ma fren.	I will love my friend.
A go sabi di pikin.	I will know the child.
A go nid di moto.	I will need the car.
A go nid di moni.	I will have the money.
A go ste di tawn.	I will stay in the town.

Perfect

A don de haws.	I have been home.
A done layk nyam.	I have liked yams.
A don feel kol.	I have felt cold.
A don luv ma fren.	I have loved my friend.
A done sabi di pikin.	I have known the child.
A done nid di moto.	I have needed the car.
A don get di moni.	I have had the money.
A don ste di tawn.	I have stayed in the town.

Habitual

A de de haws.	I am always home.
A de layk nyam.	I always like yams.
A de feel kol.	I always feel cold.
A de luv ma fren.	I always love my friend
A de sabi di pikin.	I always know the child.
A de nid di moto.	I always need the car.
A de get di moni.	I always have the money.
A de ste di tawn	I always stay in the town.

Works Cited and Bibliography

Algeo, John. "External History." In *The Cambridge History of the English Language, Volume VI: English in North America*, edited by John Algeo, 1–58. Cambridge: Cambridge UP, 2001.

——. "Vocabulary." In *The Cambridge History of the English Language*, vol. IV 1776–1997, edited by Suzanne Romaine, 57–91. Cambridge: Cambridge UP, 1998.

Allen, Ward, ed. *Translating the King James Bible: Being a true copy of the only notes made by a translator of King James's Bible, the Authorized Version, as the Final Committee of Review revised the translation of Romans through Revelation at Stationers' Hall in London in 1610–11*. Nashville: Vanderbilt UP, 1969.

Alsagoff, Lubna and Ho Chee Lick. "The Grammar of Singapore English." In *English in New Cultural Contexts: Reflections from Singapore*, edited by J.A. Foley, Thiru Kandiah, Bao Zhiming, A.F. Gupta, L. Alsagoff, Ho Chee Lick, Lionel Wee, I.S. Talib, and W. Bokhorst-Heng, 127–51. Singapore: Singapore Institute of Management/Oxford UP, 1998.

Austin, Frances. "The Effect of Exposure to Standard English: The Language of William Clift." In *Towards a Standard English 1600–1800*, edited by Dieter Stein and Ingrid Tieken-Boon van Ostade, 285–313. Berlin and New York: Mouton de Gruyter, 1994.

Australian Bureau of Statistics. www.abs.gov.au. Accessed 22 August 2016.

Bailey, Charles James, and K. Maroldt. "The French Lineage of English." In *Langues en contact: Pidgins, creoles = Languages in Contact*, edited by J.M. Meisel, 21–53. Tübigen: TBL Verlag, G. Narr, 1977.

Bailey, Richard W. *Speaking American: A History of English in the United States*. Oxford: Oxford UP, 2012.

Baldi, Philip. *An Introduction to the Indo-European Languages*. Carbondale, IL: Southern Illinois UP, 1983.

Baugh, Albert C., and Thomas Cable. *A History of the English Language* (5th edition). Upper Saddle River, NJ: Prentice Hall, 2002.

Beal, Joan C. *English in Modern Times*. London: Arnold, 2004.

Bede the Venerable. *History of the English Church and People*. Translated by Leo Sherley-Price. Revised by R.E. Latham. New York: Penguin, 1987.

———. "Ecclesiastical History of the English People." In *Beowulf*, edited and translated by R.M. Liuzza, 183–85. Peterborough, ON: Broadview P, 2000.

Benson, Larry Dean. *The Riverside Chaucer*. Boston: Houghton Mifflin, 1987.

Bickerton, Derek. *Roots of Language*. Ann Arbor: Karoma, 1981.

Boorstin, Daniel J. *The Americans: The Colonial Experience*. New York: Random House, 1964.

Boroff, Marie, trans. *Sir Gawain and the Green Knight*, edited by Marie Boroff and Laura L. Howes. New York: Norton, 2010.

Brook, George L., and Roy F. Leslie, eds. *Layamon*, edited from British Museum Ms. Cotton Caligula AIX. and British Museum Ms. Cotton Otho C.XIII. (Early English Text Society, 250, 277). London and New York: Oxford UP, 1963, 1978.

Buchanan, James. *The British Grammar*. Menston, UK: Scholar P, 1968 (first publication 1762).

Burgess, Glyn S., and Keith Busby, eds. and trans. *The Lais of Marie de France*. New York: Penguin, 1999.

Burnley, David. *The History of the English Language: A Source Book* (2nd edition). Harrow, England: Pearson, 2000.

Bybee, Joan, Rever Perkins, and William Pagliua. *The Evolution of Grammar: Tense, Aspect, and Modality in the Languages of the World*. Chicago: U of Chicago P, 1994.

Campbell, Gordon. *Bible: The Story of the King James Version 1611–2011*. Oxford: Oxford UP, 2010.

Campbell, James, Eric John, and Patrick Wormald. *The Anglo-Saxons*. New York: Penguin, 1991.

Cartlidge, Neil, ed. and trans. *The Owl and the Nightingale*. Exeter: U of Exeter P, 2001.

Cassidy, F.G., and Richard N. Ringler. *Bright's Old English Grammar and Reader*. Fort Worth, TX: Harcourt Brace Jovanovich, 1971.

Caxton, William. Preface to Eneydos. Edited by Jack Lynch. http://andromeda.rutgers.edu/~jlynch/Texts/eneydos.html. Accessed 14 September 2017.

Cheshire, Jenny. "Variation in the Use of Ain't in an Urban British Dialect." *Language in Society* 10.3 (1981): 365–81.

Chicago Manual of Style (16th edition). Chicago: U of Chicago P, 2010.

Clark, Eve. "Locationals: Existential, Locative, and Possessive Constructions," in *Universals of Human Language, Volume 4: Syntax*, edited by Joseph Greenberg, 85–126. Stanford, CA: Stanford UP, 1978.

Cooley, Marianne. 1992. "Emerging Standard and Subdialectal Variation in Early American English." *Diachronica* 9: 167–87.

Crystal, David. *The Cambridge Encyclopedia of the English Language*. Cambridge: Cambridge UP, 1996.

DeCamp, David. "Toward a Generative Analysis of a Post-Creole Speech Continuum." In *Pidginization and Creolization of Languages: Proceedings of a Conference Held at the University of the West Indies, Mona, Jamaica, April 1968*, edited by Dell Hymes, 349–70. Cambridge: Cambridge UP, 1971.

DeGraff, Michael. "Against Creole Exceptionalism." *Language* 79.2 (2003): 391–410.

Dillard, J.L. *Black English*. New York: Random House, 1972.

Donne, John. "Ignatius his conclave." 1611. Luminarium. http://www.luminarium.org/sevenlit/donne/ignatius.htm. Accessed 14 June 2017.

Elstob, Elizabeth. *The Rudiments of Grammar for the English-Saxon Tongue, First Given in English: With an Apology for the Study of Northern Antiquities*. London: W. Bowyer, 1715.

Evenden, Elizabeth. "The Impact of Print: The Perceived Worth of the Printed Book in England, 1476–1575." In *The Oxford Handbook of Medieval Literature in English*, edited by Elaine Treharne, Greg Walker, and William Green, 90–110. Oxford: Oxford UP, 2010.

Faraclas, Nicholas. "Nigerian Pidgin English: Morphology and Syntax." In *A Handbook of Varieties of English: Vol. 2, Morphology and Syntax*, edited by Bernd Kortmann, Kate Burridge, Rajend Mesthrie, Edgar W. Schneider, and Clive Upton, 828–53. Berlin/New York: Mouton de Gruyter, 2004.

Fasold, Ralph. *Tense Marking in Black English*. Washington, DC: Center for Applied Linguistics, 1972.

Filppula, Markku, Juhani Klemola, and Heli Paulasto. *English and Celtic in Contact*. New York: Routledge, 2008.

Fischer, David Hackett. *Albion's Seed: Four British Folkways in America*. Oxford/ New York: Oxford UP, 1989.

Fisher, John. *The Emergence of Standard English*. Lexington: U of Kentucky P, 1996.

Fisher, John Hurt. "British and American Continuity and Divergence." In *The Cambridge History of the English Language, Volume VI: English in North America*, edited by John Algeo, 59–85. Cambridge: Cambridge UP, 2001.

Friedman, Lauren A. "A Convergence of Dialects in the St. Louis Corridor." *University of Pennsylvania Working Papers in Linguistics (Selected Papers from New Ways of Analyzing Variation)*, 21.2 (2015): 58–68.

Fulk, R.D., Robert E. Bjork, and John D. Niles, eds. *Klaeber's Beowulf and the Fight at Finnsburg*. Toronto: U of Toronto P, 2008.

Geoffrey of Monmouth. *The History of the Kings of Britain*. Edited and translated by Michael Faletra. Peterborough, ON: Broadview P, 2008.

Gilbert, Glen G., ed. and trans. *Pidgin and Creole Languages: Selected Essays by Hugo Schuchardt*. Cambridge: Cambridge UP, 1980.

Gildas. *De Excidiae Britanniae*. Medieval Sourcebook. In *Six old English chronicles, of which two are now first translated from the monkish Latin originals*, edited by J.A. Giles. London: G. Bell & Sons, 1891.

Giles, J.A., trans. *Six Old English Chronicles*. Henry G. Bohn: London, 1848.

Gillingham, John, and Ralph A. Griffiths. *The Oxford History of Britain: The Middle Ages*. Oxford: Oxford UP, 1998.

Goddard, Ives. "Pidgin Delaware." In *Contact Languages: A Wider Perspective*, edited by Sarah G. Thomason, 43–98. Amsterdam: John Benjamins, 1997.

Green, Lisa. *African American English: A Linguistic Introduction*. New York: Routledge, 2002.

Hamer, Richard, ed. and trans. *A Choice of Anglo-Saxon Verse*. Atlantic Highlands: Humanities P, 1981.

Heine, Bernd and Tania Kuteva. *World Lexicon of Grammaticalization*. Cambridge: Cambridge UP, 2002.

Holm, John. *Pidgin and Creole Languages*, 2 vols. Cambridge: Cambridge UP, 1989.

Howarth, David. *1066: The Year of the Conquest*. New York: Penguin, 1977.

"I sing of a maiden." MS Sloane 2593. c. 1430. Luminarium.org. Accessed 18 August 2016.

Jenkins, Jennifer. *English as a Lingua Franca: Attitude and Identity*. Oxford: Oxford UP, 2007.

Jespersen, Otto. *A Modern English Grammar on Historical Principles, part V*. Copenhagen: Ejnar Munksgaard, 1940.

——. *Growth and Structure of the English Language* (with a foreword by Randolph Quirk). Chicago: U of Chicago P, 1982.

Kachru, Braj, ed. *The Other Tongue*. Oxford: Pergamon, 1980.

Keynes, Simon. "The Vikings in England, c. 790–1016." *The Oxford Illustrated History of the Vikings*, edited by Peter Sawyer, 48–82. Oxford: Oxford UP, 1997.

Kibler, William. *An Introduction to Old French*. New York: The Modern Language Association of America, 1984.

Krapp, George Philip, ed. *The Vercelli Book*. ASPR 2. New York: Columbia UP, 1932.

Krapp, George Philip, and Dobbie, Elliott Van Kirk, eds. *The Exeter Book*. ASPR 3. New York: Columbia UP, 1936.

Krueger, Roberta L. "Marie de France." In *The Cambridge Companion to Medieval Women's Writing*, edited by Carolyn Dinshaw and David Wallace, 172–83. Cambridge: Cambridge UP, 2003.

Kurath, Hans. *A Word Geography of the Eastern United States*. Ann Arbor, MI: U of Michigan P, 1949.

Labov, William. *The Social Stratification of English in New York City*. Washington, DC: Center for Applied Linguistics, 1966.

——. *Language in the Inner City*. Philadelphia: U of Pennsylvania P, 1972.

Lakoff, Robin. *Language and Women's Place*. New York: Harper and Row, 1975.

Lass, Roger. "Phonology and Morphology." In *The Cambridge History of the English Language: Volume II, 1066–1476*, edited by Norman Blake, 23–155. Cambridge: Cambridge UP, 1992.

Laud Misc. 636, fol 1r, Bodleian Library, Oxford.

Leap, William L. *Word's Out: Gay Men's English*. Minneapolis: U of Minnesota P, 1996.

Leet-Pelligrini, H. "Conversational Dominance as a Function of Gender and Expertise." In *Language: Social Psychological Perspectives*, edited by Howard Giles, W.P. Robinson, and Philip Smith, 97–104. Oxford: Pergamon P, 1980.

Leonard, Sterling Andrus. *The Doctrine of Correctness in English Usage 1700–1800*. New York: Russell and Russell, 1962 (reprint).

Levine, Bruce, Stephen Brier, David Brundage, Edward Countryman, Dorothy Fennell, and Marcus Redicker. *Who Built America? Working People and the Nation's Economy, Politics, Culture, and Society*, vol. 1. New York: Pantheon, 1989.

Li, Charles, and Sandra Thompson. *Mandarin Chinese: A Functional Reference Grammar*. Berkeley and Los Angeles: U of California P, 1981.

Library of Congress. "Scandinavian Immigration." www.loc.gov. Accessed 24 November 2012.

Lowth, Robert. *A Short Introduction to English Grammar*. London: R. Dodsley, 1762.

Malory, Thomas. *Le Morte Darthur*, edited by Helen Cooper. Oxford: Oxford UP, 1998.

Millward, C.M. *A Biography of the English Language*. Fort Worth, TX: Harcourt Brace, 1996.

Montgomery, Michael. "British and Irish Antecedents." In *The Cambridge History of the English Language, Volume VI: English in North America*, edited by John Algeo, 86–153. Cambridge: Cambridge UP, 2001.

Moore, Samuel, and Thomas A. Knott. *The Elements of Old English* (10th edition). Ann Arbor, MI: The George Wahr Publishing Company, 1977.

Mugglestone, Lynda, ed. *The Oxford History of English*. Oxford: Oxford UP, 2006.

Muthmann, Gustav. *Reverse English Dictionary: Based on Phonological and Morphological Principles*. New York: Mouton de Gruyter, 1999.

Oxford English Dictionary Online. www.oed.com.

Preston, Dennis. *Perceptual Dialectology: Nonlinguists' Views of Areal Linguistics*. Berlin: de Gruyter, 1989.

Pulsiano, Philip, ed. *Medieval Scandinavia: An Encyclopedia*. New York: Garland, 1993.

Rickford, John Russell, and Russell John Rickford. *Spoken Soul: The Story of Black English*. Hoboken, NJ: John Wiley and Sons, 2000.

Rissanen, Matti. "Syntax." In *The Cambridge History of the English Language, 1476–1776*, edited by Roger Lass, 187–331. Cambridge: Cambridge UP, 2000.

Robinson, Fred C. *Beowulf and the Appositive Style*. Knoxville, TN: U of Tennessee P, 1985.

Romaine, Suzanne. *Language in Society* (2nd edition). Oxford: Oxford UP, 2000.

Sebba, Mark. *Contact Languages: Pidgins and Creoles*. London: Macmillan, 1997.

Sihler, Andrew L. *New Comparative Grammar of Greek and Latin*. Oxford: Oxford UP, 1995.

Sir Gawain and the Green Knight. Oxford: Clarendon P, 1967.

Smith, K. Aaron. "The Development of the English Progressive." *Journal of Germanic Linguistics* 19:3 (2007): 205–41.

———. "The History of *be fixing to*: Grammaticization, Sociolinguistic Distribution and Emerging Literary Spaces." *English Today* 25.1 (2009).

———. "Standardization after 1600 and Its Effects on Two Domains of English Structure." *Studies in Medieval and Renaissance Teaching* 18:1 (2011): 47–60.

———. "Historical Development and Aspectual Nuances of Ain't-Periphrases." In *Ain'thology: The History and Life of a Taboo Word*, edited by Patricia Donaher and Seth Katz, 72–94. Newcastle upon Tyne: Cambridge Scholars, 2015.

Smith, K. Aaron, and Susan M. Kim. "Colonialism: Linguistic Accommodation and English Language Change." To appear in *Teaching the History of the English Language*, edited by Colette Craig and Chris Palmer. New York: MLA, forthcoming.

Smitherman, Geneva. *Talkin and Testifyin: The Language of Black America*. Detroit: Wayne State UP, 1977.

Steinbeck, John. *The Grapes of Wrath*. New York: Penguin, 1992.

Thomason, Sarah, and Terence Kaufman. *Language Contact, Creolization and Genetic Linguistics*. Berkeley and Los Angeles, CA: U of California P, 1988.

Tacitus. *The Agricola and Germania*. Translated by A.J. Church and W.J. Brodribb. London: Macmillan, 1877.

Tieken-Boon van Ostade, Ingrid. "Lowth as an Icon of Prescriptivism." In *Eighteenth-Century English: Ideology and Change*, edited by Raymond Hickey, 73–88. Cambridge: Cambridge UP.

Tiersma, Peter. "Local and General Markedness." *Language* 58 (1982): 832–49.

Traugott, Elizabeth Clos. "Syntax." In *The Cambridge History of the English Language: Volume I, The Beginnings to 1066*, edited by Richard Hogg, 168–288. Cambridge: Cambridge UP, 1992.

United States Census Bureau. "Demographic Trends in the 20th Century." Census 2000 Special Reports. By Frank Hobbs and Nicole Stoops. November 2002. https://www.census.gov/history/pdf/1970suburbs.pdf. Accessed 20 September 2017.

Ussher, George Neville. *The Elements of English Grammar*. Menston, UK: Scholar P, 1968 (first publication 1785).

van Kemenade, Ans, and Bettelou Los, eds. *The Handbook of the History of English*. Oxford: Wiley-Blackwell, 2006.

Verner, Karl A. "Eine Ausnahme der Ersten Lautverschiebung." *Zeitschrift für Vergleichende Sprachforschung auf dem Gebiete der Indogermanischen Sprachen* 23.2 (1877): 97–130.

Webster, Noah. *An American Dictionary of the English Language*. Online edition. http://webstersdictionary1828.com/Preface. Accessed 26 May 2016.

———. *The American Spelling Book, Containing an Easy Standard of Pronunciation, Being the First Part of a Grammatical Institute of the English Language, To Which is Added an Appendix Containing a Moral Catechism, and a Federal Catechism*. Wilmington: Bonsal and Niles, ca. 1802. http://onlinebooks.library.upenn.edu/webbin/book/lookupname?key=Webster%2C%20Noah%2C%201758-1843. Accessed 26 May 2016.

Wee, Lionel. "Singapore English: Morphology and Syntax." In *A Handbook of Varieties of English: Vol. 2, Morphology and Syntax*, edited by Bernd Kortmann, Kate Burridge, Rajend Mesthrie, Edgar W. Schneider, and Clive Upton, 1058–72. Berlin/New York: Mouton de Gruyter, 2004.

Weis, René, ed. *Romeo and Juliet (The Arden Shakespeare)*. New York and London: Bloomsbury, 2012.

Weldon, Tracey L. "Gullah Negation: A Variable Analysis." *American Speech* 82.4 (2007): 341–66.

White, James. *The English Verb. A Grammatical Essay in the Didactive Form*. London: A. Millar, 1761.

Wolfram, Walt, and Clare Dannenberg. "Dialect Identity in a Tri-Ethnic Context: The Case of Lumbee American Indian English." *English World-Wide* 20.2 (1999): 179–216.

Wolfram, Walt, and Natalie Schilling-Estes. *American English: Dialects and Variation* (2nd edition). Malden, MA: Blackwell, 2006.

Yule, George. *The Study of Language* (4th edition). Cambridge: Cambridge UP, 2010.

Zeitoun, E., L.M. Huang, M.M. Yeh, and A.H. Chang. "Existential, Possessive, and Locative Constructions in Formosan Languages." *Oceanic Linguistics* 38.1 (1999): 1–42.

Index

Terms in **bold** type are explained in the Glossary, which begins at page 299.

From the Publisher

A name never says it all, but the word "Broadview" expresses a good deal of the philosophy behind our company. We are open to a broad range of academic approaches and political viewpoints. We pay attention to the broad impact book publishing and book printing has in the wider world; for some years now we have used 100% recycled paper for most titles. Our publishing program is internationally oriented and broad-ranging. Our individual titles often appeal to a broad readership too; many are of interest as much to general readers as to academics and students.

Founded in 1985, Broadview remains a fully independent company owned by its shareholders—not an imprint or subsidiary of a larger multinational.

For the most accurate information on our books (including information on pricing, editions, and formats) please visit our website at www.broadviewpress.com. Our print books and ebooks are also available for sale on our site.

broadview press
www.broadviewpress.com